Walter Lorenz

...ctives on European Social Work

Walter Lorenz

Perspectives on European Social Work

From the birth of the nation state
to the impact of globalisation

Barbara Budrich Publishers
Opladen & Farmington Hills 2006

A CIP catalogue record for this book is available from
Die Deutsche Bibliothek (The German Library)

© 2006 by Barbara Budrich Publishers, Opladen
         www.barbara-budrich.net

         ISBN 10   3-86649-008-9
         ISBN 13   978-3-86649-008-6

Das Werk einschließlich aller seiner Teile ist urheberrechtlich geschützt. Jede Verwertung außerhalb der engen Grenzen des Urheberrechtsgesetzes ist ohne Zustimmung des Verlages unzulässig und strafbar. Das gilt insbesondere für Vervielfältigungen, Übersetzungen, Mikroverfilmungen und die Einspeicherung und Verarbeitung in elektronischen Systemen.

Die Deutsche Bibliothek – CIP-Einheitsaufnahme
Ein Titeldatensatz für die Publikation ist bei Der Deutschen Bibliothek erhältlich.

Verlag Barbara Budrich Ⓑⷮ Barbara Budrich Publishers
Stauffenbergstr. 7. D-51379 Leverkusen Opladen, Germany

28347 Ridgebrook. Farmington Hills, MI 48334. USA
www.barbara-budrich.net

Jacket illustration by disegno, Wuppertal, Germany – www.disenjo.de
Printed in Europe on acid-free paper by
Paper & Tinta, Poland

Contents

Preface

There is a growing awareness among social professionals[1] in Europe that despite the variety of titles and disciplines under which they have become established in national welfare systems they do have much in common. However, the problem remains, how to get hold of what they have in common and to make sense of this variety. When I made my first foray into conceptualizing European dimensions of social work in 1994 the publisher of the English version ('Social Work in a Changing Europe') did not consider a reprint after the first edition had been slowly sold, although the Swedish and the Italian translations fared better. Since then several international journals have been launched that promote a European discourse on social work, notably the 'European Journal of Social Work' and 'Social Work and Society'. European exchange and collaboration projects produced very insightful studies that enhance our understanding of trans-national issues (e.g. Marynowicz-Hetka, Wagner, and Piekarski 1999; Adams, Erath and Shardlow 2000, 2001; Campanini and Frost 2004; Hamburger et al. 2004, 2005, 2006; Erath, Littlechild and Vornanen 2004; Littlechild, Erath and Keller 2005; Lyons and Lawrence 2006). It is particularly gratifying to see that European exchanges that included former Communist countries have spawned also intense historical research interests which trace the intricate international connections that have always been a feature of the social professions (Hering and Waaldijk 2003, Schilde and Schulte 2005). Nevertheless, I cannot claim to be able to give a summary picture of the current state of European social work, although my work has brought me very immediately into contact with various national traditions of social work (I grew up in Germany, trained and worked as a social worker in London, UK, and taught social work both in the Republic of Ireland and now in Italy). The following chapters are revised versions of publications over recent years through which I tried to lay bare some of the most significant developments in European social work at the turn of the millennium and to present them in an historical perspective. Their actuality for teaching and practice in social

---

1   The term 'social professions' will be used to refer to the range of titles and activities which in the German literature are characterised as 'Soziale Arbeit' (as distinct from Sozialarbeit), including the fields of social pedagogy, social education, youth and community work, animation and non-residential, non-medical care work. The boundaries are fluid and no 'territorial claims' are staked out with this term which was first used in the context of the First Thematic Network of the Social Professions in Europe, ECSPRESS, see Lorenz and Seibel 1999

work is underlined by two developments: The Bologna Process for the coordination of higher education structures entails not just formal changes but aims explicitly at enhancing European dimensions in university studies. If this is not to lead to superficial harmonization and standardization close attention has to be paid to the significance of differences that a closer encounter with national traditions of training and of academic discourses reveals. Equally, the European Directive on Services in the Internal Market (CEC 2004) promotes the mobility of services including the social and health field and poses profound challenges to national and trans-national service providers to declare and substantiate their standards of quality. Defining such standards is a highly complex process which needs to make reference to theory and research, but also to political, cultural and ethical considerations. This book tries to convey a sense of the complexity of the issues involved while offering a perspective on future developments.

A first revision of what I consider to be the most important papers through which I analysed key aspects of current developments in European social work was accepted (in English!) as a PhD Dissertation at the Fakultät Erziehungswissenschaften of the Technische Universität Dresden, Germany, and I want to gratefully acknowledge the encouragement and critical comment I received from Prof. Lothar Böhnisch in seeing this project through. Other friends and colleagues also played a vital role in providing me with information and contacts, comments and critique, encouragement and sustenance of many kinds, notably Anna Aluffi Pentini, Oldrich Chytil, Franz Hamburger, Karen Lyons, Hans-Uwe Otto and Friedrich Wilhelm Seibel, and I want to thank them and numerous others who will probably recognize their influence most sincerely.

Walter Lorenz
Verdings / Südtirol,
March 2006

I gratefully acknowledge permission by copyright holders to use material in substantially revised form that was previously published as follows

Chapter 4:
Lorenz, W. (1998), Social work, social policies and minorities in Europe, in C. Williams, H. Soydan and M.R.D. Johnson (eds.), Social work and minorities— European perspectives, London: Routledge, pp. 247-264, ISBN 0-415-166963-1 (copyright with the editors)

Chapter 5:
Lorenz, W. (1999), Social work and cultural politics: The paradox of German social pedagogy, in P. Chamberlayne, A. Cooper, R. Freeman and M. Rustin (eds.), Welfare and Culture in Europe—Towards a New paradigm in Social Policy, London: Jessica Kingsley, ISBN 1 85302 700 6 (copyright with the editors)

Chapter 6:
Lorenz, W. (2001), Intercultural communication and ethical commitments in post-modernity, in M. Kelly, I. Elliott and L. Fant (eds.), Third Level, Third Space. Intercultural communication and language in European Higher Education, Bern etc.: P.Lang, pp. 13-32, ISBN 3-906767-70-1 (copyright with Peter Lang AG, International Academic Publishers)

Chapter 7:
Lorenz, W. (2001), Understanding the 'Other' – European perspectives on the ethics of social work research and practice, 12th Annual Public Lecture hosted by CEDR, Southampton, CEDR and Department of Social Work Studies (copyright with R. Lovelock)

Chapter 9:
Lorenz, W. (2001), Social Work Responses to "New Labour" in Continental European Countries, British Journal of Social Work 31 (4), pp. 595-609 (copyright with Oxford University Press)

Introduction

The following analysis of the importance of the recognition of cultural diversity and the social construction of identity for social processes generally and for social work in particular has several objectives. Firstly, it seeks to demonstrate that achieving social cohesion and integration in European societies today is not a matter of finding inherent or innate similarities between members of a community and establishing them as the basis and legitimation of social bonds, as was the tendency in many European nation state developments. Rather, social bonds under the conditions of modernity can only come about as a result of elaborate communicative processes aimed at reaching consensus over the scope and the terms of social integration. Diversity of any kind, cultural, ethnic or in terms of interests and abilities, is therefore not a hindrance to social integration but constitutes the very material out of which social entities derive their strength and vibrancy to form cohesive bonds. These communicative processes are an arduous task and it is therefore always tempting to short-cut the process either by manipulation or by force. Paying attention to diversity brings with it the danger of marginalisation and exclusion, and it is therefore not enough to pursue communicative consensus-seeking idealistically and without reference to institutions and structure. Instead, the processes of communication as intercultural communication, in the private as much as in the public arena, need to be secured by rules and enforceable rights. This brings into play public and social institutions which were designed to facilitate the process of forging social cohesion in modern societies, among them the institutions of social policy and of social services, both of which currently are in the throes of profound transformations.

As these structures and practices can only be understood in a historical context, the second aim is therefore to trace the historical origins of these institutions in recent European history and to demonstrate the intricate links between the state-building and the solidarity-creation projects. Within these specific dynamics, social work and social services found their role and mandate and it would be inappropriate for the social professions to renege on this mandate and to withdraw into a kind of abstract professionalism that seeks its mandate solely in private contracts between service users and service suppliers. Social work will therefore be affirmed as a public service.

Thirdly, it is precisely this intricate engagement with political, historical and cultural processes which gives the social professions their particular character, and it is therefore not surprising that this professional group, in broad European comparisons as well as within every European country, is distinguished by a rich but also utterly confusing variety of profiles, titles, training traditions and tasks. This disunity has often been regarded as a source of weakness and a sign of the 'backward' status of the professional group, whereas in fact it needs to be regarded as its distinguishing hallmark. Together with this realisation comes, however, the task of shaping this diversity more systematically in the sense that it does not represent an arbitrary collection of traditions and positions but that the links with the surrounding cultural and political processes and institutions as well as their history are exposed. Only then can European exchanges be harnessed for the development of a shared European discourse on social work and social work methodology.

The fourth scope of this study is consequently to link these historical contingencies that led to the variety of professional manifestations with a systematic reflection on the origins and principles of social work epistemology and methodology. In this context, communication emerges as central both in terms of it being the unique methodological tool uniting all the different forms of social work practice and as a means of grounding an ethical framework for action which transcends the politically given instructions.

Fifthly, since this fundamental reflection on the importance of the grounding of ethics in communication has been largely neglected in social work research in place of a positivist orientation geared towards scientific objectivity, it will be shown that this rendered the professional field more vulnerable to political interference and misuse. Professional autonomy, where this can count as an appropriate goal at all, cannot be achieved by a withdrawal from the very processes that constitute the social professions sociologically and politically, but only by fully, consciously and critically engaging with them and asking, in whose interests research is being conducted. This withdrawal is not only a constant source of instability and self-doubt, it also directs the social professions towards a state of disempowerment at the point where new welfare agendas are being implemented which engage social work in functional, managerial solutions for problems whose social dimension is being increasingly denied.

The sixth objective is the analysis of these trends in social policies in Europe and beyond under the impact of globalisation. It has been shown that the processes of globalisation bring with them a re-definition of the functions of the state and indeed of governance which has particularly far-reaching consequences for social policy. This restructuring seems to take the form of a weakening of the state, but at the same time it places renewed emphasis on certain functions of the state, notably the social control and moral imperative functions. It is important therefore not to regard globalisation as a quasi-natural development which evolves automatically and leaves only the option of adjustment and conformity, but to recognise the precise interplay between economic and political processes and the undiminished relevance of political steering processes. Hence it is relevant to distinguish general shifts in social policy and their impact on political parties and governments of the whole spectrum of ideological positions from movements at the level of political culture which show a certain resilience against attempts at levelling their importance. Communicative competence is required precisely in this context because every act of communication defines the social relationship of the partners in interaction and therefore affords the opportunity of shaping social relations at the micro-level with clearer reference to the macro-level.

The core suggestion emerging from these studies is that social work practice, communicatively conceptualised, needs to become the practice of social policy understood as social citizenship, which means that every intervention needs to be aimed not just at the resolution of a specific problem encountered at the individual level, but also at the re-examination and re-claiming of the sets of rights and obligations that make up the social sphere and which constitute the substance of social integration. This is a crucial dimension of every social problem encountered. The biggest threat of globalisation is that it seems to create a vacuum at the level of political governance and that consequently the boundaries of social solidarity, and with that also the boundaries of identity, become uncertain. Population movements are but one indication of this new uncertainty, cultural politics and the world-wide struggles for recognition have an even more pervasive effect and threaten to weaken contractually negotiated social bonds further. One main indication of this is the so-called crisis of the welfare state where fundamentally new principles emerge in the politics of integration. But uncertainties and anxieties become much more widespread as boundaries dissolve at all levels. In this context a critical approach to social work methodology has much to contribute. The outlines of this approach can be derived from the reflection on the fundamental characteristics of successful communication, communication that recognises the existence of 'difference' and hence is always in principle intercultural communication. But beyond that recognition of difference lies a commitment to solidarity, to the creation of a stable social entity that ensures fairness and equality and safeguards the well-being not only of a power elite but of all members of a political community. Nothing less is at stake in every 'case' of social work inter-vention, nothing less is at stake in the attempts at creating a Social Europe that harnesses the rich cultural diversity of the continent and has the enhancement of the quality of life of all European citizens as its central concern.

1. The diversity of social professions in Europe – origins and significance

Social work does not represent the picture of a unified profession in Europe. While this might be interpreted as a lack of professionalisation and therefore as an interim stage which, in the course of the unfolding of its own evolutionary potential as a profession and with the help of the professional associations promoting its cause, will one day be overcome, these historical reflections take a different approach. They regard the 'incomplete professionalisation' not as a negative attribute but instead as a key indicator of the special nature of the social professions. The lack of professional autonomy, measured by the criteria of other established professions, is precisely the attribute which identifies social work as a social profession, i.e. as a professional activity that does not strive to distance itself from social processes, in the way that medicine and other therapeutic professions, psychology, the legal professions and to some extent the teaching profession managed to do, but which derives its mandate always from being based in and linked to the way in which society, not a group of experts, collectively defines, often in a most contradictory way, criteria of 'well-being', social integration, social solidarity and hence the conditions under which society can only exist. 'The social' as this ill-defined, contested and often idealised, often negated vanishing point of solidarity in modern societies, in social work attaches itself not only to its title but to its mode of operating, or rather, the fact that social work came into existence in a particular historical period. That it bears the features of a specific product of modernity with very few institutional fore-runners in pre-modern times (in contrast to the old established professions) illustrates the necessity of modern societies to organise special institutions and activities for the creation and maintenance of cohesive bonds under radically changed social, political and economic conditions. Modern societies had to 'reinvent', to 'imagine' (Anderson 1983) themselves as integrated wholes whilst experiencing the discontinuity of traditional bonds which could no longer be regarded as 'natural' and simply 'given'. As sociology knows since Durkheim (1984), the basis for solidarity under the modern conditions of the division of labour is radically different from that of a traditional society. Solidarity in modern societies requires organisation, planning, complex communication processes, the establishment of norms and laws and the organised defence against deviance. To address the task of this self-initiated integration a high degree of reflexivity was necessary, a change that gave birth to the discipline of sociology which has as its central theme this 'detraditionalisation' and the necessity of modern societies to reflect on the principles and functions of social order as constituted not by external, eternal laws but as the products of social processes (Lash et al. 1996). It is within this turn towards social reflexivity that social work, in all its many different organisational and conceptual varieties, has its origins. Social work forms one element of the constitution of social order under the conditions of modernity. The dominant form of political self-organisation became the nation state which therefore is itself not a taken-for-granted form of organisation but a highly contested product of this very process of self reflection. Its inherently contradictory nature of the nation as a concept is well characterised by Žižek:

> 'On the one hand, "nation" of course designates modern community delivered of the traditional "organic" ties, a community in which the pre-modern links tying down the individual to a particular estate, family, religious group, and so on, are broken – the traditional corporate community is replaced by the modern nation-state whose constituents are "citizens": people as abstract individuals, not as members of particular estates, and so forth. On the other hand, "nation" can never be reduced to a network of purely symbolic ties: there is always a kind of "surplus of the Real" that sticks to it – to define itself, "national identity" must appeal to the contingent materiality of the "common roots", of "blood and soil" and so on. In short, "nation" designates at one and the same time the instance by means of reference to which traditional "organic" links are dissolved and the "remainder of the pre-modern in modernity": the form organic substance acquires within the universe of the substanceless Cartesian subjectivity'. (Žižek 1991: 20)

The institutional concretisation of the transition from social organisational patterns characterised as *Gemeinschaft* to those representing *Gesellschaft* (Tönnies 1887) was this compromise, fraught with tensions, which in turn required instruments for achieving stability and structure. It is therefore important to recognise that the origins of social work are not just linked to social transformation processes at the core of the rise of modernity associated with industrialisation and democratisation with the accompanying reflexivity and the need for new lifeworld forms of solidarity, but even more so to political agendas for their systemic stabilisation such as represented by the nation state project. As such social work, in all its forms, shares in the fundamental ambiguity of modernity in general and is also caught up in the contradictions that constituted the politics of the nation state, and this regardless whether looked at as a public or as a non-governmental activity. Social work has historical and political character.

From this follows that as the role of the nation state is currently changing dramatically under the impact of globalisation and the project of modernity itself appears to be in crisis, social work is of necessity affected by these contemporary developments and needs to be subjected to a fundamental examination of its relationship with society and of its founding principles, including its social policies. It is becoming apparent that the existence of 'the social' can no longer be taken for granted as a shared concern beyond all the ideological splits over its political realisation. Instead, one of the implicit and explicit tasks in all social work interventions needs to become the (re-) constitution of the social itself in a manner that is no longer directly linked to the nation state project. The initial historical reflections which follow in this and in other chapters are therefore of immediate and immense practical relevance because they explore the possibilities of gaining a certain degree of professional autonomy for the social professions grounded in systematic scientific reflection, not for the sake of enhancing status and privilege, but for the purpose of grounding these 'inherited' activities and mandates in a contemporary analysis of the requirements of society and its citizens.

It is one of the prevailing characteristics of modern societies, particularly in the form of nation states, that they have a broken relationship to their own modernity. Sociologically speaking the at times naively nostalgic, at times blatantly power-driven hankering after pre-modern forms of solidarity – and hence of legitimation—is not so much a sign of an incomplete process of modernisation as of the often diagnosed ambivalence of modernity itself. Modernity is split between on the one hand valuing its emancipatory potential positively as a means of overcoming the restraints of dogma and irrationality and on the other hand recognising with trepidation that this emancipation was achieved largely by the instrumental use of rationality and hence power which destroys the very basis on which democratic, legitimating processes can be built (Horkheimer and Adorno 1947). Seeing social work as located within these dynamics means then to analyse its characteristics with regards to both the 'system' and to the 'lifeworld', to express this tension in Habermasian terms (Habermas 1987). In other words, social work cannot be understood fully as either a total product of social policy and hence of the system aiming at rational solutions to social problems, which would prescribe its functions minutely and treat the profession merely as an instrument for the implementation and control of social legislation, or as a lifeworld activity with references only to private forms of caring and problem-solving and the intention of keeping the grasp of the system over this domain at arm's length. Social work is rooted in both worlds and remains committed to both. At the same time, however, this dual dependency by itself could not provide a basis for professionalisation, and it is therefore understandable that early social workers, caught up in this ambivalence and confronted with the impossibility of building solidarity either by 'traditional natural processes' of the 'mechanical' kind or by means of force and control, which was the modern states' response to social instability, sought to initiate their own process of reflection and hence of training (Rauschenbach 1999, Thole 2002). The push for recognised training programmes was a means of facilitating the search for a point of view from which both types of processes could be assessed critically and an independent response be developed without however leaving the social and historical context which provided the basis for social work's mandate.

These considerations will form the basis for the following analysis of the separate yet connected effects of developments at the level of social policy, of social movements and of training traditions and academic discourses on the presentations of the social professions in Europe, which can be represented as three overlapping circles (figure 1).

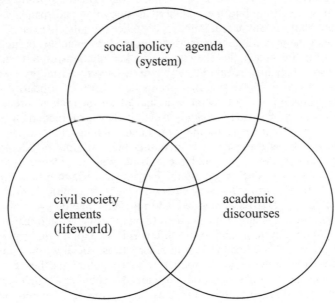

Figure 1

Of particular interest will be the intersections of these constitutive factors in both their historical and their contemporary significance. One fundamental premise is that as social work does not seem to 'fit in' exclusively with any one of those domains and cannot be defined and practised from any one of those three positions alone, this is not to be regarded as an historical limitation of the profession which has to be overcome, but on the contrary it marks the fundamental attributes of this professional activity and is indeed a characteristic to be preserved and to be developed, probably as key indicator

14

of a new type of professionalism, but certainly as the horizon for competences that characterise an advanced as against an initial state of social work. The intersections between the circles indicate that social work is engaged in and can critically influence the at times contradictory processes through which social solidarity has to be achieved under the conditions of modernity.

The segment formed by civil society and official state policies, regardless of the type of prevailing welfare regime, represents historically the nation state project, the attempt at bringing together and coordinating support structures from 'above' and 'below'. Conceptually it indicates the balance between horizontal and vertical solidarity, as shall be explained in later chapters, an attempt which culminated in the height of the welfare state development after World War II and is now being threatened by the advance of neo-liberal policies. Practically, this domain represents a crucial challenge to social work to maintain this tension, not just in its organisational structure poised between a dual mandate from service users and from the state, but also in its interventions where it constantly needs to pay equal attention to the right of equality and to that of diversity and individual identity (figure **2**).

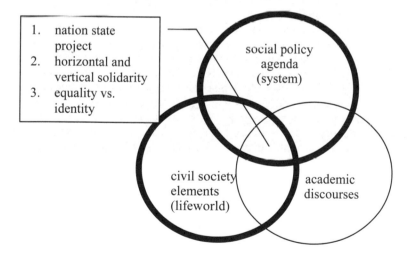

Figure 2

15

The intersection between social policy agendas at the level of the system and of academic discourses marks the degree to which social work managed to emancipate itself from the role of a 'handmaiden' to the state, an independence that was not just motivated by professional ambitions, but fostered also, at least tacitly, by the system itself. Ever since the days of the Elberfeld scheme in Germany and the attempt at systematising philanthropic assistance (Wendt 1985) the system in the form of the local municipality and later the state recognised that it required the services of skilled diagnosticians who could fine-tune the boundaries of inclusion and exclusion, not just for the benefit of the individual concerned but also for the purpose of arriving at an efficient and legitimate rationale of distribution. This central distinction between the 'deserving' and the 'undeserving' marks the boundaries of organised social solidarity and features largely again today in the re-structuring of European welfare states. The suspicion that attached for instance to case work as the archetypical social work method, as to whether its implicit individualism was designed to support the individualism characteristic of capitalist market societies or whether it was simply a scientifically derived method that gained professional acceptance despite 'accidentally' serving such political convenience repeats itself in the question over the latest methodological concepts around case management and social management which also render a professional / methodological and a political reading equally valid (figure 3).

Finally, the encounter between lifeworld processes and academic discourses represents not just a relict from the early days of the profession and hence a stage of development that has been left behind and overcome by the progress of professionalisation. On the contrary, this intersection provides a very contemporary challenge to social work as social movements are gaining in strength and are increasingly pitting the weight of personal qualities and experiences against that of formal academic qualifications. The question of identity, much neglected in social work academic discourses, is thereby posed today with renewed sharpness and vigour and this has profound

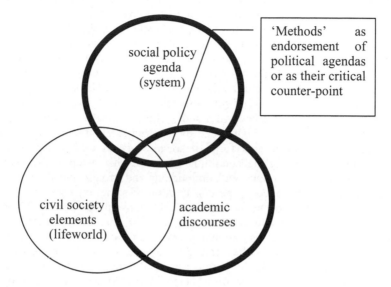

Figure 3

methodological implications for social work, not just in relation to a universalist conception of social policy (figure 4).

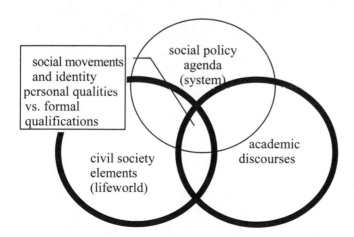

Figure 4

The recent turn towards post-modern approaches in social work methodology (cf. Healy 2005) is an expression of the belated articulation of identity as an issue for social work, but overall uncritical post-modern methodological approaches appear to provide an inadequate response as shall be argued later.

The approach taken in this book emphasises the necessity of sustaining the tensions inherent in social work's multifarious legacy and of turning them into a project for the deliberate shaping of the 'in-between spaces' in which this profession is located and in which new forms of social solidarity need to be developed. These forms of solidarity will be geared towards harnessing the social valences of lifeworld bonds whilst critically linking them to universal human rights as guaranteed by governmental structures at national and international level. This form of social work as reflexive practice is geared towards creating the conditions of social citizenship at the level of concrete social interventions with individuals and groups and thus towards underpinning the still incomplete construction of social citizenship at social policy level. In addition to mediating the relationship between civil society processes and state at national level this type of practice will increasingly have to engage with trans-national social policies and with international social movements such as they find their expression in the move towards giving the European unification project a social dimension. This programme therefore contains the outline of what could be termed 'critical European social work' in the specific historical context of Europe (figure 5).

This investigation is inspired by a conviction that the closer engagement with historical origins of the professional field can lead to a better under-standing of the nature of social work's 'dependent status' and that this reflection can make a direct contribution to a clearer and more effective strategic positioning of the profession in view of the current re-structuring of socio-political priorities and hence of the entire re-designing of the 'social sphere'.

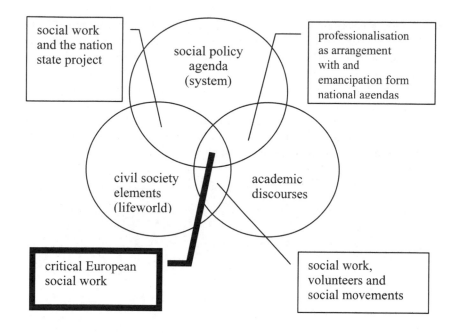

Figure 5

Only by sharpening the view of the nature of social work's 'dependency' as a necessary feature of a professional activity that is essentially historical and hence hermeneutic in its methodology can the nature of social work's brand of professionalism be properly recognised and formed. What is more, the chance of defending it against ideological manipulations and giving it an explicit anti-discriminatory practice orientation does not rest on a withdrawal from political controversy and on taking refuge in apparent academic neutrality. On the contrary it shall be shown that it was precisely this withdrawal to a position of neutrality that made the profession vulnerable to ideological misuse. The encounter with the history of the European nation state is therefore a basic condition not just for a better understanding of the origins and development of the profession, but for the development of culturally meaningful yet anti-discriminatory practices. A critical European model of social work must therefore be capable of addressing this central aspect of European cultural and political dynamics in which social work has been involved from the very beginning but towards which it has so far failed to take clear position. The following chapters will therefore systematically explore the intersections in the above diagrams as key instances for the understanding the different dimensions of this diversity from both an historical and a contemporary viewpoint. The purpose of these investigations into the disunited, historical aspects of the social professions is also to highlight the character of this kind of practice as closely related to social policies, and this underlines the proposed mandate of a European model of social work as a mandate for the micro-practice of social policies and the construction of a truly 'Social Europe' at all levels.

2.   Nation state and social work

As mentioned in the introduction, modern nation states are characterised by an inherent ambivalence regarding the principles upon which to base their internal integration and solidarity. Fundamentally it remained unclear whether the modern nation state represents the community of people who are already, 'essentially', 'primordially', and without necessarily knowing it, 'all the same' by virtue of their 'roots' or whether they are first of all different, thrown together by historical chance and economic necessity, have the right to be different but are held together by a socially negotiated contract which forms the band of their unity and identity (Brubaker 1996). This ambivalence ultimately gave social and educational services the chance to assume such an important stabilising part in modern societies. Workers in those services became automatically involved in the formation of collective as well as individual identities even though many of them never realised that identity and particularly the stabilisation of collective identities played such an important part of their work.

A guiding hypothesis of this chapter, which explores the intersection of social policy and academic-professional agendas, is that because social work discourses, until recently, failed to problematise the professions' link to the 'nation-state building project' they could not develop their actual identity-building mandate independently and accountably. For a long time, social workers tended to either work with a taken-for-granted view of identity, or ignore the question of identity and operate with some abstract notion of 'people in general'. This analysis by contrast sets out to link a particular mode of finding and defining professional autonomy in the social professions with the development of anti-discriminatory and anti-racist methods; or to express the latter positively: Professional autonomy for the social professions is not a matter of perfecting their distance from political processes and to foster personality and identity development as purely psychological processes, but to make a positive contribution to the social and political conditions under which such processes lead to social solidarity and equality in a society. By becoming engaged in the negotiation of non-essentialist, non-racist identities as part of their interventions social workers develop their actual professional potential. This form of practice shall be termed 'the practice of social citizenship' (see chapter 3).

The professional necessity for developing this perspective and for re-defining the direction of professional autonomy towards the engagement with political, citizenship and identity building processes that link the issues and discourses of identity with those of equality is becoming blatantly apparent under the conditions of globalisation. One of the effects of the process of globalisation, which shall be explored in chapter 8 in more detail, is that the nation as a reference point for identity has become questionable, a process which has triggered a new wave of nationalism. The emergence of this polarisation between the dissolution and the tightening of national boundaries and characteristics, between the global fusion of cultural boundaries and the emphasis on 'tribal' life-style choices, and between the higher esteem afforded to freedom, liberty and human rights generally and the increase in social control, discrimination and racism is an indication of the unstable compromise of ideas that historically make up the modern concept of the nation. On the one hand the concept contains a legacy of nationalism and imperialism, of inter-nation rivalries which twice in the 20th century erupted in world wars, of intolerance, racism and oppression, of the holocaust and of 'ethnic cleansing'. On the other hand the idea of a nation carries notions of democratic self-determination, citizenship and civil rights, social solidarity and social protection, and has been an important source of inspiration and emancipation in many liberation and human rights movements. It seems that the nation state as the modern custodian of the concept of freedom and equality has failed to link sufficiently the politics of collective identity creation with processes of the lifeworld where individual and collective identities are being negotiated and that the new fora where these negotiations take place (at both the sub-national and now increasingly also the European and international level) are dominated by ideologies and power manipulation not subject to democratic controls. This prevents the question of identity being made the subject of critical and informed debate and into this vacuum enter the politics of resentment which foster the rise of neo-Nazism and racism as popular movements.

The uncertainties over collective identities in the modern world manifest themselves in a fundamental paradox (Giddens 1991): on the one hand the traditional barriers between classes, cultures and countries begin to dissolve giving way to global connections and influences. The 'global village' shares the same fashions, the same tastes in music and visual entertainment and communicates via satellites and the internet instantaneously. It also shares common ecological concerns, increasingly aware of the intricate links that exist between all parts of the life sustaining system. Beyond that, awareness of the precarious social global balance spreads as contrasts between wealth and poverty become more visible and cannot be explained away fatalistically. On the other hand life-styles begin to differentiate themselves ever more strongly with a high degree of exclusivity so that regions, countries, ethnic groupings, sub-cultures and individuals define their identities in a 'them and us' manner, underlining a desperate search for a sense of belonging.

The waning of the significance of the nation state goes back to well before the effects of globalisation were felt and analysed. The experience of the last World War as a conflict unleashed by nationalism had given a strong impetus for the formation of supra-national organisations such as the United Nations, the Council of Europe and the European Common Market. Political leaders of the post-war era in Europe were determined to prevent the evil of nationalism and national rivalry from plunging the world yet again into the abyss of war, although the strategies of the military alliances of the cold war era still utilised the basic principles of competition and 'superiority' characteristic of the nation states. Economic interests within both the capitalist and the communist block relativised national borders even further. This created an interdependent territorial net of specialised production sites in the former communist states while capitalist market forces equally created economic structures that spanned distant territories and for whose operations national borders were regarded a hindrance (Wallerstein 1991).

However, during the same time of post-war economic expansion the nation state concept began to proliferate world wide and influence particularly the transformation of former colonies into independent states. It fostered notions of self-determination, sovereignty and legitimacy linked, as had been the case with the first generation of European nation states, with aspirations for competitive national economies and the hegemonic values of a distinct national culture. After the collapse of the Soviet Union a similar movement flourished in Central and Eastern Europe renewing the deep ambivalence of the nation state construct and leading for the first time after the end of WWII to bloody wars in Europe. Nationalism re-emerged at the same time as globalisation began to spread no longer impeded by bloc mentalities, precipitating the crisis of social solidarity that accompanied the apparent victory of market capitalism world-wide.

In terms of a changed public consciousness in the wake of these political and economic changes one of the most unsettling effects of globalisation is perhaps caused by media technology which causes an 'intensification of consciousness' (Robertson 1992: 8). This development allows for instant and close participation in world events in the privacy of every living room equipped with a TV screen. The 'virtual participation' in events like wars, natural disasters and political dramas in other parts of the world appeals to the conscience of the viewer in such a way that solidarity, at least momentarily, extends far beyond national and cultural boundaries as demonstrated in the 'Band-Aid' induced surge of help for African famine victims or the spontaneous relief actions for Romanian or Chinese orphans. Distant events, distant lives suddenly become a matter that can no longer be externalised emotionally with accustomed psychological defences that draw firm dividing lines between 'them' and 'us'.

At the same time globalisation and the expansion of potential responsibilities at supra-state level is accompanied by a weakening and re-structuring of the traditional bonds of solidarity at sub-nation state level. Beck's diagnosis of an 'unleashed process of modernization [which is] overrunning and overcoming its own coordinate system' (Beck 1992: 87) paints a picture of the 'detraditionalisation' of a class-based culture and consciousness, of gender and of family roles. People no longer have stable expectations of the pathways their lives and careers will take but share in a range of experiences (unemployment, luxury commodities, travel etc.) which seem more randomly allocated across class divisions in the 'lottery of life' in which individuals have to calculate their own risks. Family obligations, age and gender roles, formats of social contacts cannot draw on a clearly discernible pattern any longer forcing individuals continuously to make their own choices. The need for such choices and the concentration of gratification on having made successful choices promotes narcissistic tendencies which get further exploited by commercial interests in all spheres of life, particularly with regard to leisure activities. The results are greater social inequalities aggravated by the fact that traditional 'defensive solidarities' in terms of kinship bonds, social class or of labour organisations are losing their relevance and their influence (Taylor-Gooby 2001).

Overwhelmed by the necessity to make constant choices members of modern societies are tempted to take refuge in certainties that present themselves as 'factual' (e.g. the biology of sex differences and other genetic determinants, the physiology of ethnicity), or in forms of community that seek to revive nostalgic enclaves in the bleak and impersonal industrial, digitalised social landscape or that construct identity from 'common roots' like tribes and nations (Taguieff 1990). The renewed rise in nationalism and the growing importance of ethnicity as a reference point in political discourse are indications of this fundamental ambivalence and the seeming attractiveness of such reactive solutions.

There appears to be a correspondence between the uncertainties confronting individuals in search of their personal identities and those that characterise the political arena in defining the limits of our collective responsibilities nationally and internationally. In other words, the issues of identity and of solidarity reveal their common link in terms of the renewed priority afforded to collective identities over individual, self-chosen expressions of identity just when social policies are moving in the direction of disconnecting them and promoting extreme forms of individualism. The neo-liberal restructuring of the welfare state right across Europe (Mishra 1990, Squires 1990, Pierson 1994, Jessop 2000b) has as its aim the dismantling of the welfare consensus forged in the experience of the last world war that had been regarded as the completion of the establishment of full citizenship (Marshall and Bottomore 1992) (see chapter 8). The welfare state consensus had meant that despite all differences in welfare regimes (Esping-Andersen 1990, Leibfried 1992) the state affirmed a role in the creation of social solidarity not only as a means of ensuring greater equality but also as a source of its own legitimacy through winning the loyalty of its citizens. Social citizenship completes the social contract on which the nation-states are founded to bring the relationship between state and citizen into the domain of everyday "private" concerns over the maintenance of well-being and a decent standard of living and makes therefore citizenship a tangible element of contact and interaction between the public and the private sphere (Flora 1986). The gradual withdrawal of the state from these arrangements and the trend towards the privatisation of welfare provisions and hence of social risks means in essence that private contracts come to replace social contracts and that the principle on which solidarity is grounded generally becomes uncertain and unreliable in these social relations. Existing webs of solidarity are being fragmented beyond the limits that were so far regarded as politically acceptable for maintaining a tolerable degree of inequality within a welfare system (Taylor-Gooby 2001). The state changes its role from providing to activating (Lorenz 2002, Dahme and Wohlfahrt 2002, Esping-Andersen 2002, Dahme et al. 2003) and this alters the conditions of solidarity from collectively-ensured to individually-earned. It also turns welfare into a set of obligations primarily to private institutions such as the family, the community or commercial insurance companies (Culpitt 1992).

These uncertainties over the specific boundaries of national solidarity and responsibility and their underlying principles lead right back to the historical roots of the European nation state and the assumptions which guided its development. It will be argued in the following that the fundamental flaws and unresolved contradictions of those assumptions, which gave rise to an ideology of nationalism infused with racism, are now contributing to the fragmentation of solidarity. Central to the instability of the nation state and hence to the weakness of the welfare state is this construct's basic inability to accommodate cultural, ethnic and ultimately also physiological diversity within a framework of social equality and justice.

A parallel ambiguity also besets the process of European integration and is building up to an irreconcilable set of contradictions on which particularly the expansion project is likely to founder. The process of European integration has many similarities to that of the development of European nation states that were faced with the task of uniting diverse cultural regions and systems of political allegiance, despite (or because of) the caution against not declaring the European Union a de-facto state (Delanty 1995). The organisation of a system of shared social solidarity among the nations of Europe is a central factor in this process, just as it was in the history of nation states and with a similar time lag that makes European social policies appear an after-thought to economic policies, but an after-thought vital for the legitimation of the project (Leibfried and Pierson 1994). What is at stake (and awaits therefore the active participation of those working at the grass-roots of inter-cultural social issues) is whether the social policies of the European Union will ultimately reproduce the nationalist principles characteristic of national welfare or whether they can draw on the lessons of the national experience and square diversity with equality in a newly grounded and actively practised form of European citizenship (Pieterse 1995).

In these processes two strategies of defining the boundaries of solidarity and identity and hence of citizenship are competing, each with its history in nation-state developments and each presenting its own set of problems (Bauman 1995b). One is the pragmatic attempt of acknowledging that the shape and contents of any collective identity are arbitrary to some extent and a matter of collective choice. The form of mutual solidarity people or societies choose to contract with each other requires no 'substantive' base in their inherent sameness and is in that sense indifferent to and independent of their personal identity. This position accepts that all boundaries are historically contingent and treats identity and obligations as a matter of pragmatism and convenience made secure by contracts. This liberal solution appears to suit a modern mind set that values freedom from traditional bonds. Its limitations are, however, that solidarity negotiated in this 'unconditional' way can always be withdrawn, rules can change, obligations, for instance in the inter-generational contract over pensions, can be cancelled as political alliances shift. The liberal, civic approach seems incapable of accommodating a psychological need for continuity, for substance behind unifying symbols and cultural norms and for collective identities. Its formalism reduces equality to a symbolic claim which not only leaves the question of substantive differences and the experienced inequalities resulting from them unresolved but actively encourages the competitive, free play of interests as constitutive of the formal identity thus established.

The other, 'essentialist' solution to establishing a common identity concentrates on the definition of a 'common core' and searches not for negotiated outer perimeters but for the 'centre' in which a common identity might be anchored or rather 'discovered' as being 'given' (in nature or in lineage) prior to all political negotiation. Concordance with this core of essential characteristics decides then over membership to the whole and for those regarded as 'belonging' solidarity is unconditional. This approach has an appealing simplicity and 'naturalness' about it promising the confirmation of a substantive identity and within it equality. Being of the same nation was indeed associated with the aspiration for an end to class and regional discrimination, and nationalism founded its appeal very much on this prom-ise. However, on closer examination all such given 'essentials' turn out to be fictions, myths constructed for political ends, and belie their appearance of

26

stability and continuity. Furthermore, the solidarity of the 'included' invariably excludes those lacking in those essential characteristics all the more harshly as it affords them no chance of 'entering' and of ever belonging fully.

As shall be shown, in the development of the European nation states both strategies featured, with the latter frequently becoming the dominant influence in the form of nationalism. It is important in the assessment of the social function of education and social services that they played an important part in the realisation of these strategies and are therefore implicated in the transmission of core values concerning the nature of citizenship and the conditions of 'belonging'. The concept of the nation contains itself the fundamental and for many fateful ambivalence between both approaches to a collective identity (Hroch 1985) and brings with it the constant danger of a racist resolution of this tension.

In tracing the history of the European nation states Hobsbawm (1990) distinguishes between a 'revolutionary-democratic' version of the nation which emphasises the form of the contract between free and independent citizens as the basis of their rights, associated with the French Revolution, and a 'nationalist' version which builds cohesion and integration on a 'common cultural heritage' as in the Italian or German tradition. The revolutionary construction of the nation did not and could not rely on a pre-existing notion of cultural homogeneity or ethnic "purity" of a people; at the time of the French Revolution only about 50% of the population spoke French (Balibar 1985) and the 'social contract' negotiated between citizens affirmed explicitly the right 'to be different' (in terms of religion or life style) but emphasised all the more legal equality as the basis of national unity. What united the new French nation was not so much a common past but a common task, the ending of traditional privileges. Nevertheless, cultural heterogeneity soon became a problem for the French revolutionaries as it threatened stability, and citizenship was in fact far more than a pure formality: it soon became conditional on the knowledge of the French language and thereby on being able to participate in the 'official French culture', a criterion of 'cultural and civic collectivism' (Greenfeld 1992) which still has enormous integrative power in France to this day (Brubaker 1990).

In the fundamental re-ordering of the political map of continental Europe which followed the Napoleonic wars a curious mixture of ideological-mythical and rational-economic criteria gained prominence to determine the territorial outlines of all those new political entities which became the nations of Belgium, Denmark, Greece, the Netherlands, Norway, Portugal, Sweden, Spain and later Ireland which had not existed before, at least not in that form. Nation states were by no means products of mere cultural aspirations but had to be big enough to be economically viable, according to the famous pragmatics of Mazzini (Hobsbawm 1990: 31), so that not every wish for national independence, formed by nationalist and romantic movements in the wake of the anti-Napoleonic resistance, came to be satisfied. However, all those national identities that came to be seen as the basis of nation states (but were in fact products of the establishment of political sovereignty) were informed by two overriding principles: the difference to a neighbouring culture (Swedish/Norwegian, Spanish/Portuguese, Danish/German, French/ Dutch etc.) and the claim for the 'antiquity' of one's own culture (Hroch 1993).

In the course of the nineteenth century European societies became increasingly nationalised (Balibar 1991). 'Nationalism played the role of the hinge fastening together state and society' (Bauman 1992: 683). The 'nationalist' version of the nation state, choosing as its unifying principle a common cultural and increasingly also genetic essence and a common past, established itself as the dominant model in Europe exemplified by the national projects of the unification of the states of Italy and of Germany. In both those countries the internal amalgamation of diverse kingdoms, each with their very different histories, traditions and language-versions into one nation state required considerable intellectual and educational efforts so that Massimo d'Azeglio, one of the chief ideological architects of a united Italy, could say at the opening of the first Italian parliament, 'We have made Italy, now we have to make Italians' (Hobsbawm 1990:44), and similar 'formative efforts' applied in all new nation states. The Austro-Hungarian monarchy and the Russian empire were perhaps the only big continental European entities which managed to resist, in the case of Austria till the end of the First World War, in that of Russia one could say until the 1990s, the emerging identification of nation and state. Yet in those countries national independence movements, inspired by romantic intellectual campaigns searching for 'cultural roots' and spurred by new political elites sensing opportunities for power, could eventually not be contained sufficiently by those multi-cultural and multi-ethnic colossuses on account of their despotic structure that allowed no space for the democratic negotiation of cultural diversity within a framework of equal rights.

Contrary to the impression nurtured by the new nation states that their modern political form (and the associated territorial claim) was the manifestation of a historical destiny, a realisation of ancient dreams just waiting for their moment in history, the European nation state is not the product of cultural or ethnic unity and purity. Instead 'it is the state that makes the nation and not the nation the state' as the Polish 'liberator' Jozef Pilsudski pointedly remarked (quoted in Horsman and Marshall 1994: xviii). For instance, many national languages, from modern Greek and Italian to Czech, Flemish and Romanian were either 're-worked' from prevailing vernacular but non-standardised versions or refined and elevated from the status of dialects to that of official languages by the efforts of academics and philologists. In other words, the nation and all the mechanisms for its constitution and maintenance, are thoroughly modern phenomena that merely couch their modern traits in 'traditional' forms and symbols. This spells a fundamental ambiguity that time and again impedes the development of political processes at the public and the civil society level capable of responding to the challenges of the integration of diverse cultural traditions and identities in an overt and democratically accountable manner.

Towards the end of the nineteenth century nationalism became the predominant means of consolidating and securing the new political entities of the European nation states whose boundaries were notoriously difficult to justify 'on historical grounds'. The crucial ally in this national project, and indeed in the opinion of some historians (e.g. Hobsbawm 1990, Balibar 1991) its driving force, was industrial capitalism which derived its conquering power from the concept of 'national economies' competing with each other (Wallerstein 1991). Even in countries like Great Britain where liberalism was the prevailing ideology the state had an essential role in giving private enterprise the required support and protection in vital areas like education and, more gradually and reluctantly, social services. But both came to be recognised as vital instruments of social control that could be applied to secure the good behaviour and the 'loyalty of the masses' and thereby their commitment to the national cause, which seemed threatened above all by the inherent internationalism of the labour movement. This strategy left business free to transcend the boundaries of traditions and of territories where it suited its capitalist interests in this early manifestation of capitalism's globalising tendencies and its accompanying divisive effects.

As nationalism began to dominate the political agenda of the nation state the 'emancipatory component' of the idea which had inspired and continued to inspire many national liberation movements, the fight against 'the arbitrary rule of princes and small aristocratic elites' (Mommsen 1990: 215), gave way to new forms of power being exercised through the hegemony of a 'national culture'. National culture became not just an ideological symbol of external superiority over 'rival cultures' but also an instrument of internal domination over a country's own ethnic and cultural minorities (Mommsen, ibid.). The means of legitimating and of bolstering this assumed superiority soon reached beyond cultural arguments and the creation of a common language to incorporate new means of affinity and exclusion. It is in this context that in order to argue for the uniformity of a nation the 'second-degree fiction' of a common race (Balibar 1991: 99) became activated. By grounding the 'togetherness' of a nation not primarily in solidarity (which requires an act of will by the individuals) but in 'blood and soil', in something that we are born into, it removes belonging from the sphere of choice (Bauman 1992). Collective identity becomes destiny, secured with references to the findings of modern science. Darwinism and the first scientific speculations of genetics were utilised to assemble a pervasive ideology of racism which conveniently filled the gaps left by scientific evidence with ideology disguised as science. Where the superiority of the white race over black races cannot be based on biological evidence the cultural argument takes over, the claim of the greatness of one's own 'civilization' proving itself through its rise to imperialist world domination. Indeed racism of this kind, tried and tested within the colonial context, served the power elites within Europe itself to class themselves as superior over those, for instance, of the Jewish, the Gypsy or the Irish people, and indeed over the sub-stratum of a 'residuum' of society defined by their 'deviant' behaviour. The 'substance' which was presumed to constitute a European nation changes from political to cultural and eventually to ethnic and racist criteria (Miles 1989), producing a particularly lethal bonding of nation and race in the case of German nationalism and Nazism.

Within this ideological framework the European nation state depended for its stability on the creation of homogeneity, and in the production of this cultural conformity it employed the ideological assistance of nationalism. The dynamics of this nationalism expanded the nation state project globally. Its aggressive energies spilled over the edges of Europe to reach for the furthest corners of the world in the form of colonialism. The political agenda of colonialism exceeded the 'economic necessity' generated by the expansive tendencies of capitalism in its ideological pursuit of the idea of wanting to civilize the world (Fryer 1984). Colonial rule became a paradigm for new forms of internal social control which allowed the exercise of power to be advertised as being 'in the best interest of the ruled'. Cultural hegemony on a world stage further legitimated the hegemony of the dominant culture 'back home', whether it manifested itself through the education system, the civil service or indeed the testing and perfecting of methods of community development which came to be one of the tools of social work. European culture was 'destined' to rule the world, such is the logic of 'progress' to which it conformed.

Within the logic of progress and superiority racism found its particular niche in modern European national, cultural and economic politics and the aggressive forms of nationalism provided it with rich nurture. For the belief in progress was self-limiting where the incorporation of 'natives' and their traditions into Western belief systems either did not work (because of their 'stubborn resistance') or could turn into a threat to White superiority (on account of their 'cleverness in learning'). Colonial rule came to 'ring-fence' certain aspects of other cultures which it sought to control and to legitimate these with racist arguments where this helped to maintain clear boundaries. It set up race-separated political and administrative structures (for instance with 'tribal chiefs' in Africa) thus paving the way for elaborate systems of apartheid (Miles 1989). In this way colonialism structured the encounter with the 'dark continent' and 'primitive societies' to create the Black Person as the archetypical 'other' precisely in order to underline a fundamental, essentialised distance between superior and inferior populations generally. In the process it also united the disparate characteristics of 'whiteness' into a coherent whole characterised by its intrinsic, unassailable superiority (Said 1994). Racism served to eliminate the cultural, subjective and ultimately arbitrary basis of the construction of difference and superiority and to quell any lingering doubts and uncertainties with 'facts' backed by science. It became a means of avoiding discourse and debate and therefore a way of continuing (and thereby totally subverting and corrupting) the educational project of cultural unification of the nation state with other means, with the means of oppression. Henceforth education and socialisation methods centred on taken-for-granted notions of 'the national' could draw on racist arguments. Once tried and tested in the colonies, this educational formula came to dominate also internal social and educational policies.

The nascent nation states where potentially as heterogeneous as the colonies and as much in need of integration and stability in view of the accentuated social divisions created by industrialisation. They depended on instruments of stabilisation of which the conceding of limited political citizenship rights was one branch, the gradual expansion of social and educational measures another to secure the loyalty of its citizens. Gellner goes as far as to postulate that these universal nationwide cultures which became the hallmarks of nations were an essential requirement of industrialisation itself. 'A modern industrial state can only function with a mobile, literate, culturally standardized, inter-changeable population' (Gellner 1983:46).

This standardization exercise was not confined to the establishment of a compulsory education system, although in most industrialising countries this took precedent. The whole project of creating a national heritage of standardised behaviour as the foundation of a national culture became the criterion by which it could be decided who was to belong properly to the nation, not just in relation to foreigners. Parallel with the school system the social organisation of both the public and the private sphere drew on patriotism for their inspiration and legitimation: sports became the means by which not only the physical health of the (male) nation could be improved in functional readiness for war, it became a forum for the dissemination of national fervour, a means of incorporating especially the young population which was always regarded as a potential source of instability and disaffection. As 'Vater Jahn', the chief ideologue of German national sports during the nineteenth century, expressed it: 'The rights of citizens are dependent upon the activity of such citizens. That citizen loses his rights who deserts his flag, besmirches his Fatherland in foreign countries, or loses his reason' (quoted in Greenfeld 1992: 369f).

31

At the civil society level philanthropy and countless charitable organisations unfolded an unprecedented 'crusade' against destitution in what amounted to a national effort at rescuing people from the margins of society, bringing those aboard who had been left stranded despite the rising tide of national progress (Fraser 1973, Wendt 1985). The bourgeois side of the women's movement in the nineteenth century derived much of its energies from patriotism. Philanthropy helped to express women's desire to have a publicly acclaimed part to play in the affairs of the nation (Rowbotham 1977), equivalent to the part men were called upon to play through military service (which itself formed an essential plank of the nation-forming exercise).

The incorporation of the masses into the nation state was by no means unconditional. The process operated at the social level with the blunt and often brutal instrument of distinguishing the 'deserving' from the 'undeserving', used as a moral category of old to set limits to solidarity and moral obligations, but now revived in 'modern' form as a curious mixture of functional and ethical criteria. A binary system, allowing only for unitary identities that can be clearly and scientifically distinguished, began to be practised. The moral institutions of the state, the schools, workhouses and prisons, were themselves 'setting examples' of where the line between acceptable and unacceptable behaviour was to be drawn. That boundary became questionable when it permitted the 'wrong kind of people' to be punished or excluded or indeed when 'the wrong kind of people' came to enjoy the protection of society. The rescue efforts of all the blossoming welfare societies of the Victorian age, in Britain and in the parts of Europe following Britain's industrial lead, had as much a practical as a symbolic significance for the consolidation of the nation state (Jones and Novak 2000). They showed that the boundaries of the nation state could run through every community and every family in the sense that membership of society and citizenship depended on the willingness to be conforming and worthy members of that entity. Welfare and education services ultimately draw the boundaries of solidarity under modern conditions in industrial societies where traditional community and family bonds and allegiances have become suspended in a massive upheaval of social and geographic mobility. The nation constitutes its identity through these educational efforts, through not leaving the socialisation of its young to chance, through setting up and enforcing internal boundaries of acceptable behaviour and by standardising those criteria. 'Let us simply say that schooling is the principal institution which produces ethnicity as linguistic community' (Balibar 1992: 98).

By this device workers in these emerging educational and social services become hitched to the national bandwagon whether they are employed in the public or in the private/voluntary sphere. What obscured the realisation of their place within a national agenda for most of them, to this day, is that they sought to deliver their service precisely not from an overtly political position but from a perspective of professional autonomy and 'neutrality'. Professionalisation was indeed vital to the legitimation of their functions since the state, as a modern state, was keen to advertise its 'attractiveness' and hence its conditions of solidarity largely not through coercion and arbitrary authority but through the principle of rationality. Participation in the national project, choosing to 'behave properly' were ultimately to be seen as functions of reason and those failing to exercise those rational choices where either impaired in their mental functions (in which case they needed treatment) or lacking in insight (in which case they needed education). Rationality therefore had to inform the methods and principles applied by the professionals operating the educational and therapeutic services in a very fundamental way, and only the use of methods, developed in a process of systematic and scientific reflection could lend their action legitimacy.

For the social professions the reliance on rational principles of intervention was an ambiguous tool. On the one hand it helped to overcome the vestiges of moralism which had marred the pioneer phase of social services where volunteers set out in a patronising way to teach the poor how to manage their affairs better. The individualism implicit in this form of instrumental rationalism, the method of diagnosing each case according to its particular circumstances, also acted as a restraint against the whole-sale stereotyping and condemning of categories of 'problem populations' as inferior. But on the other hand it operated with principles and values of 'normality' derived largely from positivist notions of mental health and social adjustment which allowed for little engagement in a cultural discourse on the subjective meanings of 'differences'. Even Marxist models of revolutionary social intervention, of which there were sporadic 'experiments' in youth work and residential care in many parts of Europe early in the 20th century (Lorenz 1994: 58), were constructed around a fixed model of a desired state of society which seemed oblivious to perspectives of gender and ethnicity.

Social services developed quite rapidly in all countries of Europe in the 1920s and 1930s with increasing direct support by the state. As social service staff came more directly under state control the position of value neutrality demonstrated its blindness to political misuse most catastrophically in Hitler Germany. That regime had elevated nationalism to the status of a central political device not just of its foreign but also of its social policy programme. Most Western European countries (and the USA) had sympathised with the technical and rational solutions to social problems suggested by the fledgling science of genetics as promoted by 'Eugenic Societies' which advocated programmes of sterilisation in the case of a broad spectrum of medical conditions considered hereditary (Proctor 1988). Despite extremely tenuous scientific evidence a sweeping range of mental illnesses and disabilities, including alcoholism and epilepsy, were assumed to have a genetic basis and the case was made that if science could not cure these diseases in the present generation it could at least prevent them from burdening future generations. Nazism seized avidly on those ideas and as soon as it came to power in 1933 enacted as one of its first pieces of legislation a law permitting and promoting the involuntary sterilisation of people with conditions deemed hereditary, 'where necessary' on an involuntary basis (Klee 1985).

The urgency and speed with which this law was passed underlines its central ideological function within fascist social policy which aims at the complete segregation of those worthy to belong to the nationalist state and the unworthy rest (Lorenz 1994: 64f). Nazism did not stop at symbolic, partial and temporary physical segregation; disguising its ideology as science it swept aside the 'sentimentality of half-measures' constrained by 'moral scruples' and proceeded to constantly and consistently select and segregate in all its policies with the sterilisation, with the incarceration in concentration camps and with the extermination of 'unworthy life' as its infamous 'final solution'. The racism of Nazi social policies against 'weak members of society' runs parallel to and becomes at times indistinguishable from the racism perpetrated against the Jewish, Roma and Sinti and other minority populations. The 'ethnic cleansing' culminating in the holocaust engulfed not only the millions of people classed as racially inferior but additional thousands of children, women and men diagnosed as 'inferior forms of life' on account of their disabilities, their homosexuality or perhaps their social conditions as vagrants or delinquents (Aly et al. 1985). This was not an evil afterthought of a regime losing its sanity in the desperation of a war it had unleashed; it was the deliberate, calculated and well prepared implementation of an overall policy design with nationalism as its pinnacle.

This machinery of segregation and extermination was operated not only by people who would commit the final atrocities of killing but also by those 'experts' who would assist in 'drawing the line' between the 'deserving' and the 'unworthy' by virtue of their diagnostic skills. In this insidious way a whole range of professionals became implicated in the system: doctors, social workers, health visitors, care staff, teachers and many others were providing evidence for the courts so that in a charade of legality these could issue orders, for instance denying marriage certificates to people 'posing a threat to the health of the nation', or for compulsory sterilisation or for admission to institutions. The system relied on all welfare personnel filing case reports in which they listed the family histories of epilepsy or alcoholism, assessed the chances of rehabilitation of offenders or of children with learning difficulties. Sticking to their professional task with the air of value neutrality and scientific detachment (especially after the 'non-conforming', 'politically active' workers had been sacked or imprisoned) they did not feel responsible for the consequences of their assessments and may indeed not have become conscious of the full implications their work had in 'the national context' (Otto and Sünker 1989, Kappeler 2000). This diagnostic service was not only provided by statutory services; the main voluntary welfare organisations of Germany, with the exception of the socialist one, continued to operate under Nazism, but on condition that they 'support the national cause'. While some individuals and some organisations offered resistance at enormous personal risk, all institutions of German civil society, including the churches and their welfare services, de facto supported national policies, de-sensitised by the fact that, seen from a functional perspective, this system appeared merely to continue and perfect the incorporation of welfare into the national interest which had been the intention of the nation state for some time before (Schnurr 1997).

After the defeat of Fascism the programmes for 'democratic re-construction' instigated by the United Nations, the United States and Britain targeted very explicitly the welfare services and their personnel for re-training in 'democratic approaches. But they ignored the element of 'scientific value neutrality' as a fatal chain of Nazi dis-welfare. Values were confined to appeals to self-determination in case work which became the dominant social work paradigm, and in group work where 'democratic', self-directed styles replaced hierarchical notions of group leadership (for details see Lorenz 1994:76). But these efforts were not accompanied by a fundamental critique of positivism and its function in diagnostic categorisation. It was not recognised that the evil of a fascist approach to welfare had not emanated primarily from its collectivism and from the imposition of ideologically determined forms of practice (which social workers usually knew how to get round) but rather from the disjuncture of the political and the professional discourse that prevented the 'ordinary welfare workers' from fully facing up to the consequences of their actions. The individualist consensus of a 'social pathology' discourse (Mills 1943) which prevailed in the social sciences of the 1950s and 60s left social and youth workers inadequately equipped to launch a radical critique of welfare agendas which continued to be ideologically infused with nationalist assumptions.

This became evident above all in the area of education and youth and community work in European countries confronted once more with cultural diversity in a manner reminiscent of the nation-founding period. The massive population displacement of the war combined with labour shortages had made many countries of Europe recipients of migration and thereby locations of a new cultural and ethnic diversity. Whereas in earlier periods emigration was often treated as a kind of cleansing process to reduce diversity, by sending convicts to penal colonies and by forcing those to leave the country who potentially constituted 'social problems', diversity now appeared on Europe's own doorstep, forcing the nation state to confront the issue of cultural diversity which it had sought to displace (Joppke 1999) (see chapter 4). The welfare consensus after the Second World War had been built on the myth that new social policies had eliminated structural poverty so that those individuals and families still not able to cope were cast in the light of people who had 'problems of adjustment', who required treatment or education in order to be able to fully participate in society. And in analogy of the treatment of those who came to the attention of educational and welfare services those members of recently arrived migrant groups (e.g. from the British New Commonwealth, from former French colonies or from Mediterranean countries as *'Gastarbeiter'* in Germany) were also regarded as in need of help with their ability to adjust. Indeed, 'integration' and 'assimilation' became the initial chief objectives of 'remedial responses' in all European countries (Miles 1993). Spurred often by the wishes of immigrant families themselves who wanted their children to adopt the language of the host country as quickly as possible these early strategies aimed at 'levelling differences' by 'bringing newcomers up to standards'. In all these social practices the normality of the national standards remained unquestioned or became affirmed even more strongly.

The treatment of ethnic minorities has paradigmatic significance for the inability of social work at professional and methodological level to take critical position towards its incorporation into national agendas across the whole spectrum of social work fields. Integration and assimilation as methods of dealing with cultural diversity were a first-line pedagogical response in virtually all European countries but did not fulfil their declared objectives of establishing 'racial harmony' (Mullard 1982). Rather, they contributed to the interest ethnic minority groups took in affirming their own separate identities, as was later also the case with certain user groups like people with special needs. A second phase of responses which can be classed as the 'multi-cultural approaches' recognised this autonomy and the value of plurality; many of these initiatives went as far as celebrating cultural diversity and suggesting that many of the 'foreign' cultures contained an exotic promise or a truth lost to the 'indigenous' culture and that they therefore represented a source of renewal. This phase would correspond to a degree of 'cultural and gender sensitivity' that influenced social work methods discourses in the 1980s. These responses failed to deal with the actual process that define cultural, ethnic and social boundaries, the power acted out in the conflicts not so much over particular cultural contents but over their hierarchical ranking (Todd 1991). In other words, a critical social policy dimension was given insufficient consideration in the development of academic and professional discourses in response to the growing awareness of cultural diversity, even though the effects of the new practice quite clearly underlined the necessity to consider both spheres in conjunction, as emphasised in the first chapter.

It was left to social and civil rights movements to place the issues of identity and of the right to be different on the political agenda in the last three decades of the twentieth century in an interesting historical parallel to the role such movements played in the latter parts of the nineteenth century. With social movements such as the peace movement, the women's liberation movement and the ecology movement, the importance of 'civil society' as the site of political action became evident once more. Their significance for the political process was first of all that all those movements cut right across the concerns of national politics to forge very strong and immediate international allegiances, and secondly that they had their issues defined by the participants in the political process themselves. Before any experts could tell a group of women or a group of black young people 'what was good for them' they sought to define their own agenda for change and in this process came to identify and challenge the structures of discrimination which had kept them deliberately out of the political process.

The methodological implications for youth and social work of this radically changed agenda are far-reaching, particularly in the context of globalisation which simultaneously impacted on the role of the nation state and combined with fundamental changes in national welfare state policies. It is important to highlight in this historical overview that the significance of this change towards a rights discourse and the key to overcoming the serious limitations of previous programmes lies not in finding a new social work method but in the closer and more consistent analysis of the political context in which education, social work and the struggle against racism need to be related to each other (Macey 1995). In other words, only by re-examining their relationship with the national agendas can youth, welfare and educational workers start their search for appropriate methods.

The national agenda, in the context of the contradictory trends outlined at the start of this chapter, is now at the crossroads. On the one hand its influence and power is being weakened by new forms of economic, cultural and political internationalism. European unification, international treaties and conventions and an international human rights awareness which begins to set common standards across nation states, all necessitate changes in the way welfare is being conceptualised and delivered. Many improvements in the position of oppressed groups in European countries came about as a direct result of European or international standards being brought to bear on national legislation through treaties or rulings of international courts in what has been described as the 'cosmopolitan project' (Held 2002). On the other hand new forms of exclusion are becoming apparent at national and international level. The treatment of migrants and asylum seekers by the EU itself has become much more selective and restrictive as 'fortress Europe' erects perimeter controls around its territory in a sinister symmetry to the functions of the former Iron Curtain (Miles 1993). Additionally, social citizenship is becoming ever more restricted and conditional on welfare recipients making an active effort of showing themselves 'worthy of support'. These types of consolidation and protection policies mirror ominously the strategies of exclusion and of racism by which the nation states shaped themselves. 'Unification for Europe', in the words of Lyotard (1993: 159) may yet also come to mean 'unification of its hatreds'.

And while a 'European nationalism' being established at the level of the European Union itself is perhaps too remote a possibility, the power of 'national nationalism' has become again a pronounced item on the political agenda, and not just in the programmes of explicit right wing and neo-fascist parties which saw a frightening resurgence in Europe. In response to the insecurities caused for personal and collective identities by globalisation, nationalism advertises itself as a safe solution which takes recourse to sensible, popular certainties within the construct of a binary world-view of identities: them/us, bad/good, enemy/friend. National sentiments are once more presented as 'natural feelings', not necessarily genetically determined but 'available' as the guarantee of a sense of belonging. National belonging as a sentiment, centred always on a set of taken-for-granted contents, appears to offer stability and continuity where identities are threatened with fragmentation and discontinuity.

Seen in this historical context the crisis of national identity in Europe is not a product of migration and 'imposed', growing diversity. It is a crisis of collective solidarity stemming from the inherent instability of the nationalist construction of the nation state which, however, manifests itself in the responses to migration particularly forcefully. Signs of this crisis of solidarity are as much the fragmentation of the welfare consensus when certain groups of citizens like the young unemployed, pensioners or homeless people can no longer rely automatically on a minimum level of support guaranteed by the state, as in the numerous political conflicts where regions within nation states and indeed small communities make claims for cultural and often also political autonomy (Wieviorka 1994a: 180). These conflicts became exacerbated by the ending of the Cold War which re-focused political concerns from an East–West to a national agenda and thereby on all the ambiguities of the nation state solidarity. In the attempts at rescuing the nationalist agenda, migration and the 'threat of cultural alienation' become political instruments that divert attention away from the need of negotiating diversity which had always existed in every nation state, away from the need to extend the boundaries of solidarity beyond the borders of the nation state and beyond assumed, imagined 'natural communities' (Anderson 1983). Racism and xenophobia become negative substitutes for the ability to face up to changing, developing and multiple collective identities.

This also highlights the necessity of the anti-racist and black identity discourse to go beyond a taken for granted notion of 'Blackness' which has itself at times led to oppressive forms of homogenisation (Gilroy 1992). While the strategy of turning the label 'black' from a racist ascription into an emancipatory self-referent may have been an important step in the struggle of oppressed people to re-claim the right to self-definition, it brings with it the danger of 'essentialising' Blackness within a dichotomised agenda still dictated by existing power interests. In this regard international dialogue within the anti-racist debate has been most fruitful in recent years in promoting a 'de-centring and de-essentialisation of "race" and "ethnicity"' (Rattansi 1994: 58).

This critique is not to deny minority groups the right to define their own identities and to have those identities more visibly represented in schools, services, community centres, political parties. But in all those 'representations' the danger of culture becoming an instrument of exclusion and oppression needs to be monitored against the historical background of Europe's experience with nationalism in constant affinity to racism. In the search for non-exclusive, non-repressive forms of representation and identification it may help to return to the as yet under-utilised emancipatory version of the idea of the republican nation and its unrealised potential. This version of the nation implies sets of citizenship rights which constitute mutual obligations precisely on the basis of differences. The need for negotiation, for putting into practice the human right to equality of all members of a community, which is ultimately a political and not a biological postulate, arises only once diversity has been fully recognised, and the ensuing political and legal arrangements, once they secure such equality, are in turn the basis on which cultural, ideological and indeed biological differences can be recognised and evaluated and given a negotiated social significance.

In recognition of the lessons from the history of the European nation state and the crucial crossroads which its development seems to have reached it becomes necessary to strengthen the critical political function of social work and social pedagogy. The development of anti-racist approaches is not an issue for specialists in preparation of social work with minority groups. Anti-racism has come to signify the resistance all youth and social work has to offer to the pressure of becoming subsumed, unwittingly or deliberately, under a nationalist political agenda (Dominelli 2006). But the anti-racist agenda goes well beyond the strengthening of this resistance and searches for the positive contents of collective, inter-cultural, non exclusive identities and their realisation within negotiated rights of citizenship. The conditions for social citizenship will therefore be explored in the next chapter as a precondition for a form of social work practice that faces up to the challenges of the transformation of European societies.

3. Welfare regimes and the practice of social citizenship

The first European Directive on the mutual recognition of higher vocational qualifications (89/48/ EEC) was a vehicle for the harmonisation of social work qualifications. However, as the experience of the First EU Thematic Network for the Social Professions (ECSPRESS) showed, comparisons and exchanges will always be affected by the profound differences not just in social work titles, but in distinct social policy reference points and traditions which European unification will leave untouched (Lorenz and Seibel 1999). This chapter elaborates further on the historical analysis of the development of professional social work in relation to the nation state project given in the previous chapter and takes a closer look at the impact of specific social policy models on the practice of social work.

A superficial glance at social work services in Europe up to the 1980s showed a clear polarisation between countries where they were mainly run by the state (e.g. Denmark, Finland, Ireland, Norway, Sweden, UK) and countries where they were predominantly non-governmental (e.g. Germany or the Netherlands), with the rest of the countries showing a mix of arrangements. Since then significant shifts have taken place (see chapter 9) but in general social work everywhere is still represented in both sectors. However, the significance of the organisational patterns for practice can only be determined from an analysis of the social policy traditions behind the arrangements. Recent developments in social policy which point towards services generally being 'contracted out' or 'privatised' seem to indicate a convergence, but in reality fundamental differences remain. One of the basic characteristics of social work is that it is always concerned with mediating the complex relationship between public and private responsibilities and that it carries both a public and a private mandate, no matter whether its statutory responsibilities are located more on the public or on the private side. It is therefore not surprising to find that social work activities are regulated to highly varying degrees by national law, with some countries like Germany defining explicitly and extensively the duties and functions of social workers in law, while others still do not even mention the profession in law. In addition, different policy frameworks induce social workers to apply the law in very different ways, as is best exemplified by comparisons in child care and protection practices in Europe. In some countries social workers have a narrow margin of professional discretion and have to bring first indications and suspicions of child abuse before a court prior to taking further action, whilst others see the role of social workers in avoiding the involvement of legal procedures in all but the most severe cases (Hetherington et al. 1997, Hetherington 1998).

One further indicator of fundamental differences between social work functions relates to welfare benefits. For British social workers, as for their colleagues in the Republic of Ireland, the handling of welfare payments is not regarded as part of their professional duties (Becker 1987) and the profession always carefully avoided taking on official responsibilities in this regard. It is as if the danger of becoming closely associated with the control functions of the state through the administration of welfare benefits was so threatening for the autonomy of the profession there that it had to be avoided totally. There is no parallel for this absolute separation in other European countries, although this indicator has to be taken again in a wider social policy context. This means that it is imperative to examine to what extent the practice of social work in different European countries reflects the nature of the relationship between citizens and the state, or in other words the extent to which social work is a manifestation of social citizenship and hence needs to be practised as applied social policy.

It is of relevance to social work practice, for instance, that the concept of 'the state' in Britain is very little developed by comparison with continental Europe. As Dyson observes,

> 'The composite character of the English idea of parliamentary sovereignty, an idea that comprises King, Lords and Commons and represented an appeasement or settlement between these traditional powers, contrasts with the integrated 'public power' of continental Europe, a rationalist conception which was the product of the attempt to achieve peace by offering an explicit defence of public authority in abstract and impersonal terms' (Dyson 1980: 19).

This means that the powers of the state in the continental concept are on the one hand more visible and manifest, on the other hand they are more explicitly prescribed and, at least in principle, subjected to the continuous scrutiny by 'the citizen'. The state, distant though its central seat of power might be in highly centralised nations such as France, is regarded by the citizens of those countries as an everyday reality with whose structures they interact visibly and almost continuously. It controls them, haunts them at times with the spectre of a police state, but it does so with the legitimation that it is the citizens who control the state ultimately. This sentiment and the basic features of these continental European relationships, which usually are devolved in federal structures or regional units, are enshrined in the constitution of these countries (or equivalent fundamental laws such as the German Basic Law, *Grundgesetz*). Britain by contrast has no written constitution and its citizens, up to recently, resisted having to carry identity cards.

Continental notions of the state, far from being homogeneous however, are themselves broadly differentiated between the Roman-catholic tradition of deriving authority from divine or natural law which needs to pay less attention to securing the allegiance and legitimation by the general population, and the protestant tradition which holds those in authority to have a duty for the general well-being of the ruled and for the maintenance of a 'neutral' public order.

The state tradition in France for instance is characterised by a profound contrast between a strong, rationally constructed central authority, dating back to the late 16th century and the Edict of Nantes when the state became accepted as the carrier of 'nationhood', and equally strong collective (emotional) societal movements which challenge this authority periodically (Jouhy 1984). Consequently 'conceptions of nationhood and citizenship bear the stamp of their revolutionary origin. The nation, in this tradition, has been conceived mainly in relation to the institutional and territorial frame of the state: political unity, not shared culture has been understood to be its basis' (Brubaker 1989). The decentralisation of services in France in the wake of the unrest of 1968 was a further manifestation of this basic political tension and its 'settlement', of which social services are 'carriers'.

The birth of many continental European nation states is associated with the growth of capitalist industrialisation which had the effect of 'commodifying' people through the division of labour. 'In pre-capitalist societies, few workers were properly commodities in the sense that their survival was contingent upon the sale of their labor power... Stripping society of the institutional layers that guaranteed social reproduction outside the labor contract meant that people were commodified' (Esping-Andersen 1990: 21). The nation state represents the attempt to counteract or at least compensate for this commodification. Loyalty to the state is based on principles different from those operating in the market, and 'social citizenship', the granting of welfare and security irrespective of the person's position in the market, came to be recognised as a most useful ingredient in building this national solidarity and in legitimating the state's power.

'Social integration spread from the sphere of sentiment and patriotism into that of material enjoyment. The components of a civilised and cultured life, formerly the monopoly of the few, were brought progressively within reach of the many, who were encouraged thereby to stretch out their hands towards those that still eluded their grasp. The diminution of inequality strengthened the demand for its abolition, at least with regard to the essentials of social welfare. These aspirations have in part been met by incorporating social rights in the status of citizenship and thus creating a universal right to real income which is not proportionate to the market value of the claimant' (T.H.Marshall in Marschall and Bottomore 1992: 28).

But just as political citizenship, for instance through the extension of the franchise, was being gradually realised albeit in a manner that reproduced inequalities of gender and property, social citizenship was extended, selectively and cautiously but according to distinct patterns which were to set the scene for the various types of welfare state. Political citizenship, in other words, necessitated social citizenship sooner or later, but the realisation of social citizenship was not a matter of policies alone. Each system depended for its legitimacy on the 'fine-tuning' of those policy arrangements, which means on the individualisation of the conditions through which social citizenship can be established and justified. From the very beginning social workers or their pre-professional ancestors came to be placed on the frontline of those micro-processes that decided on inclusion or exclusion from social citizenship and simultaneously on the commodification or de-commodification of people's needs within the wider social policy parameters which social workers therefore came to represent to their clients. In all nascent welfare systems case by case assessments had to be made as to whether and on what conditions poverty, handicap and behavioural deficits could be overcome by 'reintegrating' the person affected into the labour market, by granting them public or private subventions or indeed by excluding them by leaving them to their own devices and to the impersonal harshness of institutions (workhouses, asylums, prisons), which invariably imply a suspension of full citizenship. For instance in Britain the tightening of the Poor Law in 1834 ruled out 'outdoor relief' and 'treated the claims of the poor, not as an integral part of the rights of the citizen, but as an alternative to them' (Marshall 1992: 15).

But the pedagogical effects of the work house deterrent never worked automatically and never produced the required cost savings. 'Outdoor relief' sooner or later became a necessity, mostly by default and against the declared intentions of the state to limit public assistance to workhouse measures. But in countries like Germany a more proactive role of the (initially the local) state was accepted, thereby signalling a different conception of the state-citizen relationship from the liberal ethos prevailing in Britain. Here early models of systematic poor relief committed public funds more readily to such 'outdoor relief', which meant in turn that 'case assessors', as the forerunners of social workers, were given an 'official' role on behalf of the local government authorities (and later by the state) right from the beginning instead of them doing their work on behalf of a voluntary, non-governmental relief agency such as the Charity Organisation Society.

An early manifestation of the individualised application of public welfare obligations was the 'Elberfeld System' of providing personalised financial assistance to the poor on which public welfare in Germany came to be modelled. In Elberfeld, a rapidly industrialising town on the river Wupper in Germany, the middle class citizens devised in 1853 a coordinated, efficient approach to alms distribution. The system divided the town into 252 districts or quarters and allocated a voluntary supervisor to each who had a 'caseload' of up to four families. Applications for support would be dealt with by these volunteers who had a duty to assess the individual circumstances in great detail and according to guidelines laid down by the town administration (Wendt 1985).

The significance of this systematised practice of poor relief for the future development of German social work derives from the fact that these proto-case-workers were not actually volunteers, free agents of private charities, but had a public mandate. In those days all citizens entitled to vote also had to make themselves available to the town council for administrative duties of which the supervision of paupers was but one type of commitment (regulations quoted in Sachße und Tennstedt 1998: 218). In Strasbourg in 1905 the Elberfeld system of combined care and public surveillance was further developed and adjusted to the conditions of rapid urbanisation by creating bigger districts, teams of volunteers and staffing the central administrative and decision making office with paid, and increasingly also trained employees. A format became hereby established which combined and coordinated voluntary and statutory activities (Sachße und Tennstedt 1998).

German conservatism was hence prepared to grant the state a much more comprehensive role in relation to the daily lives of the citizens. In contrast to the laissez-faire principles of liberalism the 'social question' became an explicit challenge for the state after the bourgeois revolution of 1848 through which it could manifest its historical presence (Geisen 2001). In his speech to a congress in 1872 which led to the founding of the 'Association for Social Policy', Gustav Schmoller, a member of the conservative group of national economists known as 'lectern-socialists', declared: 'The state is the most marvellous moral institution for the education of the human race'. As part of his strategy of unifying the until then independent German kingdoms into the German Reich, Bismarck advocated that the state take the initiative 'to call ever increasing portions of our people to participate in the cultural, educational and material wealth [of the nation]' (both quoted in Wendt 1985:181).

Bismarck's pioneering and 'pre-emptive' introduction of social insurance schemes in the 1880s was not a sudden conversion to socialist beliefs (he simultaneously declared the social-democratic party illegal) but the shrewd recognition that his strategy for the construction of a strong German nation required for its legitimation and for the further strengthening of a paternalistic state tradition a carefully targeted package of public welfare commitments (Tampke 1981). Bismarck's ideas were expressed in an official address by Emperor Wilhelm I on 17 November 1881:

'Schon im Februar dieses Jahres haben Wir Unsere Überzeugung ausspre-chen lassen, dass die Heilung der sozialen Schäden nicht ausschliesslich im Wege der Repression sozialdemokratischer Ausschreitungen, sondern gleich-mässig auf dem der positiven Förderung des Wohls der Arbeiter zu suchen

sein werde...' (,As already declared by us in January of this year we are convinced that the cure for social ills cannot be sought solely by means of repressing the excesses of social democracy but simultaneously through the positive fostering of the well-being of workers' (own translation) (quoted in Diehl and Mombert 1984, p. 185).

These political initiatives provided a lasting framework for the structure of German social services which until this day remains based on the close relationship between public and private services, statutory and voluntary work, case orientation and policy concerns. Conceptually this exemplifies the interplay between subsidiarity (see below in this chapter) and social solidarity, with all the ambiguity this entails.

Just how early the differences in social work practice were determined by the nature of national political cultures, even where it was practised outside the state system or where actual social policies took only a rudimentary form, is illustrated by the developments of 19th century Britain which paralleled those in Germany. When the Charity Organisation Society in Britain, influenced directly by the Elberfeld model, instituted its system of 'friendly visitors' and created an archetype for the interplay between the Poor-Law authorities and private charity during the last decades of the 19th century, the responsibilities of the 'visitor' differed in Britain in one fundamental detail from Germany. Octavia Hill, one of the pioneers of 'organised, individualised charity' in Britain, states in 1874:

> 'The important difference between the Elberfeld and the Marylebone systems is that, whereas in Elberfeld the volunteers themselves decide on the parochial relief, our volunteers have no such authority committed to them. It would be a fundamental change of the gravest nature to throw any share of such responsibility on the visitor ... The large discretionary power exercised by Guardians under our English Poor-Law (which contrasts with the very definite scale for outdoor relief in use at Elberfeld) would make it an additional difficulty to place the decisions as to grants in the hands of visitors' (Hill 1883: 73).

Using 'discretion' is therefore not primarily a methodological concern but a consequence of social policies. In the handling of welfare benefits different state traditions, and more specifically different approaches to citizenship manifest themselves, which only subsequently were re-worked as 'methodological' differences in the respective social work discourses at academic and professional level.

The history of social services in the Netherlands represents yet another type of state–society relationship. This nation state was shaped by a series of struggles for independence in which religion on the one hand and bourgeois liberal ideals on the other were important factors. The struggle strengthened the internal solidarity of the various fractions and resulted in finely balanced compromises and relative tolerance between them (Ellemers 1984). Since the late 19th century the state came to be regarded as resting on separate 'pillars',

46

collective yet sectionally divided structures representing civil interest groups (Catholic, Protestant, Jewish, socialist and humanist). The right to have not just schools and hospitals that reflect one's own religious or ideological 'sense of belonging', but also trade unions, political parties, newspapers and radio stations led to the 'sectorisation' or 'pillarisation' (*'verzuiling'*) of Dutch, and to a large extent also of Belgium public life and society (Schendelen 1984; Roebroek 1989; Branckaerts 1983). In relation to welfare and particularly in relation to personal social services this principle meant until relatively recently that most organisations developed as 'sectoral', privately managed but mainly publicly financed initiatives (*'particulier initiatief'*), and the local authority would only set up its own services if no such initiative had taken root. While much of this structure has been overtaken by privatisation and marketisation (Laan 1998, 2000), these later trends nevertheless continue the theme of a differentiated, self-determining civil society.

According to T.H. Marshall's classical analysis the welfare state represents the third step in a sequence from civil rights to political rights and finally to social rights in the organisational differentiation of modern societies (Marshall and Bottomore 1992). 'The modern welfare state is a European invention—in the same way as the nation state, mass democracy, and industrial capitalism. It was born as an answer to problems created by capitalist industrialisation; it was driven by the democratic class struggle; and it followed in the footsteps of the nation state' (Flora 1986: XII). This means that in the work of welfare personnel complex sets of relationships between state and citizens are being acted out even where they are employed in the voluntary sector. The different forms of 'welfare regimes' (Esping-Andersen 1990) that developed in Europe correspond to the various types of state traditions only to a degree and introduced additional independent variables affecting social work. Each type of welfare regime interprets the notion of social citizenship differently and extends it to a different range of people. 'The welfare state is not just a mechanism that intervenes in, and possibly corrects, the structure of inequality; it is, in its own right, a system of stratification. It is an active force in the ordering of social relations' (Esping-Andersen 1990: 23).

All typologies of welfare states are abstractions which cannot do justice to the complex historical relations that make up each national system, but the following signposts might help to give a general orientation. By combining Esping-Andersen's analysis of 'welfare regimes' with Leibfried's typology (Leibfried, 1992: 254) the post-war welfare states of Europe can be seen as broadly conforming with the following models:

1) The universalism of the Scandinavian model is predicated on employment as a primary entitlement provided or at least sponsored, if the need arises, by the state. Its fundamental assumption and political

legitimation is that if the well-being of citizens can be secured through having access to jobs and a regular income, the state needs to rely less on redistributory measures outside the labour market. 'The enormous costs of maintaining a solidaristic, universalistic and de-commodifying welfare system means that it must minimize social problems and maximize revenue income. This is obviously best done with most people working' (Esping-Andersen, 1990:28). This strategy is of particular benefit to women as it aims at actively facilitating their full participation in employment and reduces particularly their dependency on welfare payments.

Within this model, most clearly exemplified until recently by Sweden, social workers are mainly employed by state agencies and are part of dense networks of multi-disciplinary services which have taken over a considerable proportion of the informal caring functions traditionally associated with women in the family. According to the Swedish Social Services Act of 1980 the role of social services is to promote democracy and solidarity and public assistance are regarded as an entitlement. The structure and the resourcing of municipal social services not only allows but compels social workers to be directly involved in evaluating, adapting and developing these services in line with changing needs of their users and in an integrated manner. The emphasis on public employment has led to a high participation rate by women in the labour market, not least in the social services themselves, and day care services for children are a high priority. All this amounts to social workers enjoying a relatively high status in society and the stigmatising effects of their interventions being kept to a minimum. Nevertheless, the central role of the state in the financing and providing of services is also changing in Scandinavian countries under the impact of New Public Management models and a new distribution of responsibilities between public and non-public services becomes established (Sunesson 2000, see chapter 9).

2) By contrast the residual model of welfare focuses on supportive measures outside the labour market which makes the 'means test' a pivotal device in ensuring both minimum subsistence levels and the willingness of the population to work. Measured by its income maintenance system the UK conforms to this model 'because the new middle classes were not wooed from the market to the state' (Esping-Andersen 1990: 31) and they therefore continue to seek to cover their needs by means of private (commercial) arrangements. The universalism once envisaged by Beveridge in his comprehensive design of a welfare state that was to have 'rewarded' in the post- WWII peacetime the loyalty of a nation united in war was eroded by the in-built dualism of state and market in insurance, housing, education and now also in the privatisation of health and community care services. The principle of universalism was never fully realised and private schools, insurance and pensions schemes (though to a much lesser degree private health, until the Thatcher years) continued to play an important role.

Personal social services as the 'fifth social service' in the British welfare state according to the Beveridge model (besides education, health, housing and income maintenance), have had more than their fair share of the divisiveness characteristic of the residual model. Social workers' attention in particular remained focused almost exclusively on poor families (and latterly even more exclusively on their children) and they inherited the 'last resort' image of the Poor Law. Their official mandate rarely extended to pro-active, inclusive and universal initiatives. These much more 'attractive' (i.e. less punitive) areas remained the domain of the voluntary sector and of other professional groups like youth workers.

The current preoccupation with child protection responsibilities which dominates the work of public service social workers in the UK has accentuated the 'social pathology' orientation of British social work which is perhaps the most direct result of the residual welfare concept within which it is made to operate, with statutory workers bearing the brunt of the political dilemma (Parton 1991, Corby, 1991, Dingwall et al. 1995). They are not only made to draw the line between acceptable and unacceptable child rearing practice but also to weigh up the rights to citizenship between parents and children while not being able to command the resources that would secure the social rights of both.

Thus the residual framework (and the further 'residualisation' of social services in the wake of neo-liberal politics) leads almost inevitably to a more pronounced polarisation of care and control. In the eyes of the users of services and of the public at large state social work has the character of controlling measures which become activated only in crisis situations while non-statutory services provide care. British social work has consequently also born the brunt of public criticism over child protection decisions precisely because it is associated so directly with a model of the state that determines the boundaries of social rights in a pragmatic case by case fashion and relies for social cohesion of the 'lower social classes' more on coercion than on endorsing civil and social rights.

3) Compensation is the key principle of social insurance on which Bismarck built his strategy of national and social integration in Germany. This principle ensures that the right to social security for people incapable of earning a living through labour has the character of a private contract which places the compensation received beyond the field of public stigma and disapproval. The state presents itself as a 'social state' by procuring and safeguarding these contracts but it does not compensate directly nor does it guarantee a right to work. The state as a corporatist state delegates welfare and above all insurance responsibilities as much as possible to occupational, religious and other 'voluntary' organisations thus preserving status and class differentials in the structure of society while safeguarding basic welfare rights. Exponents of this welfare regime are Austria, Germany, the Nether-

lands and Switzerland with France and Italy showing also signs of this corp-oratist-statist legacy in Esping-Andersen's view (1990).

'Subsidiarity', recently elevated to the rank of catch-all formula for the salvaging of European integration, is the key to understanding the inter-play between the statutory, the voluntary and indeed the informal sector of care in this welfare regime. Historically it resulted from the confluence of secular corporatist ideas about the 'organic' relationship as one body with many parts between individuals, families, communities, interest groups and the state on the one hand and catholic social philosophy on the other. The latter is embodied in the 1931 Encyclical of pope Pius XI 'Quadragesimo Anno' (referring back to the Encyclical 'Rerum Novarum' of 1891 with which the Catholic Church had sought to formulate an alternative to both socialism and liberalism and states

> 'just as it is wrong to withdraw from the individual and commit to the group what private enterprise and industry can accomplish, so too it is an injustice, a grave evil and a disturbance of right order, for a larger and higher association to arrogate to itself functions which can be performed efficiently by smaller and lower societies. ... Of its very nature the true aim of all social activity should be to help members of the social body, but never to destroy or absorb them... The State therefore should leave to smaller groups the settlement of business of minor importance, which otherwise would greatly distract it; it will thus carry out with greater freedom, power and success the tasks belonging to it alone, because it alone can effectively accomplish these: directing, watching, stimulating, restraining, as circumstances suggest and necessity demands. Let those in power, therefore, be convinced that the more faithfully this principle of subsidiary function be followed, the greater will be both social authority and social efficiency, and the happier and more prosper-ous the condition of the commonwealth.' (Pius XI 1931: sections 79-80)

In Germany the principle of subsidiarity forms the cornerstone of social policy. The priority it bestows on the powerful voluntary associations in the field of welfare over equivalent state services was upheld by a decision of the constitutional court in 1967 and is reflected in all social legislation. This means that in terms of volume and of diversity of services the voluntary sector commands a leading position. Its six blocks, the welfare organisations of the Catholic, Jewish and Protestant religions, the Red Cross, the association of the labour movement and the independent association (*Paritätischer Wohlfahrtsverband*) are represented nationally and across all fields of services and draws largely on public financial resources with only a small proportion of funding coming from voluntary donations. For subsidiarity in Germany (in contrast to countries like Ireland which operate a 'rudimentary' version of subsidiarity consisting only of the delegation of responsibilities) was always linked to the principle of social solidarity: the 'smaller unit' can claim the support of the 'bigger unit' to fulfil its tasks appropriately, while retaining the control over its activities. Only solidarity and subsidiarity in combination can form the 'social state' (*"Sozialstaat"*) which 'refers to a state whose legal, economic and social system is founded on the principle of social security (avoidance of material distress for the citizen), social justice and social equality (of opportunity)' (Dyson, 1980:21). Social work in countries conforming to the corporatist model generally reaped the benefit of the resultant diversity of services, commanding considerable resources for the professional quality of service and enjoying the stability of a statutory framework that covers also many functions in the voluntary field. 'Pillarisation' in the Netherlands consolidated the social work professions and made them flourish in their diversity (Nokielski 1989). Their influence in turn was initially so great that the traditional interest groupings had to give way to functional, task-oriented 'social services' administered by professionals, based on social rights and entitlements rather than on charity and geared towards the rational implementation of universal social policy aims (Brenton 1982).

While much of the 'competition' between different non-statutory agencies enhances creativity and innovation, specialisation and ideological impositions derived from the distinct 'charity tradition' of the agency can create deep divisions in this system. Social workers get absorbed in 'sectoral responsibilities' which can easily reproduce and magnify social inequalities and which also make it difficult to develop a community approach. Specialisation can lead to relative inaccessibility, as was reported of the Dutch system before its more recent re-organisation (Roebroek 1989).

4) As 'rudimentary welfare states' can be classified Portugal, Spain, Greece and also Ireland and some regions of Italy in as much as for a long time they instituted no or only minimal legal rights for social security (Leibfried, 1992). In these countries the development of social services was patchy and often uncoordinated. Full employment was never considered a realistic goal with emigration offering an escape route politically and economically. At the same time the promise of a future comprehensive welfare system remained a strong political factor in securing loyalty and staving off disaffection.

The employment situation of social workers in countries representing the 'rudimentary' welfare model is hard to quantify. In countries like Ireland or Spain (Sabater 2005) plans had existed in the late 70s for a decisive expansion and the full professionalisation of public social services, but they were thwarted by the economic crisis affecting public expenditure at the very moment when the expansion was set to take place. Nevertheless, social services have now steadily expanded, largely under the impact of public disquiet over cases of neglect of childrenand the demand for more decisive action on the part of the state (Ferguson and Kenny 1995, Skehill 1999). As a result most professionally qualified social workers in those countries are to be found in public employment. Because of the blurred distinction between informal and formal care and between the competences of different professional groups a large part of personal services is still however being provided by the voluntary sector which utilises unpaid volunteers, and by professionals with other qualifications. The post-dictatorship Spanish constitution of 1978 declared Spain to be a 'democratic and social state based on rights' (article 1) and details the social obligations of the state (articles 39ff) but in practice other laws making relatives primarily responsible for assisting family members in need ('*Alimentos entre parientes*') have more effect (Zaragoz 1991: 32).

Social policy regimes therefore form the structural basis for the various forms of social citizenship which in turn defines the margins within which social work can operate. Nevertheless there are great similarities in the daily practice of social workers across different models of the welfare state. For the regimes are by no means static and just as social workers are products of and representatives of different versions of social citizenship, they are also engaged in the shaping of the actual practices of social citizenship and hence of social policy. 'It is an intrinsic feature of the Welfare State as it was built and planned, through conflicts and compromises, that it implies both acknowledgement and displacement of needs, both support of social rights and new forms of social control through the enforcing of rigid regulations and the increasing power of professionals and bureaucrats' (Saraceno 1987: 61). In no European country has social work become associated entirely with state services, nor does it indeed operate anywhere totally privately and outside a statutory framework. This indicates that while the profession certainly carries out functions of the welfare system and above all interprets it by individualising its provisions, it also acts potentially as a corrective in taking its mandate from the users of services or from its own professional standards. To quote Saraceno again, 'Paradoxically, we might say that the more social rights are acknowledged, the more individuals and groups become aware of their partiality and ambivalence; not only because their private lives and responsibilities have been eroded by the state, but because through the state's acknowledgement of their needs they become able to develop a fuller and richer consciousness of themselves as subjects of rights and needs' (Saraceno 1987:61). These dual dynamics played a role even under those political conditions which denied the existence of social problems and hence the need for social work, which need to be recalled briefly.

The existence of social work during the period of state socialism in eastern European countries, albeit under a variety of 'disguises', is further evidence that the state, even a socialist totalitarian one, requires the assistance of additional 'steering mechanisms' performing the task of translating public problems into personal issues. 'It was maintained that with economic growth based on socialist relations of ownership social evolution would soon get rid of all kinds of problems, such as delinquency, alcoholism or mental illness, poverty and even economic hardship' (Ferge 1979: 63). Officially, the concern for material subsistence had been taken care of by the socialist state regulating employment, housing, education, health and income maintenance universally. But even within the logic of this approach, leaving aside for the moment its feasibility, there remained the need for the function of 'fine-tuning' the state measures to the needs of individuals, or indeed the adjustment of individuals, their attitudes and abilities, to the collective interests. This necessitated the growth of a stratum of workers in official or semi-official capacities, but also on a voluntary, in-official basis, who dealt with such issues of 'adjustment', thereby fulfilling the role of social workers without carrying their official title (Zaviršek 2005).

Much of this work traded as 'rehabilitation' as the term 'social work' would have meant the acknowledgement of social problems. Rehabilitation was strongest in the field of guiding people back to a productive life after physical illness or accident and in 'conductive education' for young people with congenital disabilities. Professional competences spanned the range of medical, physio-therapeutic, educational and counselling skills. But rehabilitation also extended to work with people suffering from addictions and to delinquents, where the parallels to western type social work were even more apparent. Rehabilitation and education as conceptual (and ideological) reference points allowed for the emergence of explicit 'welfare workers' particularly in Hungary, East Germany and Poland who were employed in welfare centres advising parents on child rearing problems, dealing with substitute care arrangements or with material hardship and coordinating the work of voluntary organisations (Ksiezopolski and Sienko 1988: 300). Georgy Konrád's veiled autobiographical account of such work in Budapest in his novel The Case Worker (Konrád 1977) highlights the universality of everyday dilemmas across the ideological state barriers.

At the same time, party and trade union officials also carried a mandate for some types of welfare work, particularly in relation to housing, job transfers, marital difficulties, alcoholism and minor forms of delinquency. This was partly due to the lack of other support structures, partly in response to the desire to get away from the stigmatising effects of charity when support and insurance schemes handled by 'the people themselves' through their representatives were meant to underline their self-help and rights character (Ferge 1979).

The work of unofficial volunteers was organised mainly through the churches and their respective welfare organisations whose assistance was publicly disapproved but practically prevailed upon by the official welfare workers for instance in Poland (Medical Post-graduate Education Center in Warsaw 1978). These organisations had often been re-constituted after their original banning with secret approval by the government, an ideological slide of hand which allowed for the utilisation of existing informal welfare networks without however giving official approval to the continued existence and thereby publicly demonstrated necessity of 'bourgeois' welfare support services (Kantowicz 2004).

Together these formal and informal welfare workers had to fill the gaps remaining between officially proclaimed and actually existing social rights. They could not publicly articulate the existence of these gaps thus demonstrating the fundamental discrepancy between social rights on the one hand and civil and political rights on the other. 'By far the most important factor … which ultimately led to the downfall of these regimes, was that the real enlargement of social rights (even though unequally distributed among different groups in the population) was accompanied by a severe restriction of civil and political rights' (Bottomore in Marshall and Bottomore 1992: 62).

These latter considerations are of particular significance in the reconstruction of social policy and social services in former socialist countries under capitalist conditions. A similar rupture looms when market principles are introduced both for economic activity and for social service delivery in the wake of neo-liberal social policies. This ideology claims that economic market principles alone would take care of the steering processes of social development. Under that ideological dictate social work is bound to be relegated to a secondary, auxiliary function of redressing imbalances, compensating for the lack of rights, gate-keeping at the boundaries of entitlements, and general social control if the political systems do not secure the comprehensive implementation of civil, political and social rights. The momentum for such a development of comprehensive social rights can only be generated in a vibrant civil society which asserted itself briefly and effectively in the overthrow of communism but which subsequently requires more support and stimulation, not least through social work in the form of community action, to sustain its momentum. The following thoughts on the role of social policy in society, formulated during the dying years of the Polish communist regime, retain their validity in principle after its eventual collapse:

'The state has an untransferable responsibility for the welfare of its citizens. This does not mean that the state should take over responsibility from the people but that conditions should be created to enable people to manage by themselves, in co-operation with the family, other citizens, local communities, social organisations and, of course, the state. People have to regain a subjective role in the creation of a social policy on all levels of the decision-making process as well as in the realisation of its goals. Without these changes it would be impossible to direct social policy towards awakening a feeling of affiliation with a community, towards promoting mutual aid or social work motivations' (Ksiezopolski 1987: 105).

Since the disappearance of communist states in Europe the relative stability of Western European welfare states also begins to give way to fundamental changes. Significantly these were first heralded by changes in the administrative structure of social services, justified often with the intention of bringing them closer to the citizens and enabling more participation, but increasingly the underlying ideological interests of greater control over the behaviour of citizens and above all of cost reduction became more apparent (see chapter 8). Recent social policy changes therefore amount to a fundamental questioning of unconditional citizenship guarantees, and this not just through the restrictions on entitlements for migrants and asylum seekers (Humphries 2002), but also through the enforcement of citizen obligations for national recipients of welfare. It is therefore worth tracing the main lines of this shift from paternalist welfare positions to efforts at granting greater participation and rights and finally to consumerist welfare ideologies.

In response to the demands expressed by New Social Movements for self-determination and participation, fostering solidarity and endorsing formal democratic rights proved to be particularly difficult for those European countries with highly centralised governmental structures. Their weakness was exposed in the wave of protest movements 'from the basis' which swept Europe (and much of the rest of the world) in 1968. It speaks for the political significance of social services that some countries like France, Italy and Greece (after the end of the dictatorship), in seeking to address their deficit in political credibility without wanting to yield power, made efforts to change over to accessible, community-based social and health services, thereby triggering similar developments in other countries in the 1970s which had profound effects on the nature of social work.

In Italy, the trend towards decentralistion had a variety of origins; mutual aid associations and particularly co-operatives had always been a strong feature of Italian life and the political demands for participation and greater immediacy were articulated both from radical sources such as Marxism and feminism and from catholic social teaching. Italy's law 833 of 1978, which launched the radical reorganisation of health services, designated the local 'district' or borough (*'comune'*) as the political and administrative level for the provision of services. The over 8,000 *'comuni'* with usually 20,000 to 50,000 inhabitants (but sometimes less than 1,000) set up local health units ('Unità sanitaria locale', USL) which may combine health and social welfare responsibilities (Cigno 1985).

The Italian achievements in terms of decentralising state services are considerable given the complexity of Italian state-citizen relationships. Local service committees confront politicians, who are proportionally represented on them, with the practice dilemmas caused by their politics (Cigno 1985). But the initial agenda of *'gestione sociale'*, management by the collectivity, aimed at more direct representation of citizens but failed to address their dependency on bureaucrats and professionals. Government backing for local initiatives often had the effect of 'demobilising' the social movements and burnishing the caring image of the state (Ergas 1982). The dominance of the political culture impeded actual progress in service delivery systems, and subsequent reforms, like law 328 of 2000 which aimed at closer cooperation between public and private services at local level, had little impact (Gori 2004). Without a fundamental change in the relationship between citizens and the state tinkering with administrative structures does not suffice.

Compared to the Swedish system of local social service committees, which are similarly composed but operate in a political context that emphasises the legal and universal entitlements of service users, the Italian experience with decentralisation always played into the hands of the old patronage system ('clientelismo') which is deeply engrained as a pattern of dependence (Ascoli 1987). There were striking parallels at the time in this regard with the situation in Greece where clientelism is also very much part of the political culture. Stathopoulos (1991) describes the limited effect legislation promoting decentralisation and citizen participation at local and regional level (laws Nr. 1262 of 1982 and Nr. 1622 of 1986) had in rural Greece. Political power always returns into the hands of central government and of political parties. The newly created participatory structures were quickly seized by members of national political parties seeking to 'promote their own party's interests at local level' (Stathopoulos 1991: 124). Consequently, local people were inclined to measure the usefulness of community workers by their ability to open up funding, channels of political influence and access to government. The political culture yields very slowly to the sense of empowerment community workers seek to engender in the local population.

In France decentralisation officially came about with the law of 1984 when the Mitterand government sought to radically alter the centralised structure of France. The path had been prepared through participatory initiatives in the 1970s, notably in the sphere of social services: Well over 100 social centres ('Centres Sociaux') sprang up all over the country, financed from both governmental sources and the French 'private' health funds with the explicit brief of applying the principle of user participation in the running and the direction of the centres. Triggered by the political events in France of 1968 this movement meshed with the typically French system of sectoral 'caisses', funds for old age, sickness and family welfare, which have consumer representatives on their boards. But it also activated new forms of social and cultural work which de-emphasise a problem orientation (Chamberlayne 1992) in the newly created methodological frame of 'animation' (which of course has traditional roots in settlement work). This facilitated forms of interaction between workers and community representatives on the causes of need instead of concentrating solely on delivering state responses to these needs (Cannan 1991). Overall however, the complexity of local government structures and the dual responsibilities of social service centres (to state and private organisations) failed also in France to increase their direct democratic accountability to service users (Wallimann 1986).

The very fact that governments in the context of their decentralisation policies frequently called upon the services of social workers to 'make it work' reveals the ambivalence of decentralisation. It has been argued (e.g. Mayer and Müller 1984) that overall, the 'enmeshment' of private lives with the institutions of the state was not been reduced at that time. Subsequently, a separation came about as a result of reforms from the opposite political spectrum to the first wave of centre-left initiatives at decentralisation. The growing complexity of these relations and the emphasis on cost effectiveness were used to divert attention away from the state and the arena of politics towards economic and local management issues within the framework of neo-liberalism. Professionals like social workers, priding themselves on their autonomy but tending to ignore their political mandate, now become once more pivotal in lending legitimacy to new, cost-cutting principles of resource allocations with their 'objective, professional diagnoses'.

> 'Whatever new levels and forms of decentralisation can be observed, they are part and parcel of a system growing in complexity... In many areas of health and social services the individual meets the State mediated through the professionals charged with the provision of care and services. It is ironic that the individual as client on whose behalf the whole system is said to be organised has so few opportunities of taking part in a more active sense' (Nowotny 1984:11).

The trend towards decentralisation and 'consumer choice' contains therefore an ambiguous message in terms of the conditions for social citizenship. Decentralisation can on the one hand turn into an opportunity of client participation, into a questioning of the taken-for-granted basis on which welfare and welfare services are structured and organised in a society and in a manner that was demanded by the social movements of the 1980s. But the concept of 'participation' can also lead to a more insidious form of control, a greater presence of the state and its agenda in the lives of citizens under the guise of 'choice', and to greater inequality as user groups compete among themselves for scarce resources. Shifting services from official agencies to voluntary groups, informal networks, 'the community' and indeed to 'the family' has now a well established place on the neo-liberal political agenda that may lead to new forms of capitalist exploitation and hegemony (Chamberlayne 1992). There is therefore a clear role for social workers to assert their professional autonomy critically in the context of these developments, not as a widening of their power position, but as a critical and independent reflection on the political consequences of their 'fitting into a given agenda', no matter how closely this agenda appears to meet the fundamental principles of client self-initiative and participation that underlie social work. The task of empowerment is by no means achieved by merely mechanically applying an official participation agenda.

The 'crisis of the welfare state' and the subsequent rise of New Right policies which exploited and deepened the crisis led western European countries into a similar dilemma to that being confronted by Central and Eastern European countries after the fall of communism and brought about profound changes in all four types of welfare regimes. In fiscal terms, the Keynsian mechanism of public investments boosting economic expansion had exhausted itself under the increasingly costly burden of re-payment commitments arising from public borrowing, which in turn exacerbated the unemployment crisis (Carter 1998). Full male employment as the economic basis of insurance-based welfare systems began to crumble just as women started to question their marginalisation in the labour market, their increasing dependence on assistance and the lack of public and economic recognition of their care and domestic functions (Esping-Andersen 1996). Unemployment associated with the fundamental restructuring of industrial and agricultural economies in the 1970s combined with the demographic effects of an aging population, and a loosening of marriage and family ties simultaneously placed heightened demands on welfare services. At the same time social security regulations were altered in the direction of limiting and tightening social insurance conditions thus driving more and more recipients of social insurance benefits to draw on social assistance. This in turn resulted in more means-testing of social benefits generally, not just in the traditional area of social assistance, a phenomenon generally referred to as 'workfare' replacing 'welfare' (Saraceno 2002). All this caused the relationship between the generations, between social insurance and social assistance and the boundary between self-help responsibilities (voluntary, private and commercial) and the responsibilities of the state to become redefined. Assistance was made to cover risks and sectors of the population for which it was never intended. Through these developments the state's controlling functions in welfare matters became more visible as such social control measures added to the alienation experienced by recipients of welfare. At the same time the bifurcation of the labour market into those enjoying relatively stable, well-paid employment and those in marginal, temporary and discontinuous employment turned the mutuality principle of insurance schemes on its head so that insurance schemes became 'bastions of corporatist privilege from which the most vulnerable were increasingly excluded' (Chamberlayn 1992:7).

At the ideological level, the political left with its traditional advocacy for institutional universal welfare measures changed its key demands for equality and universal services, even in Scandinavian countries and in Austria, where social democratic governments had decades of power, and began to woo the middle class voters within an agenda dominated by the New Right rationale of lower taxation and social costs. In this climate the 'Swedish model' of relying largely on state services was being curtailed since 'the national efforts to solve the economic problems seem to develop local social problems that create, in the long run, heavy structural costs for the public sector' (Nilsson and Wadeskog 1988: 37). The Italian efforts of moving from a rudimentary to a more egalitarian though still corporatist welfare state experienced a 'jamming up' under bulging public expenditures and divergent consumer interests (Donati and Colozzi 1988).

In the Netherlands the dismantling of its traditional welfare structure by the conservative-liberal government in the 80s coincided with the gradual dis-establishment of social work just as a comprehensive, pro-active, profession-led concept of welfare was within sight. The politics of retrenchment exploited the growing demands for 'basis-democracy' which had also turned against the power vested in professional organisations and extolled the virtues of the 'caring community' (*'zorgsame samenleving'*, Nokielski 1987:122). Nevertheless, the Netherlands for a long time remained an example of at least the attempt at the 'needs-led' structuring of social services: local authorities grant-aid (albeit according to measures of cost efficiency) private non-profit making organisations ('stichting') set up around particular fields of need and social problems, notably in areas like mental health, family work, homelessness and drug dependency. Only one project catering for a particular area of need per local authority receives assistance in a process of competitive tendering and the performance of the winning agent gets monitored annually (Laan 1998).

In this third phase of restructuring not just social service structures, but the entire social policy orientation, the UK has perhaps embarked on the most fundamental restructuring of community care of any European country. Under the banner of choice for the users of social services the role of local authorities as providers of social services was dismantled by the rigorous neo-liberal policies of the Conservative governments of the 1980s. Comprehensive service-providing departments were replaced with evaluation teams that have to purchase the most cost-effective services from non-governmental suppliers. This split between 'purchasers' and 'providers' (Harris 1999) not only divides the profession according to interest positions dictated by a virtual and actual market situation, it also fragments social solidarity in general as users of social services are only seemingly in control of the process and are in fact banded into risk groups on a gradient of 'worthiness' according to the cost-effectiveness of budget-driven intervention methods (see chapter 8 where this third phase is analysed in more detail).

The progressive erosion of the principle of equality in social welfare heightened the crisis of legitimation the nation states experienced since the 70s. Social workers came once more to stand in the frontline of political pressures to maintain the appearance of the state system's legitimacy by providing a 'caring image' to society. More acutely than ever before did they have to mediate in the conflicts between an increasingly vociferous service user population and political objectives which aim at individualising or particularising social resources to selected 'vulnerable groups'.

But citizenship issues feature now also at the supra-national level with the more explicit development of a social policy agenda of the European Union through the Social Charta and the Amsterdam Treaty. The various programmes of the Social Fund are designed to foster a sense of European citizenship and belonging, in close parallel to (and sometimes, as in the case of the Combat Poverty Programmes, in actual competition with) the social policy aims of the nation states (Ginsburg and Lawrence 2006). Social workers in all parts of the EU, but particularly in 'peripheral' countries and 'regions of industrial decline', work in projects financed through these programmes and have to tailor their project objectives to the EU guidelines. This describes a situation where opportunities for tangible citizenship in the EU are either being created or denied, depending on the conditions of funding but also on the 'interpretation' those conditions receive at the local level. 'In the short run, the structural funds appear to be competitors to any emerging focus on social citizenship' (Leibfried and Pierson 1992: 340). Yet the struggle for citizenship has to be taken on, not so much by the professionals but by the users of services themselves. Networks are being set up between different user groups right across Europe which take self-advocacy directly to the level of lobbying the EU institutions and MEPs. Their experience is that the politics of the funding process no longer conform to the channels of local and national government structures but show an interesting propensity for 'short-cuts' directly to Brussels. 'Eurolink Age' for instance maintains an office in Brussels, the Single Parent Action Network (SPAN) is forging cross-national links as is FEANTSA, a Europe wide campaign on homelessness (Baine, Bennington and Russell 1992).

There remains ample scope for scepticism: 'For the moment there is not a single civil right which is defended by the European Community. There is not a single basic right of citizens which has anything to do with the Treaty of Rome' (Dahrendorf 1992: 85)—and European integration confronts social workers once more, like in the history of each nation state, with the alternative of developing social services as compensation for the lack of social rights or as the vehicle for the full rights of citizenship. The un-coupling of welfare benefits from market principles will be the single most crucial task to be achieved not by the EU bureaucracy, but by the nascent European civil society in which social work must become a driving force.

When Pinker states, 'it seems obvious—to me at least—that problems of a personal nature do exist and that people are quite capable of being the architects of their own misery' (Pinker 1990: 93) by way of calling on social workers to concentrate on these personal issues instead of 'meddling in political issues', he misses the point that the political mandate social workers carry out within all the welfare systems is to locate and define first of all the boundary between personal troubles and public issues. The dichotomy between case work and social action as two distinct methods treats that boundary as given, whereas the actual core skill of social workers lies in the ability to leave the choice—and the mix—of methods open and to give clients a say in the choice. It is the hallmark of modern societies that this boundary can no longer be regarded as fixed, that it has become problematic and the subject of political negotiations, just as the boundaries of social solidarity and the principles on which solidarity can be based have become uncertain. The fact that every modern state has developed some system of public welfare and that the EU is being drawn, very reluctantly, into ever more expansive social policy areas bears ample witness to this. Society is implicated not just in issues like people lacking resources, education, jobs or housing, but also in every case of fatal child abuse, in the death of a pensioner from hypothermia, in the plight of a homeless person. In counselling people in their personal grief, helplessness or outrage it is essential for social workers to open up the official, taken-for-granted definitions of the boundary of 'the personal' and in particular to resist the translation of public wrongs into personal troubles, but equally not to deny the people immediately affected their share of responsibility for their condition (and the necessary changes) which constitutes their human dignity. The different European welfare systems and the process of European integration itself do have an immediate bearing on the practice of social work, and the mode of every intervention contributes to the version of social citizenship, at national and European level, that is yet to become a lived and practised reality, not just in social service transactions. It is precisely this ability to define 'social service work' as a matter of shaping social politics which is under threat from the advance of neo-liberal politics, and it therefore becomes necessary to explore the nature of the relationship between social work and capitalism in a later chapter (chapter 8).

Having established the cultural origins of the different versions of citizenship and their continuing influence in terms of distinct welfare regimes and hence of distinct forms of social work practice, the issue of cultural diversity within nation states becomes now a focus of attention and needs to be analysed. Methodological unity and national cultural homogeneity appear to be intricately linked and are, as ideological constructs that tend to be withdrawn from critical debate and scrutiny, inherently instable and troublesome. The next chapters examine therefore 'minority issues' from cultural, political and also methodological perspectives, not just on account of the increased exposure of social work to immigrant groups and their cultures, but because the constitution of identities and the respective rights and obligations form an inalienable element of the social work mandate.

4. Minorities and cultural diversity—challenges to the nation state project

'In 1990 21.2% of the population of Greater London were black, "foreigners" (excluding foreign-born citizens) constituted 16% of the resident population of greater Paris ... in Amsterdam at the beginning of the 1990s 22% of the population were "foreigners"—and half of the primary school population -, in Frankfurt about 25%, and in Brussels some 28%' (Therborn 1995:50). Cultural diversity had certainly arrived in the urban centres of Europe by the last decade of the 20th century, at levels comparable to those prevailing in New York. Europeans find this astonishing, sometimes alarming; they had become accustomed to considering their territories as ethnically homogeneous and now regard the rising number of ethnically distinct groupings in their urban centres as a disturbance of this 'established' pattern—forgetting, on the whole, that their presumed homogeneity was of quite recent origin. Viewed from a longer term historical perspective, not before 'around 1950 had the states of Europe achieved an unprecedented ethnic homogenization of their populations' (Therborn 1995: 47). No wonder therefore that the question of ethnic and cultural identity did not appear on social work's methodology agenda till well into the 1980s when the intersection of civil society processes and academic discourses, outlined in chapter 1, had to be re-worked entirely. This chapter explores the history and consequences of that encounter without which contemporary European social work methodology cannot be understood.

It is often conveniently forgotten that this relative homogeneity had come about largely as the indirect or direct impact of Nazism on Europe and the world, its racist policy of the extermination of whole populations, its aggression against countries near and far. It had been compounded by a WWII armistice settlement that, while not exactly repeating the Wilsonian doctrines of the Versailles peace treaty that had concluded the First World War, nevertheless gave renewed impetus to the idea, that cultural and political boundaries should be made to coincide as a means of identification and for purposes of their political utilisation. This temporary demographic homogenisation had been the result of the deliberate, politically motivated displacement of minority populations, most notably by Nazi Germany in the territories it occupied, and through the backlash after the war against the German populations of Eastern Europe, creating among them some 10.7 million refugees (Niethammer 1991). Immediately after the Second World

War population movements happened on a large scale, and not only in Germany; Austria and Finland for instance received 6% and 10% respectively of their populations in refugees, Italians were expelled from Dalmatia and Istria (Therborn 1995: 46). With the exception of the Soviet Union, Yugoslavia and Switzerland the European nation states came to consider themselves as mono-ethnic, although the realisation of this 'ethnic' homogenisation had been veiled by the global re-ordering of political alliances along the lines of the cold war divide into communism and capitalism. Political block mentality superseded and 'dampened down' the potential and actual nationalism contained within this order, an example of which was also the creation of the European Economic Community.

This political recipe to ensure peace in large parts of Europe after the devastation of the Second World War was in this sense strangely reminiscent of the formula of appeasement which had produced the welfare state consensus: it, too, regarded society as basically homogeneous or at least constituted by common needs and interests, and solidarity as something that could be achieved therefore through the coalition of former adversaries who forget their differences on the grounds of shared rational interests superseding former irrational cultural (or class) barriers. Ethnicity as such initially played an inferior role. Homogeneity was constructed around behavioural assimilation. To conform to the concept of national unity was equivalent to behaving normally, rationally and any deviation from the rational norm of 'good citizen behaviour' was treated as a matter of individual pathology. The refugees that arrived during that time and had to be 'integrated' counted as in essence 'indigenous' on account of the rational, sensible choices they had made in a political sense: Germans who had escaped an alien, i.e. communist regime; refugees from the uprisings of Hungary and Czechoslovakia and who quite 'naturally' belonged to 'our side', even if at a cultural level of everyday encounters mistrust and conflict was all too apparent. But at the 'official level' their belonging to the national community was founded on the acknowledgement of the choice they had made. The position of these political refugees stood in contrast to that of economic migrants who started to appear in western (and to some extent in eastern Europe) a decade or so later, who were not regarded as refugees and instead, in countries like Germany and Switzerland, were made to retain their status as foreigners over several generations.

Historically speaking, cultural homogeneity of major cities in Europe certainly was an anomaly. Therborn calculates that in Central and Eastern European countries the proportion of the population of capitals which by today's criteria would have represented the typical, dominant national ethnicity in the decades before the First World War as ranging from as low as 36% (Prague), 38% (Bratislava), 40% (Bucharest), 46% (Helsinki) to 62% (Warsaw), 75% (Zagreb), 85% (Vienna) and 89% for St. Petersburg (the highest 'indigenous' proportion for those capitals, Therborn 1995: 44). The 1950s therefore completed a process of social homogenisation constructed increasingly around ethnic concepts. This tendency had set in with the political transformations of Europe in the post-Napoleonic era, had been fuelled by the patriotic movements which gave rise for instance to German and Italian unification in the latter half of the 19th century, had spread into global rivalry in the period of aggressive colonialism, had resulted in the break-up of the remaining multi-ethnic empires at the end of the First World War, flared up again in nationalism, fascism and Nazism in the inter-war period and plunged the world into cataclysmic destruction in the Second World War.

One indication of this process is that Europe is world-wide the continent with the lowest concentration of languages and hence has become a special case where language bonds and their technological and political significance can forge hegemonic coalitions:

Table 1: World languages by category of size (Haarmann 2001: 73)

World region	Total number of languages	Number of languages spoken by > 1m people	Number of languages spoken by < 1m people	Number of languages spoken by very few people
World total	6 417 (100%)	273 (4.2%)	4 162 (64.8%)	1 982 (30.8%)
Asia	1 906	126 (6.6%)	1 549 (81.3%)	231 (12.1%)
Africa	1 821	92 (5.1%)	1 607 (88.2%)	122 (6.7%)
Pacific	1 268	1 (0.1%)	507 (40%)	775 (61.1%)
America	1 013	10 (0.9%)	428 (42.2%)	575 (56.7%)
Australia	273	-	18 (6.6%)	255 (93.4%)
Europe	143	44 (30.7%)	69 (48.3)	15 (10.5%)

Ethnic diversity and rivalry in the era of (assumed) homogeneity after 1945 had by no means disappeared, but it was not made thematic. The Cold War confrontation saw to that in east and west, as did the determination behind the western European integration efforts not to let nationalist rivalry become ever again the fuse that set the world ablaze. The Franco-German accord between De Gaulle and Adenauer was symbolic for this; it facilitated an unprecedented flow of contacts especially in the form of exchange programmes which brought the new generation of French and Germans youth closer than they had ever been. A united Europe suggested itself to the immediate post-war generation as 'the solution' to old rivalries, as a quasi-country with which young Germans (and not only they) could identify without shame, without the tyranny of a domineering culture and of stuffy traditions.

A similar political agenda contributed to the integration of the refugees in Western Germany, officially called 'out-settlers' (*'Aussiedler'*), 'German nationals' from beyond the Iron curtain who came to constitute 16.4% of the population of the Federal Republic of Germany (Castles and Miller 1993). In popular perceptions they differed little from the customary 'refugees' (*'Flüchtlinge'*) which often was a means of referring not only to East Germans, Poles and Sudeten-Czech, but in southern Germany also to everybody who had migrated within Germany and spoke with a 'posh' northern-German accent. The cultural diversity they created implicit but rarely made thematic: language patterns shifted, the difference between Protestant and Catholic regions levelled, culinary traditions were exchanged, folk customs from far-away places occasionally became visible but were contained in museum-like structures. Generally the diversity was framed in such a way that it was 'neutralised', subsumed under the much more important 'greater identity' of being German, or rather, of being Western, being an inhabitant of 'the free world'.

During the first two decades after WWII two types of population movements coincided in western Europe: the displacement and reception of refugees mainly from central and eastern Europe whose arrival was given deep symbolic significance in that it served as a constant reminder of the repressive nature of the socialist regimes, and the recruitment of workers from Mediterranean countries and the Caribbean to fill vacancies in the labour market for the reconstruction of the European economies. The myth of homogeneity could be maintained by considering both phenomena transient pending the 'return' of the migrants to their place of origin, despite the fact that the fall of communism seemed ever more utopian and the work migrants had been joined by their families. The rhetoric emanating from annual gatherings of ethnic groups in Germany (*'Volksgruppen'*) and 'people displaced from their homeland' (*'Heimatvertriebene'*) enforced that notion of an eventual return. The refugee-settlers from Eastern Germany, Poland, Hungary and Czechoslovakia were nevertheless quietly regarded as permanent members of western societies. By contrast the permanency of recruited migrant workers was never accepted. Their relationship as 'guest workers' with the 'host society' was considered as purely instrumental, a contractual arrangement with little implications for political and social integration and the acquisition of residency and citizenship rights.

It is against this historical background that the contemporary role and range of methods of the social professions in relation to issues of personal and cultural identity have to be evaluated. As was shown in chapter 2, the traditional mandate of social service staff within the nation state project was to legitimate the boundaries of solidarity of a society, to ensure that solidarity is being extended only to 'the right kind of people' and that as many as possible of those remaining on the margins of society are either being 'converted' into 'the right kind of people' or their exclusion is being legitimated on the grounds of their refusal to conform (Mynott 2002). The assumed ethnic and cultural homogeneity of post-WWII European societies suggested to social service operators that this task could be solved primarily through the recourse to psychological methods. The excluded were distinguished by behavioural or cognitive deficits, which prevented them from fully availing of that solidarity, a pattern of responses best illustrated by the 'rediscovery of poverty' in the 1970s until which time poverty had been treated as a matter of personal (mis-)adjustment. Either the clients could be helped to adjust personally or they could not be helped and were left to the care (and control) of institutions. Behind the then prevailing principle of 'client self-determination' in social work methodology stood a whole range of measures and pressures, which lay outside the range of social work but ensured conformity and assimilation. Social workers were keen to 'treat people as people', to express their professional integrity and impartiality by disregarding cultural and ethnic diversity as a source of possible bias and prejudice and to thereby remain 'politically neutral', without questioning the very specific political assumptions and interests that surrounded and instrumentalised this neutrality and assumed universalism.

It is not surprising, therefore, that the articulation of ethnic diversity in European societies which occurred during the 1980s and 90s raised fundamental questions not only about social work methods but also about the role of social work in society. With this in mind the more detailed look at social work in relation to migration can serve as an opportunity for the comprehensive assessment of social work's position in such societies which are becoming acutely aware of their cultural diversity and of the diminishing significance of the nation state.

As the immediate experience of the Second World War fades from memory and the 'block-thinking' of global confrontation disintegrates after 1989, the nature of political crises in Europe and in the wider world changes fundamentally. They can no longer be subsumed under established patterns or lines of confrontation. The boundaries between 'them' and 'us' have become uncertain and unpredictable. An immediate response to this uncertainty in relation to collective identities is the reference to the earlier experience with migration, which had set a pattern of distinction between political and economic migrants. This distinction is being invoked as a regulatory principle for the treatment of refugees at both national and European level even though this very distinction has become totally blurred and superseded by the even greater enmeshment of economic and political issues in the age of globalisation (Castles and Miller 1993).

This results in an escalation and a short-circuiting of measures between national and European policy decisions which amount to a much tighter restriction on entry to the EU for political refugees and a relative openness to selective migration suited to or demanded by changes in the economy and indeed in demography. The latter applies not only to the active encouragement of the internal mobility of labour, which is one of the central tenets of the European economic integration process, but also to a relative toleration of illegal immigration in parts of Europe like Italy (Vasta 1993) and Spain and the persistent recruitment drive in response to labour shortages in Germany, France and the Netherlands in certain parts of industry, notably the building and construction sectors, the electronic industry and increasingly also the personal and care services sector at informal and formal level. The European Union is winding its twisted way around the GATS conditions (Fritz and Scherrer 2002) whose aspirations of the free mobility of services it supports and at the same time fears. The so-called Bolkestein Directive (Commission of the European Communities 2004) is a highly controversial initiative to introduce a liberal trade in services within the European Community on terms largely dictated by the GATS criteria, although some member countries, notably France, strongly oppose their implementation.

Migration calls into question not only the myth of homogeneity of a society whereby insecurities and anxieties become exposed and defensive reactions activated; it also thereby tests the boundaries of solidarity. All responses, including humanitarian responses to the arrival of refugees are politically sensitive because they expose the precarious nature of the prevailing rationale for the existing boundaries of belonging, social responsibility and the conditions of citizenship and all their inconsistencies and weaknesses (Kushner and Knox 1999). It was the concept of the nation state which determined those boundaries, and it was the nation state that was responsible for the creation of 'minorities' in the first place: 'It is the state, which as nation state produces "national minorities" or the pseudo-national (ethnic, cultural and vocational) minorities factually. Without its legal and political intervention they would have remained virtual' (Balibar 1993, p 151). In the context of the globalisation not just of the economy but of social relations generally (Waters 1995) national boundaries assume an ever more arbitrary character and become irrelevant for the purpose of defining the limits of social responsibility. This transition is reminiscent of the upheaval at the beginning of capitalist industrialisation when the system of territorial parish responsibility for the poor and destitute was still being invoked to deal with personal hardship even though it had become totally abstract and untenable in an industrialised nation state that required labour mobility and had de facto severed to link to the parish of origin. That marked the transition between, in Durkheim's terminology, mechanical and organic solidarity with the state becoming the new organising principle for the latter. Today's transition from the national to the global scale of organised solidarity patterns and relationships can equally not rely on a pre-existing institutional framework (Beck 1994). The emergent patterns of relationship and responsibility are open and therefore constantly prone to premature closure. Yet individual consciences are instantly implicated in world events. The media present wars and disasters in far away places with unprecedented immediacy. People respond personally to crises like famines or the plight of orphans in other countries or other continents by becoming emotionally and often very practically drawn into giving direct help and the work of non-governmental organisations in international aid contrasts markedly with the slow and cumbersome organisation of governmentally organised humanitarian aid. The spread of ecological awareness illustrates further the connectedness of all world systems and the relativity of geographical boundaries as organising principles for the ecological husbandry of the earth as such. And yet there are no longer any agreed guiding principles with which to limit this potentially infinite burden of responsibility and to legitimate limits of responsibility and solidarity, let alone effective systems of governance to deal with global issues. The arrival of the new refugees on the Western doorsteps is inescapable evidence of the fact that economic and political problems can no longer be externalised, that no society can isolate itself from world events or deal with them from a distance. Their arrival is so uncomfortable for Western societies because it highlights the sliding loss of control by First World societies over the process of boundary drawing, a form of control which they have come to take for granted and through which they had exercised their global power.

The crisis of the geo-political limits of solidarity, precipitated by global-isation and by the collapse of the Soviet regime, also represents a crisis of collective and individual identity and triggers an 'identity panic' (Balibar 1993). This led directly to a new preoccupation with ethnicity in social and political debate (Bastenier 1994) as an apparent means of finding clarity and identity. The (re-)ethnification of social relations in Europe after the dissolution of block-thinking post 1989 had two fundamental aspects. On the one hand this process helped minority groups to articulate their cultural identity more vigorously and visibly in a political arena which had become sensitised to cultural differences. This allowed them to recognise and utilise the collective assertions of power invested in claims to distinct ethnicities, particularly where they were associated with claims to national independence (Rex 1993). On the other hand, using ethnicities as markers of the boundaries of community and solidarity re-activated nationalist mechanisms which had been so powerful (and disastrous) in the history of European nation states. Ethnicity in this sense always implies hierarchical orders of superiority and inferiority (Wieviorka 1994b).

The re-emergence of nationalism and neo-fascism in popular movements and party politics directed in aggressive forms against foreign and minority populations, as happened in almost all European countries during the 1990s, has the effect of ethnifying social and political conflicts further. Neo-fascist ideologies suggest 'simple solutions' which ultimately amount for their victims to the 'choice' between assimilation (on the terms dictated and controlled by the dominant group) and ethnic separation, expulsion or the re-drawing of political boundaries (Radtke 1994). But ethnicity cannot be treated as a 'natural category' to be recovered and retrieved from historical oblivion by means of objective, science-based definitions as its advocates claim; ethnicity is a means of social classification and as such a construct of very specific historical conditions and political interests.

The ambivalence of the ethnic argument exposes the contradictory premises on which solidarity as national solidarity is predicated. It suggests nationality as a taken-for-granted reference point that distinguishes nationals from foreigners on the grounds of some assumed intrinsic qualities. In European history the dominance of a nationalist construction of citizenship and national integration has come to imply an ethnified concept of the nation (Hobsbawm 1990) and thereby renders the qualities and prerequisites of 'belonging' non-negotiable and places them beyond the reach of political discourse (see chapter 2). At the same time nations are notoriously unable to substantiate the assumed equivalence of ethnic and national boundaries (Gellner 1983) as the still remaining multiplicity of ethnicities and languages in every European nation state demonstrates. There are strong indications that European identity and thereby solidarity is also being fashioned according to the recipe of the nation state, through closure constructed on (quasi-)ethnic lines which confirms a Fortress Europe mentality, and not just in relation to asylum seekers (Pieterse 1995), but also for instance in view of the accession negotiations with Turkey. The fundamental changes in the nature of the welfare states and the selective manner in which a European social policy agenda is being developed point also in that direction. It no longer suffices to be born into the community of a nation which entitles to a minimum of support. Today this support has to be 'earned', not necessarily financially but in terms of an investment in loyalty to the nation and conformity with its standards. Fortress Europe is being erected not just against foreigners, but also against homeless people, single mothers, all people on the margins who seemingly brought about their own hardship (Humphries 2002). For economic reasons the 'contract between the generations' which had ensured the payment of old age pensions from contributions paid by those presently earning a wage is being questioned. Solidarity no longer exists automatically between the economically active and those in retirement who get constructed instead as a separate cultural group on lines akin to those of ethnicity. Both on the inside of nation states and on their external boundaries, fortified by the European unification process, boundaries of solidarity are being mapped out anew, but the criteria by which these boundaries are being determined have long lost their universal validity and legitimacy. Solidarity reveals itself as a whimsical, fashion-driven, media-dependent, ultimately arbitrary game. The encounter with migrants and refugees is not the cause of this fragmentation of social solidarity within European societies, but it activates those existing uncertainties in localised, everyday, inescapable contexts and interactions.

What is more, the ambiguity in the actual meaning and operation of national boundaries is indicative of a fundamental re-ordering of the command over time and space in the course of globalisation, with immediate consequences for social work practice, not just in relation to work with migrants. The process signifies the intensification of a global interconnected-ness at every level, economic, cultural, political and technological. In the analysis of Giddens and Harvey, accelerating trends in post-modernity or late modernity (as they prefer to call contemporary developments) have completed a process of 'distanciation' of time and space, which had started with early industrialisation and resulted from the formation of international sets of relations by the nation states; the emerging national economies of the 19th century and the concomitant technological achievements further advanced this distanciation (Giddens 1984, 1991, 1994; Harvey 1989). Time and space today have not only separated from each other and have become independent of a locality, but the technology to 'shrink' space and to create virtual simultaneous encounters across the globe is having the effect of a dramatically increasing time-space compression. This is not an inevitable linear development of history; it is the direct result of the power to command the use of time and space, a power that accumulates in the hands of an elite. In other words, globalisation according to this analysis is about the re-distribution of time and space, about their very unequal re-distribution. The rich and powerful occupy more and more space, which they claim as their own (while running out of time in the process which has to be utilised ever more efficiently as the global stock market never closes) whereas the dispossessed have 'time to kill' and are being squeezed out of economically usable space to become ghettoised in wastelands (Bauman 1997). This is the motor for global migration patterns which drives jobseekers from declining national rural regions into the same contested metropolitan arena as migrants and asylum seekers from distant places. Globalisation is about a forceful and rapid rupture within the ordering of space and time. Additionally, it reduces the migrant population and the 'indigenous' excluded to an over-reliance on time: They are being eliminated from the present and relegated to the past, made to carry around with them an oversize baggage of history of which they are being constantly reminded. They are being identified with traditional forms of behaviour as former peasants, as leftovers of a working class culture, as settled nomads who have never left behind their habits and who are therefore by definition not capable of arriving in the present. In a similar vein one of the mechanisms of excluding women is still their identification with traditional values and roles as bearers not only of children but also of

71

historical continuity and a particular type of traditional social order. This identification prevents such groups from ever fully participating in the present and laying claim to a piece of contemporary territory. It also sets them in competition with each other as different groups of dispossessed populations and reveals another insidious aspect of the sporadic popularity of neo-fascist ideas among disaffected youth and insecure sections of the working class: By clinging to their ethnic identity they can easily become hooked on a selective, tendentious version of history and thereby remove themselves from the economic battleground of the present. Consequently, they can only make their presence felt in violence and provocative actions.

It is therefore not surprising that conflicts over the unequal distribution of resources erupt with increasing frequency into open violent conflicts over territories. Seen from this perspective, conflicts ranging from inner-city riots to neo-fascist agitation and certain forms of violent crime share with the wars in former Yugoslavia, in different parts of the former Soviet Union and Northern Ireland the same underlying connection to the re-distribution of time and space. They are extreme means of settling the boundaries and conditions of belonging. Their appearance as 'untimely relics from the past' belies the logic of their acute contemporary significance as manifestations of globalisation. The distinction between political and civil conflicts becomes as tenuous as the distinction between economic and political refugees. Populations can become a 'threat' to each other without being physically on the move, at least not at the moment of the conflict. Once the right of one part of the population to fully 'belong' has become contested, references to past migrations and displacements become moral justifications on the dominant side of such conflicts for claims of having 'been here first', no matter how arbitrarily such historical data are chosen. These conflicts and wars represent a new type of phenomenon which is linked directly to the changes in the nature of the nation state and they are marked by new forms of organised violence as the inversion of processes of solidarity (Kaldor 2001). 'The goals of the new wars are about identity politics in contrast to the geo-political or ideological goals of earlier wars' (Kaldor 2001: 6). These conflicts represent desperate attempts to re-connect time and space, territory and culture with reference to a reified past unity. Ethnic cleansing is evidence of a fundamental contemporary conflict over the disappearance and the symbolic reconstruction of criteria for social and political solidarity (Brubaker 1996). The message of 'simple, self-evident' and thereby deeply racist solutions it contains is bound to set the scene for endless future conflicts because it localises a problem that is in fact global. The exclusion from territory and the denial of contemporary time go hand in hand, and the new forms of guerrilla-type wars in turn create a wide-scale displacement of populations.

What is now the significance of this analysis for contemporary European social work? Quantitatively, direct social work with refugees and asylum seekers is of marginal importance to the whole field of the social services. Social workers are not even necessarily in the front line of intervention in reception centres and refugee camps. The problems that have to be dealt with primarily, issues of financial assistance, housing, search for contacts, advice on entitlements and legal matters, normally require other specialists, specific questions around psychological trauma of displacement and possibly torture and difficult relationships were dealt with by counsellors and therapists (Veer 1998). But gradually mainstream social work came to be involved since, as with all social problems, the complexity and the interrelated nature of these problems calls for a comprehensive perspective. But with this more general involvement issues of cultural understanding, not just at the linguistic level, moved centre stage. But with such a broader involvement the wider political questions emerged: are people whose citizen status is unclear entitled to such comprehensive assistance or only to such measures that help them to find the basics for existence pending the clarification of their status. Are they to be helped to make the transition to the receiving society or would this only be an additional complication in the event of their being deported back to their country of origin?

A particular borderline case in this context is constituted by unaccompanied refugee children. Social workers seem unsure how to respond to the extent that in most countries it took some time for the issue to become even identified (Okitikpi and Aymer 2000). When it is recognised responses vary widely from attempts at fitting the treatment of such children into the pattern of procedures for non-immigrant children, in which case often difficulties arise over finding suitable homes or foster places that recognise the children's' cultural identity, and treating them to different standards in view of usefulness of informal networks among migrant communities. Here it becomes clear that acting 'in the best interest of the child' cannot take recourse to fixed universal standards but that child care practices in particular are bounded by national standards and expectations (Christie 2002). These new areas of involvement challenge the profession ethically and methodologically to re-consider what constitutes the basis on which assistance is being offered to any service user and at the same time to clarify its socio-political reference points for intervention generally. The work with migrants, with all people whose citizenship status is in doubt, tests the relationship of social work with the project of the nation state and its possible over-dependence on it (Lorenz 1996). Is it still the national agenda that frames the social work mandate to ensure solidarity, to patch together a national unity so that conformity with national standards of behaviour extends as far as possible? Has the distinction between the 'deserving' and the 'undeserving' cases, which was always part of the profession's patriotic, nation-building, nation-purifying legacy, really disappeared and given way to a universal, critical, objective, scientifically based approach to diagnosis and intervention? Or can social work face up to the realities of multi-cultural societies and ground solidarity in a human rights approach that negotiates with minorities their cultural preferences without taking national standards as the decisive yardstick? Can the social professions find an operational space between total relativism and indifference to standards on the one hand and fixed, essentialist assumptions about standards of behaviour that leave no room for negotiation and development?

The contradictory effects of national (and indeed European) social policies in relation to migrant populations are indicative here. These policies oscillate broadly between attempts at 'integration through dispersal', through the avoidance of ghetto formations and the ensuing stigmatisation and discrimination (e.g. in France and to some extent the UK), and strategies directed explicitly at special needs and the acknowledgement of separate ethnic, cultural identities (e.g. the Netherlands and Sweden) (Castles and Miller 1993). Both strategies are aimed at integration and the avoidance of conflict, but the experience has been quite universally one of 'unintended consequences': dispersal encounters the resistance by the migrant or ethnic groups concerned against the implied disregard for their collective identities (with reciprocal reactions on the part of the 'indigenous' population), while specialised attention creates grounds for stigmatisation and can cause new inequalities in comparison with other marginalised groups.

These political dilemmas have their equivalent at the level of direct personal interaction. Social work and social pedagogy methods that have been developed specifically in relation to ethnic minorities, refugees and migrants are subject to the same ambiguities. The initial approaches in most countries were well-meaning attempts at helping those groups to integrate better through tuition in the language of the receiving country, information about institutions and habits and assistance in coping with formal require-ments to gain access to resources. But preventing discrimination by means of reducing cultural differences and basing integration on assimilation invariably triggers defensive reactions on the part of those who fear that their identity is being transformed or cancelled. This realisation triggered often a second set of approaches which instead of reducing cultural differences 'celebrate' the diversity of cultures as enrichment for the receiving country. These multicultural methods focus on bringing about understanding and tolerance through making cultural differences visible in festivals, customs and the revival of a cultural heritage. In both cases, culture was made the main focus of inequality, and this particularly in countries like France and Germany where culture has such a central role in the constitution of the nation state (Abye 2001). 'The pedagogical discussion in Germany has, without much critical debate, settled on a central interpretative formula that suggests that the problems of migration are simply or primarily cultural conflicts' (Hamburger 2001: 97). The underlying assumptions about the monolithic and static nature of culture further traps migrant groups in modes of interaction which can always serve racist forms of exclusion as 'justification' (Aluffi Pentini 1996). The 'essentialising' of cultural characteristics ultimately renders inter-cultural dialogue and critique of values and standards impossible and can led at times to unreflected forms of practice like the formula of same-race fostering and adoption. Only in subsequent phases did methods emerge that reflect a more dynamic model of culture. The general title of 'intercultural' approaches signified the need for cultural positions to be questioned in both directions (Auernheimer 2001) and opened up new ways of understanding and counter-acting processes of discrimination. This led in some countries to the development of an explicit anti-racist focus of intervention (Dominelli 1998). This was particularly pronounced in the United Kingdom where black activists reminded the established social work profession of the presence of racism especially in institutional practice, as was confirmed in the landmark report of the Stephen Lawrence enquiry (Macpherson 1999). In most continental European countries, as shall be explained in the next chapter, there was no widespread acceptance of the concept of anti-racism, mainly out of fear that racism was too narrow a focus in the fight against discrimination. Instead, the concept of the 'management of diversity' found more acclaim in a broad spectrum of responses, particularly in the Netherlands (Hoffman 2001), some of which still maintain a more 'educational' orientation, whereas others highlight the political nature of discrimination against minority and migrant groups and advocate structural changes in rights and entitlements accordingly.

It has now been recognised in most European countries that developing social work methods for work with migrant groups and ethnic minorities is therefore not primarily a matter of concentrating on migration or on cultural differences as the specific causes of the social problems to be dealt with, nor can such methods be designed by way of ignoring those specific conditions and reverting to a 'treating people as people' approach. Rather, the tension between the specific forms of exclusion encountered by those groups and the general nature of actual and potential exclusion encountered by all users of social services has to be explored in both directions. All forms of social work are liable to either bringing pressures to bear on people to assimilate to prevailing norms or of 'othering' clients, of arresting them in their categorical otherness and thereby confirming, even legitimating their being excluded on the grounds of their being so different.

The reflection on the impact of racism on social work practice in several countries helped to bring out these connections in the discourse on social work methods. But it does therefore not follow that anti-racist methods developed under the specific conditions of a country and a particular historical development can simply be exported to other countries. Seeing methodological developments as linear reflects a mono-cultural bias, as if for instance other European countries would have to wake up, sooner or later, to the necessity of applying the anti-racism approaches that have become a feature of some aspects of British social work. The engagement with racism and exclusion needs to recognise the multifaceted and constantly changing manifestation of contemporary racism and the historical dynamics of exclusion. In particular, the discourses over social work's role in and use of anti-discriminatory and anti-racist methods need to take account of three reference points in coming to such specific responses, as becomes evident in the literature review by Hummrich, Sander and Wöbcke (1997):

a) The different academic and disciplinary traditions prevalent in the social professions; for instance, social work in the form of community work is not inherently more political than that in the form of social pedagogy or counselling, and yet each academic discipline and methods discourse can make visible different political and structural mechanisms and consequences of exclusion. In most of these traditions, there are tensions between a merely person-oriented and a context-oriented strand of theories.

b) The differences in political culture that exist in different countries, particularly in relation to the degree and kind of mobilisation of civil society; there is no formula by which we can determine on principle whether state or non-state services and agencies are less discriminatory. What is important is instead the way the relationship between citizens and the state is mediated by associations and self-help movements within a particular tradition, which might be based on assumptions not shared by immigrant or minority communities. Being in the hands of the state or in those of a voluntary organisation per se is no guarantee for its anti-discriminatory orientation.

c) The different legal conceptions regulating 'citizenship' as the manifestation of national solidarity, for instance the principle of *ius sanguinis* in Germany as against the *ius solis* and the emphasis on cultural integration as an expression of citizenship in France. Social work practice relates directly to these differences, as outlined in chapter 2, since social workers intervene on behalf of society as a whole.

The encounter with users of social services whose basis of 'belonging' to a given society and nation is in question on psychological, cultural and legal grounds gives occasion to reflect on the need for a critical, 'multi-layered' approach to social work methods generally. Responses particularly in the area of dealing with ethnic and cultural diversity need to acknowledge explicitly the interplay between personal and political factors, and any attempt at reducing its methodology to one or the other level has grave consequences not only for the reputation of the profession, but above all for the effectiveness of the intervention.

It is through this combination of perspectives and skills at personal and political level simultaneously that social work has an important contribution to make to the development of a critical social policy perspective in Europe generally. Social policy, particularly at European level, is no longer just a matter of top-down developments but contains a growing bottom-up element in the form of new forms of participation and representation. At European level the distinction between political refugees or asylum seekers and of migrant workers is becoming ever more tenuous. Principles of solidarity with people in other parts of the world suffering political persecution and economic hardship are being replaced by considerations of economic convenience. This means that practices of selective exclusion, which had prevailed in the formation of nation states, are now being reproduced rather uncritically at European level. Just like at the time of the workhouse economic usefulness determines not only moral acceptability but reception into mainstream society. The convergence of European immigration policies from the Schengen agreement to the Dublin convention and their ratification in the Amsterdam Treaty of 1997 was intended to strengthen the perimeter fence around Europe while allowing greater mobility between EU countries. Measures taken concentrated on negative aspects, on keeping out 'undesirables', and it is very significant that the Schengen criteria treat refugees and immigrants from outside the EU broadly in line with drug traffickers and terrorists for the purposes of controls and surveillance. The intergovernmental committees dealing with such questions operate under a cloak of secrecy and are not subject to effective democratic controls. Social workers know that it will not be possible to 'manage' the tensions arising from this criterion with their standard repertoire of methods and see themselves increasingly used for purposes of social control. Immigrants in several countries are now obliged to pass tests not just of proficiency in the native language but of familiarity with national institutions and values and social work in its various forms is being enlisted to make the system work when tensions arise. Politically, defining 'Europeanness' by means of exclusion will in any case not produce a sense of European social solidarity or European citizenship. European social integration requires a broad consensus on the principles by which to construct such solidarity positively and needs to move therefore the concerns for a social Europe centre stage.

Simultaneously, however, neo-liberal social policies within the European member states mimic the defensive, excluding and discriminatory fortress mentality towards non-EU foreigners. The better off in society, the coalition of high level earners, feel under siege from welfare claimants as their wealth appears threatened by high levels of taxation and redistributive policies. This means that the link between political and social citizenship that was at the core of the European welfare state project is being weakened as welfare is becoming privatised and citizens are left to make their own provisions for the danger of social hardship. Full citizenship rights are being denied to undesirable migrants and to unacceptable natives who do not conform to the work ethic. The everyday practice of citizenship particularly between citizens and state officials, between clients and professionals, between claimants and service providers defines the nature of citizenship overall. This is the point where the political dimension of social work comes to bear much more than in campaigning and being explicitly politically active. In these 'street level' interactions 'substantial' citizenship in the distinction of Bottomore (in Marshall and Bottomore 1992) is either established or denied. The exclusion of minorities is not primarily effected by processes of migration but by processes of social construction and definition which can cause people to find themselves on the wrong side of a divide without ever having changed location. Skin colour, religion, language, appearance generally and life style are arbitrary markers in this process of social allocation. Institutions, once linked to and legitimated by the nation state, are in danger of warding off arbitrariness with new means of objectified closure, and this is where racism offers itself as a tool always ready to be used, structurally and institutionally. 'As globalisation threatens the existing balance between objective closure and subjective assumptions, we can observe a resurgence of symbolic struggles about racialized classifications. This "racism of globalisation" is not a relic of the past but a flexible and efficient answer to the border problems of modern institutions in a globalizing world' (Weiss 2006: 135). These are precisely the internal boundaries on which social workers operate and these are the construction processes to which their actions can contribute explicitly or implicitly if they do not take position critically to their allocated role.

'The migrant' is therefore a paradigmatic test case for social work. The encounter with displaced, dislocated people challenges social work to examine whether its values are rooted in or related to nationalism or racism, ideologies which restrict the right to belong and to be cared for to the identification of innate cultural or biological qualities. 'Migrants', non-citizens, challenge European societies to declare on which principles they want to ground citizenship and solidarity. 'Old Europe' has to face up to diversity not as a new phenomenon, but as an inherent, precious and crucial part of its own history which now needs to be affirmed and fostered through new social contracts at national and international level. Principles of progress, liberty and solidarity on which the 'civilising process' was premised not only require new definitions, but also new practices. Social work has been an intricate, small but important part of this civilising project. It now sees itself questioned in that role and plunged into post-modern and post-national uncertainties. Its social responsibility in the face of this uncertainty does not rest with the use of technological means that operate with positivistic notions of efficiency and social engineering. Instead, social work's central contribution to the construction of a Social Europe is linked to its ability to negotiate solutions that create understanding and solidarity without eliminating difference and uncertainty. European migration policies and social policies today represent 'attempts to burn out the uncertainty in effigy—to focus the abhorrence of indetermination on a selected category of strangers (immigrants, the ethnically different, vagrants, travellers or the homeless, devotees of bizarre and thus conspicuous subcultures) while hoping against hope that their elimination or confinement would provide the sought-after solution to the problem of contingency as such and install the dreamt of routine' (Bauman 1995a: 128).

In Beck's analysis (Beck 1994) societies find themselves on the threshold of a second phase of modernity which has direct and very specific implications for social work. The reflexivity, core characteristic of modern societies (Giddens 1991), becomes conscious of its own insecurities, of the unreliability of the norms of rationality in which modernity had invested so much. Overburdened by this need for constant reflection and unable to get to grips with it, many sections of modern society retreat into constructions of 'counter-modernity', into 'fabricated, manipulable self-evidence' (Beck 1994: 473). Territorially defined ideas of identity abound and with them the fallacy that identity could be made something simple, unequivocal, the product of simplified dualisms (in or out, acceptable or unacceptable, them or us). The ethnification of social relations therefore has to be regarded as part of this counter-modern backlash. The warning examples of the consequences of such simplifications under Nazism and its 'final solution' are not sufficient to avert the dangers of neo-nationalism and neo-fascism in Europe. The conflicts and complexities arising have to be re-worked in the present context, albeit with historical references. And this is where a refusal by social work to become drawn into schemes and programmes based on dualistic assumptions and a sustaining of radical reflexivity become crucial.

Positively and building on the experiences of anti-racist social work, these proposals go in the direction a dual strategy around which social work methods capable of engaging with 'Europeanisation' and globalisation can be constructed. This applies not just to the work with migrants and refugees but to the full range of social work tasks in today's multi-cultural, diverse societies. One requirement of such a strategy is that it fosters psychological security through competence in, rather than withdrawal from, reflexivity, allowing individuals to fully accept their multi-layered identities in the context of 'fluid' communities. This creates anxieties and uncertainties, but to respond to them with simple solutions would be irresponsible and counter-productive for the fostering of new forms of solidarity that acknowledge diversity. The other is that these re-negotiated identities and the conflicting demands on others that arise from them are worked out collectively in groups of mixed composition, including both users of services and representatives of institutions which have the power to determine civil and political rights in a form of lived, practised citizenship (Lister 1998). Differentiated social groups and communities require rules, but not as externally imposed rules, but as frameworks of rights and obligations which those affected by them can shape collectively. This means for instance that in the work with offenders or perpetrators of violence their human rights become tangible reference points for all interactions and interventions, so that their ties with various sectors of the population get respected and, where necessary, re-established. In institutional segregation, where this becomes inevitable, inmates remain members of society and of distinct communities of interest and their identity must not be exclusively become defined by the institution in which they find themselves. The inability to confine people within fixed borders causes anxieties on both sides, but borders everywhere assume a new role and a new quality as points of contact and negotiation rather than zones of exclusion where worlds and communication end. Globalisation and migration challenge social work to contribute imaginatively to this required re-construction of 'the social space' which neo-liberalism had declared all but obsolete, or rather, which new social policies, with the device of decentralisation and territorialisation, seek to use for purposes of categorisation and exclusion (Otto and Ziegler 2004). The critical discourse around the notion of '*Sozialraum*' in Germany seeks to reclaim this space in an unsentimental way as the seat for local social and political action.

This re-construction is above all a moral practical question (see chapter 6), 'since it is only the *full* relationship, a relationship between spatially and temporarily *whole* selves, that may be "moral", that is embrace the issue of responsibility for the other' (Bauman 1995a: 134). In this process, continuity is centrally important, particularly for those who experienced forceful disruptions, separations and dislocations, for instance for children caught in the cross-currents of incompatible demands, but also for whole population groups exposed to rapid transition. This continuity cannot come from references to ontological qualities like race and culture, nation or blood or soil which are always a means of deception and will always render those putting their faith in them powerless and disoriented once they experience their unreliability. Continuity can only be secured in the interplay between personal freedom and social responsibilities, a process, which has found its diverse manifestations in modern notions of citizenship. Taking citizenship as a lived experience (Lister 1998), as moral practice among people who recognise each other's multi-layered, dynamic identities, could provide a reference point for social work practice not just with migrant groups, but for social work in the age of globalisation per se.

Within the prevailing politics of recognition where ethnic identities and other 'expressions of self-interest' have currency, where political correctness conjures up notions of moral righteousness, social workers are ill advised to choose the road of 'ethnified approaches' as a means of refuting the suspicion of racism and other inherent biases raised against them. Such 'partiality' alters nothing about the nature of discrimination in society and ultimately plays into the hands of power interests that utilise ethnic boundaries as markers for discrimination and exclusion. Furthermore, from an ethical point of view it locks social work into a fundamentalist framework which Giddens warns against: 'A Nietzschean view is sometimes lauded these days as allowing for that recognition of the "other"—that necessary cosmopolitanism—which makes possible a multi-national world. It does nothing of the sort. What it leads to, in fact, is precisely a world of multiple fundamentalisms; and this is a world in danger of disintegration through the clash of rival world-views' (Giddens 1994: 252). His proposals of a 'generative equality', negotiated through 'generative politics', are very much the domain of social work because such equality needs to be worked out primarily 'at the basis', at community level, as the condition of tangible, substantive, experienced, lived citizenship which matters to transient and stable populations alike.

These observations call for a more detailed examination of the relationship between the professional and the political agendas around issues of identity and their implications for contemporary social work practice, which will be the subject of the next chapter.

5. Culture and identity in generic social work practice

The question of identity and of the role of social work in the constitution of people's identity has become inescapable. The historical considerations in previous chapters gave a first indication of the reasons why social work at various stages of its development distanced itself so vigorously from operating explicitly with cultural norms and hence with the notion of identity as a valid reference point for intervention. In the contemporary context which presages a confluence of politics and of cultural movements, the various 'solutions' of the past need to be examined afresh. The analysis of the significance of issues of 'identity' for the general practice of social work, and not just for social work with migrant and minority population groups, shows the importance of considering further implications of the intersection between civil society developments and academic-professional discourses in social work.

There can be no doubt that social work interventions directly or indirectly impinge on people's identity if identities are regarded not as essentialist qualities but as sets of social relations, but it has been only from the more recent post-structural perspective that various academic analyses began to focus on how social work exactly defines and constructs the identities of its clients (e.g. Rojek et al. 1988). This explicit attention given to identities is by no means unproblematic as it contains the danger which the profession has always been anxious to avert, that through its interventions people might become labelled, confirmed in their negative identity categories as deficient, excluded from the 'normal' part of society. Social work's declared project was instead to make a contribution to the integration of society by means of practising equality and giving equal dignity to individuals. What is new since the last decades of the 20ᵗʰ century, however, is that 'differences' are being affirmed by minority groups in society ever more confidently and vociferously, labels are turned into tools for emancipation, separate identities are being re-claimed as a defence against levelling, stifling homogeneity.

> 'In the very moment when modern liberal states fully realize their secularism (as Marx put it in "The Jewish Question"), just as the mantle of abstract personhood is formally tendered to a whole panoply of those historically excluded from it by humanism's privileging of a single race, gender and organization of sexuality, the marginalized reject the rubric of humanist inclusion and turn, at least in part, against its very premises. Refusing to be neutralized, to render the differences inconsequential, to be depoliticized as "life-styles", "diversity" or "persons like any other", we have lately reform-

ulated our historical exclusion as a matter of historically produced and politically rich *alterity*' (Brown 1995: 200).

Identity, and with it cultural identity as the key to diversity, matters inside and not just between societies. At the same time, such cultural differences serve again as justifications for inequality, as arguments against the socialist aspiration of equality, as a means of unhinging the finely balanced sets of rights and obligations which had undergirded the nation state.

To raise the question of culture in social work means therefore dealing with a paradox and calls once more for an investigation of the history of that paradox. The paradox lies in the observation that for most of its history, social work strove to rise above the level of the culturally particular and reach a level of universalism as the hallmark of its professional autonomy, while it was precisely that universalism that played into the hands of particularism, in the form of nationalism (and indeed, at times, of fascism and racism) and in the form of 'unintended' mechanisms of exclusion (cf. Müller et al. 1995). Investigating the history of that paradox might indicate ways of avoiding new unintended outcomes of today's greater attention to cultural differences, namely that they would serve to justify and solidify exclusion and inequality. Culture and difference cannot be dealt with responsibly by either embracing the concepts uncritically or by excluding them categorically from practice discourses.

The renewed focus on culture and difference occurs at a time of economic globalisation. Globalisation threatens the broad welfare consensus that had developed in Western European nation states in the era immediately after WWII. 'The welfare state may be seen as a "completion" of the nation state, to the extent that individual social rights become an essential element of citizenship as the main basis of political legitimacy' (Flora 1986: XV). It substantiated the idea that belonging to a nation could become a lived experience by giving individuals a material stake in their state. The current crisis of the welfare state therefore spells also the crisis of the nation state and vice versa. While the welfare state secured a high degree of integration (at the price of conformity and uniformity with assumed national standards, which will be discussed below) internally, it depended on a high degree of differentiation of nation states externally, on their political sovereignty and autonomy in terms of policy making, particularly in the area of social policy. With the erosion of this sovereignty the seat of governance is moving away from the nation state, making room for collective identities and identity coalitions to form without reference to the nation, but also for new centres of power outside the national systems of democratic control. In a weakened nation state 'modern' forms of social integration as enshrined in the ideal of equality may become less effective and legitimacy of the political system may become based more on differentiation and 'the politics of recognition' (Taylor 1992).

Social work is deeply bound up in these processes and only a critical examination of the relationship between methods discourses and different political cultures in Europe can help to regain more autonomy and credibility in relation to cultural practices. This chapter seeks to illustrate this by focusing on the example of the development of social pedagogy as the decisive paradigm in the German context and contrasting its origins with the social science paradigm prevalent in Britain. The purpose of this comparison is to show that both paradigms were de facto ways of responding to questions of culture and identity but that their potential for recognising the political component of methodology can only be derived from such comparisons.

The nation state project, the unification of a diversity of political entities and the legitimation of political power through democratic principles, had set itself the task of creating a coherent and unifying national culture, which it did by means of its unifying cultural politics (see chapter 2). As Rattansi comments with reference to Bhabha's analysis of national narratives: 'The "people" thus must be thought of as existing in "double time", for the project of producing the nation as a community involves a tension between a "pedagogic" authority of continuity and a "performative" strategy in which the ragged, potentially transgressive cultures of everyday life are constantly brought under the sway of a narrative of what one might call a national "community"' (Rattansi 1994: 40-41).

As far as most continental European countries are concerned whose boundaries were re-drawn in the wake of the Napoleonic wars and which formed in the course of the 19th century this constitutes the paradox of the modern state as a nation state: it had to reinterpret the romantic dream of liberation and self-determination with the imagery of a community, in analogy to the family (Anderson 1983). These nations organised their cohesion increasingly by re-constructing pre-existing common bonds, instead of the mere social contract between free and therefore 'fundamentally different' individuals, which the push for democratic rights and civil liberties in the republican tradition had demanded (Lorenz 1996). But the nation state could only establish its legitimacy and its unifying power by attending to social issues, by concerning itself with the affairs of people as private individuals and families, by transforming the prevailing vertical cleavages into a horizontal community of equals and distinguishing itself from 'outsiders' (Balibar and Wallerstein 1991). This task required its own missionaries, foremost provided by the teaching profession, but social work came to fit equally into this project. It was largely an education project, carried initially by the 'lower and middle professional, administrative and intellectual strata, in other words the educated classes' (Hobsbawm 1977: 167). It was a project that operated as the patchy, anticipatory construction of social citizenship in Marshall's sense grafted on top of the emerging political citizenship grounded in the principle of democracy.

While the task was the same in all new nation states, different political and historical contexts affected the meaning and role given to the concept of culture. In relation to social work the contrast between Britain and Germany is particularly significant. In the British tradition of liberalism in which the state was initially very reluctant to go beyond the introduction of compulsory schooling and some public health measures as positive means of integration, the emphasis was on leaving the initiative to private organisations which would regulate the cultural blend of homogeneity within a version of national identity that was ultimately confident of its meaning and its boundaries in the light of the political and economic successes of the empire. Culture in Britain, like in France (where this confidence was however a legacy of the revolution and the equalising effects of a national culture) was closely associated with the notion of civilisation. 'Both [terms] were used increasingly to describe a general process of human development, of becoming "cultivated" or "civilized"' (Thompson 1990: 124).

The role of the charity workers, in contrast to the staff of the expressly punitive and exclusionary state institutions like prisons and work houses, was to patrol the margins of the nation, to see to it that 'right kind of people' were included, that the harsher social control measures of the state only affected those who were not 'deserving' of the membership of the body of the national people. What was more important in their work than the particular culture and ideological 'message' of their charitable association, was the instrumental use of 'universal' cultural reference points such as sobriety, industry and thrift which became identified with the 'rational' ideals of patriotism:

> '*Patriotismus lässt sich so durchaus als Voraussetzung eines höheren Allgemeinsinns begreifen, der die nationale Eigenheit übersteigt und als Vorstufe des Kosmopolitismus gelten konnte Der Patriot opponierte gegen Verfall, Künstelei und Korruption, und plädierte für den väterlichen Patriarchen...*' ('Patriotism can be understood as the pre-condition of a higher sense of community which transcends national particularity and could be regarded as a preparatory stage for cosmopolitism. The patriot is opposed to decay, artifice and corruption and calls for a fatherly patriarch') (Giese and Junge 1991: 273, own translation).

The actual educational task in this context was marginal and ultimately quite ineffective. 'Any such classification by merit was found to have no relation to the necessary classification according to needs... Eventually the Charity Organisation Society was driven to drop the criterion of desert; "the test is not whether the applicant be deserving but whether he is helpable", we were told' (Beatrice Webb 1926: 174). However, the 'education' was effectively but indirectly supported by, in the case of Britain, the institutions of the Poor Law which represented the boundary of exclusion visibly, and in relation to that the work of charity workers had enormous symbolic significance. The normality of the national standards of behaviour was defined from the margins, through the boundary between what is acceptable and what is unacceptable behaviour. It is on this standard that the whole range of 'culture-based' organisations and activities of British civil society had already begun to converge. In England between 1780 and 1830 'the "average" English working man became more disciplined, more subject to the productive tempo of "the clock", more reserved and methodical, less violent and less spontaneous' (Thompson 1968: 451), and this largely thanks to the Sunday school system and the effects of Methodism and other 'evangelical' movements which ultimately all enforced the same message. The service to the one nation later found its secular expression for instance in the Settlement Movement which sought to express the need for both classes to meet and mould a new sense of belonging through 'colonies' in the inner cities.

The 'border patrol', the rescue of the deserving from exclusion, and the personal attention to the poor and destitute was in particular the patriotic duty of women (and not just in their public capacity as charity workers, but also in their private educational role as mothers) in the same way as serving the country in war, in the defence of its external borders, or as administrators of the colonies was the patriotic duty of men. Women in the ambit of middle class charity work in Britain saw themselves as 'natural' carriers of the idea of the nation without having to represent it 'officially'. Octavia Hill, in commenting in the preface to her book of 1875 on the Artisans' Dwellings Bill which was going through the British parliament at that time, strongly supports the intended provision of affordable housing for the poor but adds: 'There needs, and will need for some time, a reformatory work which will demand that loving zeal of individuals which cannot be had for money, and cannot be legislated for by Parliament. The heart of the English nation will supply it—individual, reverent, firm, and wise. It may and should be organised, but cannot be created' (Hill 1983: 10).

The pronounced individualism of British charitable activities expressed in these sentiments endorsed the basic tenets of the liberal state. By 'privatising' the concern for cultural contents while invoking the notion of the nation as an organic community it also sought to curtail the political impact of an independent working class culture (Jones 1983). Working class consciousness and identity, mirroring the rationality of capital but being denied a symmetrical role in politics, typically extended across country borders and the labour movement was constantly accused of its unpatriotic internationalism through which, for some time at least until the surrender to the nationalist fervour which fuelled the First World War, it refused to be incorporated into the nation state project. Philanthropy and the state's concessions in terms of early social policy measures served to de-politicise this consciousness and to establish a regime of power into which the working class movement could be incorporated (Donzelot 1979). If the nation state were to succeed in reinterpreting those political conflicts created by glaring material and political inequalities as insignificant remnants of cultural difference within a much more important shared national culture, to which both the poor and the well-to-do could be committed, then the political relevance of the class argument could be refuted. Within this shared commitment remaining differences became re-defined as individual differences of cultural and life-style choices. Cultural arguments then, especially in the form of the ideology of nationalism, had the function of legitimating the hegemonic role of the state as promoter of a shared sense of belonging which broke the disruptive power of persistent inequality, whereas today the argument of cultural difference has the function of legitimating the minimalist role of the state and its indifference towards the worsening of inequality.

At the academic level, in the British political tradition the search for universal reference points found its goal in social science paradigms, and this despite the individualistic orientation of practice. Characteristically, in the British context these focused on the diagnosis of social deficits which prevented an adequate social functioning of individuals within the wider society. The pioneers of social work training in Britain were ultimately engaged in the creation of 'subjects' for their emerging discipline as much as for the new organisation of the modern state (Philp 1979). From this perspective cultural norms were not evoked explicitly but were instead brought in line with the principles of civilisation and its much more universal appeal, for which in turn the state was the ultimate custodian.

For the German nation, created from an array of independent kingdoms by the uniting device of war against France in 1871, culture had a much stronger and more direct collective function. Here the programme of national unification could not be grounded in a unified religion or in justifiable claims of ethnic unity, nor indeed did geography provide clear assistance in the drawing of national boundaries as did the coastline in the case of Britain (leaving aside the vexed problem of Ireland). Instead, the dominant political elite in Germany utilised selectively the cultural arguments developed by artists and intellectuals of the romantic period. Their celebration of the uniting force of the German language already spoken in dispersed countries and their idealised notions of a nation based on cultural ideals provided a rich soil of symbols while at the same time their calls for freedom and democratic national unity in the revolutions of 1848 were material carefully sidelined by the political restoration. This meant that the new, 'belated' nation state of the second German empire had to tread a careful balance between concessions to the 'progressive' national forces which had regarded national aspirations as the vehicle for democracy and freedom and the conservative definitions of a shared national culture. This emphasis on a shared cultural heritage symbolised by language placed the German nation in sharp contrast to the 'mere', superficial 'civilisations' of neighbouring countries (Zimmer 1996). On both political sides however, the concern for a cultural renewal and consolidation as the basis for a national identity was associated with the concern for 'the social question', for social solidarity expressed in social policies (a term which was already a central reference point in the decades before unification, Wendt 1985).

This gave the German state a very different role from that of liberalism in Britain: the state had to become the embodiment of an idea, it had to create its own heritage and ancestry and it had to carefully and watchfully see to it that the organisations of civil society and the potentially explosive diversity of their highly diverse cultural positions fitted into this superstructure and supported it. The strategies of corporatism and subsidiarity provided the solution and allowed Bismarck as the architect of the German Reich to launch almost immediately into decisive social policy provisions as the second corner stone of national unity (next to his aggressive foreign policy). His social policies were designed to give the state a guiding, patriarchal and indeed educational role while at the same time enlisting the 'voluntary sector' into the delivery of those services, under the close and constant inspection of the state. With the simultaneous outlawing of the social-democratic party he also eliminated what he considered to be this unpatriotic source of instability and yet he implemented de facto many of their demands for the social protection of workers (Briggs 1961).

The pioneers of social work and the intellectuals responsible for the development of a distinct German discourse around the emerging field of social practice tuned into this political context in a unique way. They found in the concept of 'pedagogy' the means of articulating the cultural agenda as a social agenda and thereby as a political agenda while retaining, on the whole, a critical distance to the mere implementation of particular governmental programmes. In this pedagogical tradition, going back to Rousseau and Pestalozzi, culture and civilisation were not exchangeable concepts but contrasts. Where civilisation for them symbolised the superficial appearance, the polite manners, the outward conformity, culture was an inherent value of people and artistic products can only be measured against the authenticity with which those inherent values are expressed. But this realisation of the innermost core of humanity is precisely not an individual act, but takes place in the context of a human community since human beings are social beings. Creating this community, rather than the need by a state system to create a uniform culture, constitutes the pedagogical mandate for social policies 'from the bottom up', although as a social programme it cannot be fulfilled without the participation of the state to ensure its equal reach to the totality of society (Hamburger 2003).

Social pedagogy as the constitutive paradigm of German social work is, in this fundamental sense, a cultural project and one that extends far beyond school pedagogy and hence the notion of 'education' in the English language. The term is normally attributed to a 1844 pamphlet by Karl Mager for whom 'Pedagogy [was] the theory of the acquisition of culture' (quoted in Kronen 1978: 223) and therefore not directed primarily at individuals but at society as a whole. The concept received its first full academic exposition in the work of Paul Natorp who used the term in 1894 in the subtitle to a book entitled *'Religion innerhalb der Grenzen der Humanität'* ('Religion within the boundaries of humanity'). Natorp's intention was to develop an alternative to both the individualised charitable projects which aimed at the rescue of individual 'cases' and the emerging procedural formality of the 'social state' in which he recognised the assimilatory pragmatism of 'civilisation' (Niemeyer 1998). Ultimately his concept requires for its realisation the (re-)transformation of society (*Gesellschaft*) into community (*Gemeinschaft*, with explicit reference to Tönnies), a community which determines its own cultural and thereby social parameters. The formation of culture can only occur *'in, durch und für Gemeinschaft'* ('in a community, through community and for community') (Natorp 1894: 85).

This approach received its most vivid and spontaneous realisation in the movement which influenced German pedagogy lastingly, the youth movement of the turn of the 20th century. This started as a bourgeois movement channelling all the disaffection which this class felt with the industrial landscape of growing urban prosperity (Hamburger 2003). The movement of the *Wandervogel* set its sights on a cultural renewal through the suspension of the effects of civilisation: hiking through the countryside, living communally in tents, connecting with the music and poetry of folk traditions became some of the signals which heralded a new sense of community and a cultural renewal in which young people defined their own parameters. Youth work organised by every sector of civil society, church, humanist and political, sprang up in the wake of this spontaneous movement in an attempt to capture the spirit it had set free.

This 'social experiment', which came to be of lasting importance in German social history, illustrates however the central dilemma of the social pedagogy approach: Can social pedagogy, by placing culture in such a central social position, make a contribution to 'the social question', i.e. to resolving the social divisions on account of poverty and inequality, and above all a contribution that is different from both the charitable attention to individuals and the social engineering and social control programme of the state with its 'civilising' educational and social policies? Or, to ask it the other way round, what are the guarantees that the process of emancipation, the authentic articulation of needs, interests and desires which the pedagogical process wants to foster in this 'bottom up' approach, will actually lead to a viable society that is not rent apart by sectional (cultural and class) agendas and by the weight of its own diversity? For academic

90

German social pedagogy in the 1920s this dilemma became all the more a challenge as the Weimar Republic took decisive measures to develop a coherent social policy and to ground its legitimacy as a democratic state in a comprehensive programme of social reforms.

The cornerstone of that reform is the *Reichsjugendwohlfahrtsgesetz* (Child and Youth Care Act) of 1922/24. Its opening article states 'the right of every child to education (*Erziehung*)' which is not an affirmation of compulsory schooling but gives expression to the institutional application of the principles of social pedagogy: all children have the right to the kind of pedagogical attention which enables them to become full and competent members of a society. This is very much a cultural programme to which academic social pedagogy had to provide the appropriate concepts and tools. Its cultural mission, which amounted indirectly to a political programme, was the identification and formulation of a higher form of culture as the basis of community, an all embracing community, which would supersede and obviate actual cultural differences and their divisive power within the nation state. It meant to formulate a compromise between the demands of the youth movement (and numerous other movements and organisations with similar aims and objectives) which insisted on giving their programmes their own distinctive cultural flavour ('youth can only be educated by youth' was one of the slogans of the youth movement) on the one hand and the institutional interests for integration enshrined in the state on the other, interests which could not allow for these differences to 'matter' too much. Above all, it offered the opportunity for social workers and pedagogues to secure a professional (and existential) foothold in the nascent welfare state institutions with a methodology which would not alienate the spontaneous initiatives led by non-professionals (Niemeyer 1998).

Conceptualising culture as a universal entity while holding on to the notion of an educational process towards 'higher' forms of culture meant grounding it in universal principles. In the intellectual climate of German academia of the 1920s two options were available which lined up to oppose each other vigorously. The positivist camp of the human sciences ventured to emulate the objectivity of the natural sciences to arrive at 'hard data' as the basis for their concepts of human behaviour and society. A key representative of this approach in the history of German (and indeed international) social work is Alice Salomon who pioneered professional training for women in the 1920s. Taking up the title of Mary Richmond's textbook of 1917, 'Social Diagnosis', she seeks to combine in her own version the social science based positivism, consisting in the accumulation of a comprehensive 'factual' picture of people facing social problems, with a pedagogical concept of learning how to overcome these problems. Diagnosis, like in the natural sciences or in medicine, 'means a short, precise and absolutely fitting explanation' (Salomon 1926: 7). But diagnosis is not an end in itself, it is a step towards using the information on causes identified jointly with clients to work towards solutions. Anticipating the principle of 'client self-determination' she cautions that this learning must be a shared process between worker and client.

This amounts for Salomon to nothing less than 'the art of living', and since insight and resources are always limited, this means 'coming to terms with one's circumstances' (Salomon 1926: 52). This comprehensive design of the helping process is for her grounded in the specific 'nature' of women outlined in an earlier key text of hers:

> (As women) 'we want to express our nature. We must help to create something new for which men do not have the necessary experience and for which aim they also have to search for new energies and ideas. Women especially are equipped for this new task with one quality. It is the sense of the totality of the people as an organism ("*Volksorganismus*"), the social idea, which grows out of the destiny of woman to be a mother and which gives her the special ability to go beyond her own interests and those of her immediate vicinity in her feelings and actions. It is this thought which has to become the foundation of the people's state ("*Volksstaat*")... There is no true democracy as long as the life of a people is split by class interests and troubled and torn apart by class movements and class war. The people's state requires citizens who place the interests of the totality above their own interests. In its true manifestation, in its ideal form it would not contain parties any longer, only vocational groups and guilds ("*Stände*")' (Salomon 1919: 10, own translation).

Salomon struggles with the dilemma of unity and division at all levels. These for contemporary ears uncomfortable sentiments have to be taken as an attempt at formulating a programme that could be described as 'universalist identity politics of social work'. They take their departure from an essentialist view of women and particularly of motherhood which they then elevate to the status of a universal criterion of welfare and national politics. Different starting points in varying life experiences and versions of the role of women in society and in the family no longer matter, just as party-political differences ultimately do not matter, once they all become subsumed under a joint objective.

The alternative model was provided in the explicit anti-positivist tradition (to be explored more explicitly in chapter 7), represented most comprehensively by Herman Nohl, the figure that was to shape the German social pedagogy discourse lastingly. For him, life as a spiritual process cannot be captured by objectifying psychological methods but only through the hermeneutics of understanding (in the sense of Dilthey). It is this life and its ultimately unifying force which Nohl identifies at the heart of the various social movements, labour, women, youth, as the autonomous pedagogical energy which social policy and pedagogical methods have to harness. The great movements of the nineteenth century have a converging meaning: 'an awareness of the crisis of our culture which lacks an inner bond with an ideal, and the will to resolve this crisis from within a new form of being human, of which the most central characteristic is a new sense of community' (Nohl reproduced in Thole et al. 1998: 126, own translation). Social policy and particularly the new youth legislation of the Weimar Republic incorporate all these movements and aspirations, not without tensions, but united ultimately in the concern for bringing about 'the humanity in human beings' as the basis for solidarity, grounded in 'knowing oneself contained within a unity of meaning which goes beyond all understanding and embraces all communities' (op.cit. 128).

Cultural differences are recognised as important in both approaches to social pedagogy. But each methodological line aims at transforming the inherent divisiveness of culture into an integrated, universal whole. For this project the state suggests itself then as the embodiment of an idealised, purified form of culture that corresponds to the 'highest' qualities of human nature. It had been the dilemma of pedagogy all along, how to reconcile the individualised or at least particularised concerns which inevitably manifest themselves when 'freedom from imposed norms' is promised, with the necessity to represent those particular aspirations in an organisational form which corresponds to all of them collectively and legitimately. If this 'coming together' of diversity into a whole is not to be brought about by force, it requires the ultimately Hegelian dialectical construct, that the historical unfolding of culture at the level of society, its 'coming into its own', corresponds to the innate educational growth, differentiation and social development of individuals over the life time. Only then can it make sense to postulate as the essence of modern social pedagogical thinking 'that all social adjustment presupposes the development of special individual capacities, that the true service for the community is only possible when human beings experience in it a certain fulfilment of their personal essence', as the social democratic pedagogue Mennicke put it (Mennicke 1930, quoted in Thole et al.: 184, own translation), whose values and beliefs later earned him a long spell of incarceration in a concentration camp.

The irony, no the tragedy was that while these pedagogues sought to overcome conceptually the antagonism between 'person-oriented' and social policy perspectives and programmes, between individuals and society, between difference and unity conceptually and by consensus, the regime that came to power in Germany in 1933 achieved it forcibly by decree—at a terrible cost. In a way the entire Nazi programme was the continuation of an education programme, highly selectively applied but nevertheless within a strong line of continuity, through a devious combination of scientific and political means (Schnurr 1997). Hitler's government did not on the whole abolish the institutions of civil society, the diversity of humanitarian and religious associations (not even the Jewish welfare association), it got them instead committed to a common national goal (*gleichschalten*). Nor did it rescind the pedagogical measures, even the 'progressive' ones that developed through the Weimar period and which aimed at reform rather than punishment. But it operated the pedagogical process with a racist criterion of 'difference' as the crucial, absolute yardstick (with absolute, lethal consequences). Racism recasts cultural differences as factual differences on a scale stretching from the superiority of the 'healthy' to the inferiority of the 'life-unworthy' (Bock 1983). The device of racism, combined with a distinct anti-individual and anti-intellectual brand of pedagogy, sought to create unity and uniformity by absolute measures of exclusion (Sünker and Otto 1997). If pedagogical institutions could explicitly and deliberately exclude and discriminate, if the whole country could 'rid itself' of 'ineducable' cases, then, so it was promised, the 'progressive' pedagogical project stood a chance of succeeding, then it would be possible to keep 'diversity' within such bounds that the stability of society was ensured. As a report on the improvement of success rates of residential pedagogical reform measures states triumphantly in 1937: 'Because pedagogical care measures (*Fürsorgeerziehung*) have changed fundamentally since the year 1933, not only by coming in line with the pedagogical principles of the National Socialist State, but also through an earlier referral of children and youth to such agencies and on account of the fact, that these are now being relieved from responsibility for the so-called ineducables (*Unerziehbare*), we can now expect that this change will continue to show positive results for the entire field of child care and that the average success rate will be further improved' (Ohland 1937: 12). This 'unsentimental', ostensibly scientific, re-building of an organic people's community (*Volksgemeinschaft*), which the German Report to the 3rd International Conference on Social Work in London 1936 kept emphasising (Hilgenfeld 1936), appeared to represent all the ideals of a correspondence between pedagogy and social policy and in the process destroyed all the principles of both pedagogy and culture to reveal its true barbarity in the systematic killing of people that did not belong into the ideological construct of a master culture for a master race (Lorenz 1994). Social workers did not necessarily have to apply racist, culture-specific and fascist criteria consciously in their work; it was enough that their seemingly value-free, scientifically based diagnostic classifications served the state apparatus to perfect its system of exclusion and elimination.

As demonstrated in previous chapters, the programme of democratic reconstruction devised after World War II by the Western allies and the UN through a whole range of training programmes, notably also for social personnel, failed to recognise the specific dilemma of the social professions under fascism. The measures were based on the assumption that fascism had brought social service personnel under the spell of collectivism, that they had blindly followed instructions, had sought to promote authoritarian obedience to a leader figure and had compromised their professional and scientific standards with ideological elements which actively promoted a master culture. Hence the emphasis of those (re-)training programmes in social, group and community work, sponsored by the USA and the UN came to be on value neutrality, individualism and client self-determination. The case work model (and the equivalent models of group and community work) studied in the USA was regarded as exportable to every country in the world because it espoused a liberal notion of formal equality and democracy in the public realm which relegated all questions of cultural differences to the sphere of the private. Re-education programmes did not recognise that it had been the assumed value neutrality of the universalism, on which the pedagogical concepts as much as the social science derivatives of early case work had been based, that had constituted the profession's blindness to the misuse of their idealism under Nazism. What gained prominence instead in the immediate post-war period in Germany, as elsewhere on the European continent, was the highly individualised notion of self-determination as a guarantee of democracy and therefore the disregard for the public importance of any kind of collective identity, be that based on national, ethnic, regional, denominational or gender criteria, at least as far as the actual methods of intervention were concerned. Case work and group work methods alike, developed under this 'democratic' precept for instance at the famous training centre 'Haus Schwalbach', aimed at bringing about freely chosen identities irrespective of any 'given' identity elements (Müller 1988). The model represented a pure form of 'the liberal conception of the public sphere' in Fraser's terms (Fraser 1995). 'This conception assumes that a public sphere is or can be a space of zero degree culture, so utterly bereft of any specific ethos as to accommodate with perfect neutrality and equal ease interventions expressive of any and every cultural ethos' (op.cit.: 290). Even the churches and the big secular welfare organisations which retained their crucial role in the delivery of welfare services in Germany after World War II did not articulate their differences in the form of distinct methods. On the contrary they were also keen to 'treat people as people' and leave their clients to seek out cultural reference points in the nature of the service as their private preferences but not as a condition for receiving a service. In fact the social professions generally were only able to re-establish themselves slowly in Germany against the widespread suspicion that the 'social' in their title was associated with 'socialism', either of the Nazi or, which in the Cold War climate was even more threatening, of the Communist type (Müller 1988). It took quite some time in post-war Germany for the re-establishment of the socio-pedagogical tradition and it was only possible under the protection of a 'universal' social work paradigm—even where this, as in the case of Gisela Konopka, Hertha Kraus and other consultants of German origin operating from their enforced US exile, this had many roots in social pedagogy (Lorenz 1994).

In an effort to avoid all references to the divisive power of cultural differences social work practice and training in Germany (as in most other western countries) became committed to a scientific programme of individual definition and fulfilment of need, which, in fact, amounted to a programme of assimilation to a prevailing cultural and political orthodoxy. The underlying assumption was that processes and forms of communal life at individual and small group level corresponded to those at the societal level, that micro- and macrocosms of social life were coherently structured. There was indeed an intriguing correspondence at the macro-political level where the bloc-mentality of the Cold War era relativised cultural differences between nations and gave rise to a widely shared but rather superficial enthusiasm for internationalism as a means of overcoming old fashioned nationalisms.

This ideological construct and the considerable integrative force it generated, not least in Germany with the relatively successful integration of millions of refugees from beyond the Iron Curtain (being a victim of communism meant being 'one of us'), wavered in the wake of new social movements in the late 60s and 70s and came crushing down with the fall of the Berlin Wall and the revolutions in former socialist regimes. The cracks in the bloc systems had already gradually given way to discourses of identity in the late 60s and 70s. Inequality had not been eliminated but had been bracketed out and the allegedly neutral public sphere was exposed as a gendered, class biased arena. Social and protest movements, though slow in affecting the social professions, eventually also exposed the vacuity of the case work approach and its democratic promise. In Germany, this concern with the nature of social conflict and inequality in turn gave rise to a re-examination of the conceptual and methodological advantages of the social pedagogy paradigm in engaging directly and critically with the political level over against that of social work with its orientation towards adjustment within given socio-political parameters.

At the level of academic discourse, pedagogy made itself at least receptive to questions of identity and culture by shifting its field of practice decisively from the 'system' (of welfare organisations, laws and structures) to the 'lifeworld', in Habermas' (1987) distinction. Pedagogy matters in 'everyday contexts' (*Alltag*, Thiersch 1986), not in carefully controlled and abstract clinical or therapeutic spaces. Questions of identity are very much part of the lifeworld, not in a precast form as the 'system' produces them, but as expressions of collective interests in dynamic yet fuzzy forms. Young people, women, parents of children with disabilities, neighbourhood groups began to claim forms of self-representation which challenged the 'universalism' of received social work definitions and triggered a 'learning process' that pitted itself against the weight of expert professional cultures in the same way as the youth movement had done at the start of the 20th century.

96

And yet, these assertions of identity by social and user movements still did not amount to a fundamental challenge of the traditional ambiguity towards the notion of culture contained in the socio-pedagogical paradigm. This challenge came from two other fronts, the presence of 'foreign populations' in Germany in the form of migrant workers, refugees and asylum seekers, and the rise in violent forms of nationalism among young people in the wake of German unification. In relation to the former, German social pedagogy, similar to social work and education in other European countries when they first encountered immigrant populations, initially made efforts to accommodate 'the phenomenon' within its conceptual boundaries (Müller et al. 1995). It concentrated its efforts first on giving assistance towards assimilation and integration, developing a special field of 'pedagogy for foreigners' (*Ausländerpädagogik*), and later, realising the absurdity of wanting to level all differences by pedagogical means, on forms of multicultural and intercultural pedagogy (Hamburger 1993). In the sudden open acknowledgement of a diversity of cultural positions and their relevance for intervention the full weight of the pedagogical tradition was brought to bear with its liberal aspirations both for the full development of the inherent potential of each individual and for the procedural respect for the equal value of 'the other'. But these aspirations also contained their own limitations in as much as they, on the whole, assumed that the imparting of better knowledge and the socialisation in the practice of tolerance would change the nature of racism and exclusion which the minority 'foreign' populations experienced in their daily lives. Undoubtedly, the shift from integrationist to multicultural concepts is significant as it brings the notion of cultural difference and of the right to an autonomously defined identity into play (Auernheimer 2001). Yet it also highlights the ambivalent political role of culture and the limitations of the traditional pedagogical project: once a plurality of cultural universes has become theoretically accepted, often to the point of an uncritical fascination with the exotic 'otherness', it renders itself powerless to fight the inequalities that hide in cultural differences and which a multicultural approach appears to even sanction. This paralysis seems to have beset the whole of German social work and social pedagogy in the context of the realisation of the impact of cultural diversity (Müller 1995).

This becomes noticeable also in relation to the second, related challenge, the rise in violence directed at non-Germans. The moral panic generated in the wake of attacks on hostels for asylum seekers and other racist violence concentrated on measures for young people and particularly on those in former East Germany. While there is undoubtedly a serious issue to be addressed and the behaviour of young neo-Nazis is by no means inconsequential, it has to be asked whether the framing of the problem betrays the historical and conceptual limitations set by the 'match' between the pedagogical and the nation state project in Germany. Firstly, it is interesting to note that the focus is so explicitly on the behaviour of young people, precisely the group that is the primary subject of pedagogy. Giving pedagogical attention to their behaviour may easily divert attention away from more widespread racism in German society, especially as the most favoured pedagogical approaches are termed 'accepting youth work' (Scherr 1994). This implies that the lack of tolerance for ethnic minorities and foreign cultures displayed by certain groups of young people should be countered by giving them, in the face of the sub-cultural features of their obnoxious, deviant behaviour, a minimum of recognition as the precondition for any pedagogical progress towards greater tolerance (Krafeld et al. 1993). The recognition of the 'coping' element in their group behaviour could then be a step towards lessening the dependence of individuals on the group. Secondly, and more problematically, their behaviour is usually framed as 'violence against foreigners' (*Fremdenfeindlichkeit*), which implies an acceptance that the specific characteristic of their victims is their status as foreigners. True as this may be in the majority of cases in the legal sense (although violence against people with disabilities occurs also more frequently), their lack of German citizenship is in itself a product of the German citizenship laws which make the acquisition of a German passport very difficult even for second generation immigrants. The 'diagnosis' therefore endorses an underlying assumption of essentialism in cultural differences which diverts attention away from the social and political construction of these differences. Thirdly, the panic concentrates on the Länder of former East Germany and singling out those parts of Germany implicitly constructs notions of a cultural lag in comparison with West Germany where a multicultural society has gained greater acceptance. Behind these assumptions lies the old zeal of a combination of the pedagogical and the national project in Germany which manifested itself for instance in the wholesale export of the entire welfare system, including the training courses for social workers and social pedagogues and most of the teaching staff from the West to the East.

At this point the critical historical reflection on the place and function of culture in social work would have been so necessary. Contrary to the main thrust of current pedagogical efforts in Germany around the issue of migration, cultural minorities and fascist violence the problems are neither of recent origin, created by the influx of foreigners and by German unification, nor are they specific to the relation between self and 'others'. Rather, the core problem is the inherent commitment of the pedagogical project to the national cause which ultimately seeks to suspend, sublimate and merge (to spell out Hegel's untranslatable term of *aufheben* in some of its components) diversity in one authoritative public norm.

This is indeed not just a German problem and social work everywhere has to confront the complex dilemmas posed by cultural diversity even in seemingly homogeneous societies like for instance in Ireland, a country which until the sudden reversal in the late 1990s from being a country of poverty and emigration to one of prosperity (at least in parts) and immigration had considered itself as culturally homogeneous, and this despite the glaring cultural divisions marked by sectarianism and social divisions between the 'settled' and the 'traveller' communities (McVeigh and Lentin 2002). Neither the withdrawal to the ostensible safety of positions of universalism and neutrality nor the uncritical acceptance of positions of cultural relativity and subjectivity will save the profession from the danger of becoming a collaborator in power politics carried out either in the name of cultural pluralism or of downright nationalism and fascism.

The scant attention paid to issues of identity not only by politically disinterested social workers, but also by politically committed social workers on the left, cannot be compensated by introducing the concept of ethnicity uncritically in the sense that different ethnic groups require different approaches or even different standards of social work. The issues posed by the 'struggle for recognition' which 'is fast becoming the paradigmatic form of political conflict in the late twentieth century' (Fraser 1998: 19) should be well familiar to social work which in its practice is constantly negotiating difference, the right to be different with principles of equality, the right to be treated the same. It is in this daily interaction where cultural norms and reference points are being taken up as part of people's historical continuity and are being transformed at the same time into often fragmented elements of bureaucratic provisions. It is also the place where the apparent clash between the politics of recognition and the politics of redistribution can yield to the practice of democracy. Laclau has argued convincingly that while 'universality is incommensurable with particularity', it is still utterly dependent on the particular for its actualisation, as becomes apparent in human rights discourses (Laclau 1995: 107). This paradox is the precondition for democracy: a modern, fair and civilised society can only emerge from the persistent and continuous attempts to reach a temporary consensus over the significance of personal identity and cultural differences.

It is significant therefore that Krafeld, one of the first advocates of 'accepting youth work with neo-Nazi youth' in Germany has recently re-framed his approach in terms of a justice perspective (Krafeld 2001). Fook (2001) speaks of 'emerging ethnicities' as a way of introducing reflexivity in the (co-)construction of ethnic identity. Identity for her signifies a dynamic process which needs to foster the competence to cope with multiple and shifting demands on different group allegiances. There are no permanent solutions to the dilemmas and clashes of interest of a multicultural, diverse society, but there are forms of social practice which promote a constructive transformation of those clashes, a transformation of personal troubles into issues of social policy and not vice versa. In refusing to become absorbed on one side or the other of the controversy between a neo-liberal and a communitarian conception of society, between the 'new binary' of modern and post-modern models of social policy (Taylor 1998), between the dilution of traditional collective identities and the stubborn, aggressive affirmation of nationalism, social work can make indeed a contribution to the realisation of cultural fairness, social human rights and human dignity in concrete, particular, everyday contexts. It can only do so, as will be demonstrated in the following chapter, with reference to reflexivity and communication as its core competence.

6. Intercultural communication in social work practice —ethics and politics

The previous chapters presented observations on the paradigmatic significance of work with migrants and on the necessity to acknowledge and foster the development of multiple identities. Social work in the light of the changes implied in these processes could be conceptualised as practised citizenship. To spell out what this could mean in practice, the question of language and communication as the central, the only tools of social work has to be examined in more detail. This chapter will re-affirm the importance of a core political orientation of social work practice as deduced from the very conditions for communicative competence in every interaction. Once more, intercultural situations will appear not as the exception but as the constructive test case for the critique of an instrumental use of language and communication in 'mainstream' social work. This also necessitates a critical examination of social work's position not just in relation to the project of the nation state, but more generally that of modernity itself and its current status as this project now appears to be also in some difficulty. Social work has a role to play in the constitution of the (post-)modern self and it needs to be able to deal with the full complexity of this task. An inter-cultural understanding of all communication processes and the fundamental principles that make communication possible are therefore constitutive for the profession.

Culture, identity and with it inter-cultural understanding have become problematic concepts in contemporary society to a degree that makes all previous doubts about the reliability and consistency of the boundaries of self and of cultural domains appear as naïve certainties. Difference and how to constitute identity in full recognition of fundamental differences have become central pre-occupations in a post-modern world in which the self has to constantly re-constitute itself through reflection and through choices of life style. 'In the post-traditional order of modernity... self-identity becomes a reflexively organised endeavour. The reflexive project of the self, which consists in the sustaining of coherent, yet continuously revised, biographical narratives, takes place in the context of multiple choice as filtered through abstract systems' (Giddens 1991: 5). This process of 'dis-embedding', as Giddens calls it, has led to an acute form of individualism which not only finds itself lost in an over-abundance of meanings but has begun, particularly at the level of academic critique and reflection, to question the very foundations of the project of modernity upon which it was founded. The self now becomes engaged in a very different relationship with culture and culture re-emerges in late modernity with a new and highly ambivalent message.

The project of modernity had set out to bring order into the seeming arbitrariness of culture understood as sets of traditions. Its mission, formulated by Kant in his emblematic clarification of the notion of Enlightenment, was to initiate a process of emancipation: 'Enlightenment is man's emergence from his self-imposed immaturity (*Unmündigkeit*). Immaturity is the inability to use one's understanding without guidance from another' (Kant 1968: 53). It spelled also the liberation from the bondage of un-reason which held sway in unexamined cultural traditions. Reason began its global trajectory from the conviction that it represented the key to a universal understanding of a code at the core of all culture, a key that would unlock the door to absolute and universal truth, both as far as the physical world and as far as the world of values was concerned. The promises were those of a 'true' universal understanding that transcended cultural boundaries and with that of progress towards the establishment of a universal civilisation which would set new standards of freedom and humanity.

The project today looks precarious. The twentieth century which produced two world wars, the Gulag and the Shoah, which has brought every corner of the earth in the grip of a global economy and generated the conditions for massive ecological disasters, concluded with a disillusioned, sceptical attitude towards reason, progress and civilisation. Western societies had to realise and realise ever more clearly that the universal understanding across cultural divides in the name of reason, where it succeeded at all, was achieved largely by force and violence. The advance of reason led to dependency, oppression and the extermination of entire cultures through technologically perfected killing machines and politically unassailable and largely unaccountable power concentrations. This realisation leaves the self disoriented in its project of self-constitution, unable to find a unifying principle (Touraine 1995), bereft of the one certainty it had clung to in the questioning of all traditional truths, which was the leadership of reason promising order and stability. In this situation, which has the hallmarks of a profound crisis infused with existential angst (Giddens 1991), two basic options seem to suggest themselves as escapes from the over-load of reflexivity:

(i) The option of cynical disregard for all certainties, values and authorities, the retreat (or break-through?) to pure, unstructured, uncensored and immediate 'experience' for which anything goes and nothing really matters (Sloterdijk 1983). On this side the de-construction of grand narratives gathers momentum, not only at the level of intellectual

102

critique and literary analysis, but also quite tangibly at the societal level: 'The decay of the Ego goes in parallel with the dissolution of the idea of *society*' (Touraine 1995: 269). This mood is captured by the political representation of neo-liberalism which questions the existence of society as a figment of sociologists' imagination and seeks to replace the solidarity vested in a state system of welfare guarantees with private, commercial arrangements between 'free individuals'.

(ii) The other option focuses on the (re-)constitution of certainties by means of calling a halt to the seemingly infinite regress of critical questioning (or by sheer fatigue). 'Factuality' in the form of common sense, of the cosiness of actually existing communities, of the empirical pervasiveness of boundaries marked by gender and ethnicity gathers its own persuasive momentum as an apparently solid and reliable, simple, comfortable and popular reference point for the constitution of identity (Habermas 1996). In all the questioning of where to belong and with whom to identify it comes as a relief to experience for instance the tangible solidarity of a crowd of football supporters identifying with a local or national team, no matter how tenuous the actual common base of this identity is. It suggests absolute (and often anti-intellectual) simplicity and takes religious affiliation, language, or skin colour as markers of the boundaries of solidarity and responsibility when national identity becomes too complex to define and negotiate in increasingly diverse multi-cultural societies. The flirtation with essentialism and the postulation of distinct cultural and ethnic identities constituted by fixed criteria of tradition and biology at a cultural and the emergence of nationalism and racism as forces to be reckoned with at a political level are not so much signs of a back-lash or of the return to pre-modern reference points. They are contemporary products of the accentuated dilemma of the constitution of the self, a 'coping strategy' that bears witness to modernity's failed project of universalism (Bauman 1995a).

These latter references to the political implications of the crisis of late modernity indicate that the radical questioning it implies cannot be treated as a matter of detached curiosity, as is frequently the case in aesthetic discussions, but as a matter of considerable practical urgency in which social work is implicated as it is concerned with people's coping strategies. Therefore the issue of inter-cultural understanding is not an additional question on the already very full agenda of late modernity, to be tackled under 'Any Other Business' once the individual self has perhaps managed to re-constitute itself and to free itself from these intense existential anxieties. Rather, inter-cultural understanding matters today as the central quest for the possibility of grounding the self in today's complex reality through competence in communication. It is the question of whether there is any chance of sustaining the challenge of diversity and of radical questioning without destroying the social basis of the existence of the self, without turning from the meaningless cacophony of complexity to the deafening silence of abstract simplifications that by-pass communication entirely and end in speechless violence.

The approach taken here implies therefore first of all that the question of the constitution of the self in late modernity, the question of how to go about grounding and expressing one's identity, is connected to the question of communication. It means secondly that all communication has to be approached basically as inter-cultural communication, or to turn it the other way round, that inter-cultural communication is a test case for the core elements of successful, good communication. It requires thirdly for communication to be treated not primarily as a matter of technical competence but as an ethical question because its success depends on a commitment to a joint cause, however minimally that might be defined. And lastly it can be postulated with Habermas that it is this ethical commitment which is the precondition of a social existence, of a social framework that can constitute something like community through the act of communicating, and that what constitutes the possibility and indeed the necessity of community in turn gives the task of grounding the self without reference to essentialism some minimal prospect of success.

From this perspective is should become clear why it is important to consider inter-personal, intra-cultural and inter-cultural communication as part of one coherent complex. Culture is meant to signify here systems of meaning which, like language, symbols and customs, have on the one hand a kind of independent, objective existence, and on the other live and function only through the subjective endorsements (and indeed modifications) of members of a cultural community (Hamburger 1990). Culture constitutes identity just as much as identity choices constitute cultural contours. But seen against the background of the introductory remarks to this chapter the criteria of culture cannot be merely of an aesthetic nature but raise the question of norms. In this way the reflection on intercultural communication might help to point a way between the cynical and the communitarian alternative to deal with the contemporary problem of identity. The practice of social work tests whether principles of inter-cultural communication can be conceptualised on a continuum of practice situations and scenarios between, for instance, the interaction with asylum seekers who arrive in a country of a different culture requiring material, language and probably also psychological assistance and the work with parents who have abused one of their own children. Referring to both situations as culturally constituted in no way endorses the theory of a 'culture of poverty' as it had been espoused by Oscar Lewis (1959) and as it still lingers in political debates on social deprivation today, just as the difficulties of migrant groups are often reduced to those of cultural adjustment. The term often implies that poverty is meant to 'reproduce itself' by means of self-imposed limitations in motivation and ambition which have become internalised by poor people living together in poverty-stricken neighbourhoods. However, lives and life opportunities in society are separated by many factors, most of which are not a matter of choice for the individuals concerned and differences in society cannot therefore be reduced to differences in life style. Cultural theories of poverty and other social problems overlook the importance of material inequality and the real limitations this imposes. But in relating both situations of social work mentioned above to a different concept of culture emphasises that the meaning of all differences, including that of material differences, is mediated by cultural norms. It is through the application of these norms that differences turn into inequality, which makes them no less 'real', on the contrary, their cultural and social meaning and significance is indeed part of their 'reality'.

Patterns of behaviour in responding to these differences are also socially constructed and mediated by language. Their meanings are always shared among groups of people, even where the violation of norms is an individual act and may have pathological origins. The 'language' of a suicidal act, even the 'language' of the pain inflicted on a child in the privacy of an individual family, has a socially defined structure and in that sense a 'grammar'. The ability to intervene in and prevent a suicide attempt or an act of harm against a child by a violent parent is ultimately related to the ability to understand such behaviour as a language, to engage with it, and to set up a communicative framework within which change becomes possible (Ashenden 2003). Bernstein's observations on the use of 'restricted' and 'elaborate' codes used among working and middle class children respectively attempted to capture such differences as cultural differences represented in different language systems (Bernstein 1971). However, he failed or was at least ambivalent in making these differences amenable to communicative mediation and change; he failed to reflect fundamentally on the inter-cultural, transformative significance of his findings.

This latter focus on the possibility of change and transformation within the discourses on culture is frequently also omitted from considerations of inter-cultural communication which make it appear as if the task of decoding alien languages and habits alone was everything. In relation to the situations of social need and conflict referred to above the attempt to understand socially unacceptable behaviour is often confused with condoning it. Trying to understand behaviour that is totally alien to one's own cultural norms creates indeed anxieties. The realisation of difference can easily become so unbearable that the alternatives indicated above in relation to the social and political constitution of the self can also become activated in the interactive, inter-personal domain: They confront social workers with the alternative of either surrendering to the impossibility of finding an agreed moral reference point from which to judge a form of behaviour as unaccept-able and thereby conceding that all behaviour, all cultural conventions, are equally valid and thereby implicitly or explicitly condoning it, or of retreating to the seeming certainties of the prevailing conventions or official rules and prescriptions that govern bureaucratic interventions. Fixed habits and customs, which gain ground also in current managerial procedures of case management, then assume the role of absolute moral principles and function as universal norms from which to judge all forms of behaviour leaving no room to really engage with 'difference', let alone at reaching a new level of understanding. In both cases the chances of achieving any change in the other person's situation are minimal or restricted to the use of power and the imposition of restraints.

In both the setting of the constitution of the self in a context of considerable uncertainty over norms and cultural boundaries and in that more general of the grounding of principles of inter-cultural understanding and interaction organisationally and practically the same kind of dilemmas seem to operate. This gives a further indication as to how intercultural communic-ation is linked to intra-cultural communication at a time when the quest for universal reference points has run into such acute difficulties. Linking the issue of inter-cultural communication to that of the constitution of the self means then, that the question of understanding fellow human beings is ultimately not an aesthetic nor a technical question but an ethical question. Or, to put it another way, the reduction of the process of understanding to a matter of taste and life-style, i.e. of aesthetic indifference or that of technical feasibility is a violation of the dignity of human actors engaged in constitut-ing their identity through communication. It furthermore denies the possibil-ity of founding social solidarity on communication and mutual understanding and instead erodes the conditions on which society is built. If it is impossible to overcome the differences between culturally constituted positions com-municatively, it becomes impossible to constitute a society from individuals, each with their own identity, whilst allowing these individuals the freedom to be different. It becomes impossible to arrive communicatively at a sufficient level of commitment by individuals to each other and of solidarity among people characterised by ostensible differences. Solidarity would then only be possible among people who are essentially the same, who share an a priori sameness, be that genetically or culturally determined, among people there-fore who would have only a minimal need to communicate.

In order to find the way back from this paralysing silence to the possibilities of communication it might help to speculatively stretch the potential for inter-cultural communication to its hypothetical limits and ask whether it would ever be possible to understand aliens arriving on earth from outer space. Communication with such aliens will not and cannot depend on technical means, on the availability of dictionaries or of computing power capable of breaking a secret code. Understanding the visitors from outer space will only be possible in as much as we have always known them already in our imagination. The possibility of understanding them will be bounded by the way in which we have reckoned on the possibility of their existence and at the same time imagined their otherness as the totally other. If they merely confirm a fixed set of ideas, particularly if they are made to confirm an available catalogue of well rehearsed fears into which all that there is to be understood about them will be subsumed, all possibilities of 'real understanding' will be lost. This means however that our meeting with them will always be partial, if it becomes possible at all and does not resort to violence as the confirmation of our pre-conceived fears. The possibility of communicating with them will be conditional on a general mutual willingness to meet and understand. It will be limited to the areas in which the willingness to meet and to share communicative efforts are reciprocated. If violence dominates the encounter, if the fear of the totally 'other' gets the upper hand, as it usually does in science fiction blockbusters (which can be taken to be cultural reference points legitimating exclusion, created at a time when racist violence is simultaneously on the increase), this violence is a perverse expression of the claim to 'total understanding', of not admitting ignorance and sustaining ambiguity. This gesture of communicative oppression is at the core of all violence.

This hypothetical thought experiment is meant to illustrate both the possibilities and the limitations of inter-cultural understanding in a general sense. Understanding is predicated on the one hand on the possibility of imagining shared interests and intentions, and on the other hand on conceding the possibility of misunderstanding all or most of what there is to be understood. Allowing for the possibility of the 'totally other' is the actual safeguard of our understanding. This 'rest' is therefore both a technical and an ethical safeguard because it concedes, or constructs, a self in the other that is the seat of autonomy and authenticity. It posits the right to self-representation without which the encounter with the other would be merely the subjection of the other to what is already known, an act of oppression, an encounter with an object whose meanings are inferred and thereby fundamentally false. This ethical moment cannot function without the ability to sustain the discomfort of strangeness as the constitutive element of inter-subjectivity (Hoffman 2001).

All communication, not just inter-cultural communication, operates at two related levels, as Gregory Bateson pointed out in his analysis of the conditions for therapeutic communication and change: 'Every message in transit has two sorts of "meaning". On the one hand, the message is a statement or report about events at a previous moment, and on the other hand it is a command—a cause or stimulus for events at a later moment' (Bateson

1951:179). From this he concludes that the act of communicating can produce meaning only in as much as it simultaneously constitutes a relationship between the interlocutors at a 'meta-level'. As people communicate about particular subject areas they also convey to each other how what is said is to be taken. They make reference to, but also modify, play with, destroy and rebuild systems of meaning which scaffold the 'contents' of their communication. This is why Bateson can state 'that the system of codification and the system of values are aspects of the same central phenomena' (Bateson 1951: 176). The level of meta-communication in conversations operates in a social context with the aid of tone of voice, body gestures, word associations and countless other signals which establish the search for and the link to a modicum of shared premises, intentions and values. It is the interplay between communication and meta-communication, between given codes and personal meanings which makes understanding ultimately possible.

Applying this in the pedagogical field Bateson operates with the notion of 'deutero-learning' (Bateson 1942) which is the ability to learn how to learn, to 'read' social situations and their inferred meanings and to build up a well tuned, autonomously managed system of meaning. Jerome Bruner finds a related aspect of language and language acquisition constitutive for the psychological development of the self: 'Just as the first steps toward learning to use a language depend upon a transactional relationship ..., so the later elaboration of language use for the negotiation of intention and meaning also requires such transactional relationships' (Bruner 1984, p 6). Pedagogical approaches based on these concepts emphasise the connection between the development of secure personal identities and the competence to communicate effectively. Learning and identity formation take place in the context of a community which in turn is constituted by linguistic interaction. They require a pedagogical space on the borders between given identities and cultural domains (Aluffi Pentini and Lorenz 2006).

Habermas' theory of communicative action elaborates on these insights into the conditions of understanding in a wider social and political context. His project is the establishment of criteria of understanding that take seriously the replacement of a philosophy of consciousness (which had postulated a self-sufficient subject confronting an objective world) by a philosophy of language, which had been formulated above all by G.H.Mead (Giddens 1985). He finds them in a universally-pragmatic version of rationality that does not start from a priori assumptions of universal criteria but rather constitutes its validity claims through the act of communicating itself, through re-claiming Kant's transcendental criteria at the level of language and communication. Validity claims must be and can only be postulated, expressed and endorsed by those engaged in communicative action (Habermas 1981). However, this requires in turn social conditions of freedom, of non-interference with the communicative process which permit those engaged in interaction to fully enter into the relativity of inter-subjectivity and through it to reach a critically examined, openly argued and non-oppressive consensus. Every interference leads to distortions, and communication, as it occurs in 'the real world', is shot through with distortions of this kind. These distortions have their origins in the separation of 'system and lifeworld' and in the subsequent dominance of power interests which are inimical not just to freedom, but to communication and understanding in their full sense (see chapter 7). The moral question of the truth of what is being communicated turns into a political question of how the moral commitment, contained in the communicative interest in understanding, can be structurally safeguarded.

Habermas' optimism that the emancipation project of enlightenment could be completed once the mechanisms of the 'colonisation of the life-world' through 'the system' are fully known and the dialectics of enlightenment, so extensively analysed by the Frankfurt School, have been critically reworked, is not without its ardent critics. Lyotard's view of 'the post-modern condition' (Lyotard 1984) points towards a definite farewell to all attempts at completing emancipation by means of grounding solidarity in universal processes of legitimation. For him the cultural differences between groups of people are simply unbridgeable. What we are left with are localised, self-referential language games in Wittgenstein's sense, and any attempt at universalising them means applying forceful, violent unifying measures: Lyotard accuses pragmatists like Richard Rorty of 'secondary narcissism', of attempting to make one's own values the yardstick of all cultural systems. This, for Leotard, opens the door for terror, for a kind of terror typical of Nazism 'whose rationale is not in principle accessible to everybody and whose benefits are not sharable by everybody' (Lyotard in Rorty 1992: 62).

This terror is indeed all too present in the form of a growing ground-swell of racism and neo-fascism as a response to the perceived threat of alien cultures to one's own fickle and troubled identity. Relying on the appeal of democracy as the formal forum in which cultural and political differences can be settled amicably and non-violently, as Rorty seems to suggest, is a weak defence against this type of terror when the democratic institutions themselves are losing their appeal. Instead, there appears to be an urgent need to focus on learning how to defend and to practice democracy, on the acquisition of competences in everyday situations and on the creation of an awareness of how much our wellbeing and our future depend on reaching a minimal consensus over the priorities of this ultimately pedagogical enterprise, parallel to the process of securing formal democratic structures and procedures. Only then can the formalities of democratic rules and processes command new legitimacy and reach a level of effectiveness. The distortions in the communicative competence potentially available in the lifeworld, of which Habermas speaks, need to be tackled very directly as the factors that also thwart meaningful inter-cultural communication. Appeals to tolerance, to understanding and awareness are insufficient in the construction of anti-racist strategies.

This means recognising the connection between the tasks of establishing meaningful personal identities and of practising meaningful inter-cultural communication by establishing the connection between the pragmatics, the ethics and the politics of communication. The isolation of any one of those factors plays into the hands of further distortions, further alienation, further exclusion.

To come back to the examples from the everyday practice of social work and social pedagogy: social workers simply cannot allow to occupy a world of its own the mind of a person who uses a position of trust with or power over children to harm them. The outcry that such behaviour causes in the general population once it becomes known, the calls for more effective intervention indicate that we cannot cancel the minimum of solidarity a society expresses for a child who is being harmed and to whom a wrong has been done in the private sphere (Parton 1991). There is a need to make the situation safe for the child, but in order to achieve this effectively somebody must try to understand 'what has been going on', somebody must negotiate the total strangeness that this situation confronts society with, because the solidarity of society as such is at stake, and this precisely because it might become necessary to control the contact a perpetrator of abuse has with children and with society. Equally, society cannot cancel solidarity with asylum seekers who have a 'genuine case', who have suffered torture and persecution, without losing an essential part of its humanity and dignity and its faith in the protective, constitutive qualities of a humane society (Humphries 2002). In conceding this minimum of understanding human beings also concede the possibility of difference within themselves as they relate to both what they can reach or at least imagine and to what remains strange in both those situations and in themselves, without resorting to the technique of 'splitting'. But it is one thing to state such sentiments in abstract, it is quite another to translate them into action, into effective and legitimate strategies of intervention. It is in these border-areas of understanding that social work is challenged to develop its actual competence, and to develop core competences as inter-cultural competences.

The following typology of approaches developed in various European countries in response to issues of cultural diversity does not so much trace a linear development of changes that build on 'mistakes', as portrayed in chapter 4, but highlights the inherent polarisation in the light of the fundamental crisis of identity in late modernity which can only be overcome with reference to communicative processes.

1. 'Simplification' can be called an approach which 'solves' the problem of diversity by denying that there is a problem of mutual understanding. In its strong, authoritarian form it imposes a universal yardstick of right and wrong, if need be by force, and cuts out all ambivalence. According to this position, values are there to be upheld and they prove their success by being able to command compliance. In pedagogical terms this approach advocates assimilation to and conformity with the dominant, indigenous culture for all minority or immigrant groups, not necessarily overtly for control purposes, but 'for their own good': it is only by adapting to a prevailing, successful culture, by learning its language and mastering its system of symbols that members of minority groups can hope to gain access to the benefits of civilisation, to share the rewards of a system of values that can claim universal validity. In its weaker version it concedes the existence of a variety of moral systems represented by different cultures and focuses more pragmatically on the validity of localised value regimes instead of making demands for universal acceptance (Hamburger 1990). But within the confines of those dispersed communities values have something equally unquestionably self-evident about them and communication works best according to this assumption if those boundaries are being rigidly maintained. Universalism may be toned down to a matter of showing sympathy for somebody's difficulties perhaps. However, 'difficulties' count only within the meaning of an already known framework of universal human conditions, a knowledge that is oblivious within its subjective perspective, and this de-personalises the specifics of the other person's distress. The 'other person' can only be understood because 'people are people' and what people are is known totally by looking at oneself. This 'colour-blind' approach to inter-cultural communication and to dealing with questions of identity also seeks to avoid the discomfort of encountering and dealing with differences as they actually present themselves. Both the authoritarian and the 'colour-blind' approach deny the 'other person' the right to define her own identity, deny the right to authenticity and agency and thereby set up highly asymmetrical sets of relationships. This in turn is indicative of a way of constituting the self in a static form, particularly as far as the 'strong' version of authoritarianism is concerned where the self either becomes defensive or indeed aggressive and violent, in total denial of the challenges to sensitivity that the encounter with the other presents. The 'weaker' version of this approach constructs a 'tolerant' self that defines the limits of such tolerance from within the position of its own tightly controlled value system and maintains thus always the upper hand in matters of definition and of understanding.

2. The 'multi-cultural position' by contrast abandons the claim to universality rather too readily and with it the concern over the difficulties and the actual meaning of establishing understanding that could lead to a negotiated consensus and hence an opening towards universally valid norms. Politically it sees no problem with a myriad of simultaneous positions entering the arena competitively just as pedagogically it celebrates diversity and revels in the freedom that the de-construction of grand narratives seemingly bestows. One reading of a text is as good as another, each culture has its own fluid values from which life-styles can be picked as randomly and as playfully as a set of always matching colour co-ordinates can be picked from Benetton's multi-cultural catalogues. The ethical questions dissolve in a celebration of a cynical nihilism for which everything is potentially equally valid (or meaningless) and everybody seeks to protect his or her interests as best as they can, privately and without recourse to a public arena or without seeing any necessity for an organising entity like the state. The position is reflected in a fragmented, ephemeral constitution of the self that has given up knowing itself and locating itself in relation to others, a self that is adrift in the sea of globalisation.

3. But the post-modern condition may ultimately yield a trajectory between the Scylla and the Charybdis of the previous positions for those who tenaciously persevere with the project of communication despite all the difficulties and disillusionment that the collapse of claims to universal validity has brought. In continuing to make the effort to communicate at all despite all those difficulties, in 'bothering' to strive for understanding and meaning despite of and in the full knowledge of the divisions which culture and identity seem to impose, the act of communication itself might release reference points for the conditions under which understanding, however partial it might be, could become possible. Such a project will not just point a viable direction but also release the energy and the commitment required to secure the chances of this approach succeeding, communicatively and politically, and hence as a basis for social work competence. One of these crucial conditions is the link between the pragmatic project of inter-cultural communication, the ethical project of truth in understanding and the political strategies of anti-racism. Together this connection could form a set of discursive-democratic principles on how the social could be re-constructed and defended against further power infringements and attempts at colonisation. This is the optimism which inspires for instance Zygmunt Bauman to maintain his idea of a post-modern morality: 'it is possible now, nay inevitable, to face the moral issues point-blank, in all their naked truth, as

they emerge from the life experience of men and women, and as they confront moral selves in all their irreparable and irredeemable ambivalence' (Bauman 1995a: 18).

These trajectories can be summarised in the following diagram which highlights the connections between psychological, cultural, ethical and political levels (figure 6):

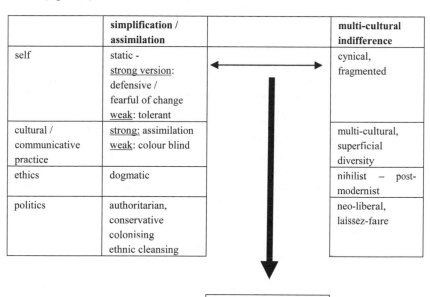

	simplification / assimilation		multi-cultural indifference
self	static - strong version: defensive / fearful of change weak: tolerant		cynical, fragmented
cultural / communicative practice	strong: assimilation weak: colour blind		multi-cultural, superficial diversity
ethics	dogmatic		nihilist – post-modernist
politics	authoritarian, conservative colonising ethnic cleansing		neo-liberal, laissez-faire

		communicative inter-cultural	
self		autonomous, multi-layered integrated	
cultural / communicative practice		intercultural / antiracist	
ethics		transactional, communicative, facing issues of morality without security	
politics		discursive – democratic, citizenship rights	

Figure 6

The choices are indeed stark. The effects of a politics of identity that aims at simplifications, at retrieving identity by violent means, at creating territories of homogeneous communities, of dividing good from evil absolutely, are all too evident. Ethnic cleansing, this epitome of the unwillingness to communicate, of violence and fear replacing inter-cultural communication, does not just happen in Ex-Yugoslavia—it happens on the territory of urban centres of population concentrations where spatial segregation is proceeding apace (Bauman 1998a). No-go areas are being claimed by groups of people who, having lost their stake in society at large, are desperate to defend their neo-tribal identities with reference to particular territories. At the same time, a globally connected economic elite defends itself also spatially with ever more elaborate security arrangements and the creation of fortresses within a hostile environment. 'The contemporary crisis is centrally located in the city and its role as a vehicle for socialisation into modernity. The resort to identity as a source of social redemption articulates this crisis. As Said observes, it bears out Fanon's worst fear ... "identity, always identity, over and above knowing about others"' (Humphrey 1996: 81).

The pre-condition and the motivation for the re-constitution of a social self, an identity that allows for otherness, both in the relation to others and in the realisation of difference in oneself, on the one hand springs from the realisation of not-knowing, the shuddering at the prospect of the total loss of meaning, the suffering from discontinuity, the despair of finding oneself lonely and abandoned in a bewildering, undecipherable world of disjointed symbols. But on the other hand it derives from the courage to sustain this void and these uncertainties for long enough so that simplifications, common sense truths, surreptitious power interests cannot colonise that moment. This sustaining allows memories of a future to emerge instead, of a security and sense of self that is constituted by being with others, being for others, not despite but because of their strangeness. We can only live in and sustain this void if we allow language to fill it, ambiguous, contingent and yet reliable, once we endow it with meaning, once we give a moral commitment to language and to understanding in the knowledge that language, or rather a particular use of language, is all that can constitute a dense social reality. Social work competence is therefore, paradoxically, grounded in the ability to sustain ambiguity and to make space for difference, rather than on the claim to definite solutions for seemingly factual problems (Jordan 1978, Parton 1998). This reliance on communicative processes in social work practice is by no means abstract idealism but is yielding concrete methodological results in the move towards critical reflection and transformative action (Fook 1999, 2004; Parton 2004). It produces practice and research that opposes the linear thinking of managerialism and neo-liberal social policies which operates with a digital approach to practice and efficiency, alien to those who handle the complexity of actual social problems.

This is not to give inter-cultural communication and inter-cultural pedagogy a privileged and unique position in resolving conflicts, overcoming inequality and creating a viable society. The provision of material conditions, the establishment and securing of human and legal rights, the development of reliable and accountable structures and systems all play an important role and the mere understanding of differences is no substitute for action and the creation of tangible structures and institutions. But these institutions and provisions are all dependent on language and understanding for their real effectiveness, for becoming factors that matter in particular ways to people with diverse interests. And the use of language for the purpose of understanding is ultimately dependent on a moral commitment, a commitment that can only be derived from the participation in communication in everyday contexts. 'Humanity is not an essence to be realised, but a pragmatic construction, a perspective, to be developed through the articulation of the variety of individual projects, of differences, which constitute our humanity in the broadest sense' (Weeks 1993: 200).

Ultimately, social work practice in all its forms and in all its fields stands in the service of this humanity. But as a specific form of practice it is particularly concerned with the social conditions necessary for the realisation of this humanity. As the conditions for establishing and practising social solidarity become ever more tenuous in late modernity and the integration of society turns into a task for specialists, it is vital for the social work profession not to approach this task in a technological manner. Grounding solidarity is something entirely different from risk reduction which is what social work is becoming increasingly saddled with through changes in social policy and the introduction of management models (see chapter 9). The refusal of this functionalism must however go hand in hand with an alternative framework both for the methodological competence of social work and its moral justification. This raises fundamental questions of the consequences of the analysis of communication processes for epistemology and research in social work which shall be examined in the next chapter.

7. Social Pedagogy—a hermeneutic paradigm for social work research and practice

The considerations concerning the grounding of social work competence in the ethics of communication lead not only to a re-examination of social work practice methods from the perspective of inter-cultural processes and principles, they also have an immediate bearing on the role of research as the basis for social work intervention. The professionalism of the social work profession has come in for serious questioning in the light of increasing demands on social workers and the greater public scrutiny and attention attached to their role according to the motto of 'evidence based practice' borrowed from medicine. Reflections on the epistemology of social work and its grounding in research become therefore an even more important part of the competence discourse. It shall be shown that the inter-cultural paradigm has relevance also in relation to the dilemmas posed by competing research paradigms and that the recourse to the basics of communication as a hermeneutic principle can map a way forward for practice-relevant social work research.

The public image of the social professions does not seem to be particularly favourable in Europe at the start of the new century, given the numerous mistakes social workers are often seen as making in childcare arrangements with fatal outcomes. It is of little comfort that other professions are also currently finding themselves in the crossfire of public critique, notably medicine, the profession social work has always tried to emulate. True enough, not every country criticises its social workers quite as much as Britain does, but social professionals still have a hard time everywhere convincing the public that they do their work efficiently and effectively. Despite the fact that social services are expanding numerically this growth is not generally regarded as a welcome sign of progress but as a regrettable indication of the decline of standards in society and an admission that services are not effective enough in the battle against social problems (Rauschenbach 1999). Societies want to put their trust in social workers as experts and yet retain a feeling that they would be better off without them, or rather without this kind of specialised expertise. Social problems ought to be resolved by 'ordinary people' – there is something unsettling about the idea that everyday life situations are less and less amenable to commons sense solutions. This ties in with a growing general mistrust of expert systems of knowledge and many self-help groups articulate publicly their conviction that having studied a problem merely theoretically leads to a different and inferior kind of knowledge than having experienced it (Williams and Popay 1994).

But on reflection the appeal to common sense is today also more contentious than ever. While appeals to common sense continue to be used by politicians and the media as a means of establishing, or rather (as they see it) of 'discovering', an already existing consensus submerged perhaps by too many divergent expert opinions, the diversification of public opinion and of special interest lobby groups also reflects an acute suspicion on the part of the public that such an underlying consensus does not exist on any of the normative issues social professionals have to deal with. As knowledge is increasingly being constructed around 'the person' and around personal experiences with the advance of 'identity discourses' (see chapter 5) confidence wanes that this will lead to commonly shared insights and conclusions. On the contrary, this recourse to personal experience inevitably leads to a greater emphasis on differences and on the rupture of fixed and closed systems of knowledge which have failed to admit such difference. This is most vividly exemplified by the demands by women to end the pretence that male-dominated professions administered and promoted a neutral kind of expertise when in fact highly subjective factors and interests bore heavily on such areas of knowledge (Oakley 2000). And if knowledge is always gendered, it is also subject to other sectional biases.

The implications of these ideas and developments for training and for employment selection in the social professions are that personal qualities are again being taken into consideration more seriously over and above formal qualifications. The issues of subjectivity, relativity, diversity, and the multiplicity of identities and therefore of theoretical perspectives are not only the subjects of abstract epistemological debate but are dilemmas in and for everyday practice. The challenge of a post-modern rupture and fragmentation of unity leaves no professional field unaffected and has its direct parallel in the growing importance diversity of identity and multiplicity of cultures have in societies everywhere (Lash et al. 1996). At the same time the pressure on all professions not only to be publicly accountable but also to 'get it right' and help society reduce and eventually eliminate all risks is also growing and professional misjudgements are being judged ever more harshly (Parton 1998).

For social work this poses a particularly serious dilemma and confronts the profession with the most fundamental questions, not about the merits and demerits of this or that form of practice but about the very possibility of accountable practice in the first place. The questions social work professionals have to ask themselves constantly are, how can they ever claim to know something about another person, something that has validity for that person and is not an imposition of their personal world view or of ideologically determined objectives? In the contemporary context, if they resort to arguments of objectivity they feel more and more uncertain about the actual

118

universality that reason and rationality can command, given the recognition of their being infused with cultural values and norms (even though the demand for 'evidence-based practice' more and more demands and constructs just such rational diagnostic criteria (Gilgun 2005)). If they resort to personal, subjective preferences they stand to lose the scientific validity of their assessments and thereby their professional standing (even though this is exactly what the demand for 'empowerment', which is being promoted so strongly as a professional practice principle, seems to imply).

Fortunately this dilemma is not new to social work, although it seems that the profession, in most European countries, has been doing its best to hide from it. The proposal here is that facing up to the peculiarity of its type of knowledge creation and the discomfort that social work professionals have sensed in the past when giving an account of their knowledge base, can form the point of departure for an epistemology and for a more confident reformulation of the principles of research that meets the contemporary critique of professional knowledge head on (Dewe and Otto 1996). This requires an examination not just of the type of knowledge used by social workers but of the processes by which such knowledge is established. In the following this overall problematic will be referred to as 'research', for doing research, thus understood, certainly involves more than working on empirical data. It also acknowledges that although in the UK, for instance, there was relatively little in the way of formal research activity in social work as such before the 1960s (Lyons 2000), social work educators certainly did not simply develop their methods 'on the hoof'. Traditionally, their primary mode of doing research was the systematic evaluation of case notes, and case studies, finding in them evidence of the implicit or explicit application of the relevant tenets of academic disciplines like sociology and psychology, formed the knowledge base of social work at the time.

It is often regarded as a deficit that social work did not develop its own independent knowledge base and 'borrowed' so heavily from other disciplines. The borrowing as such is no problem– all professions and disciplines borrow from each other and if the placing of social work training in universities is to have any meaning at all it is to underline its place in a 'universitas' of disciplines that are meant to define their approaches and their subjects through mutual exchanges. What is problematic, however, is that social work has often been wedded until recently to positivistic models of sociology and psychology, and this for reasons of gaining status and prestige within a given academic status hierarchy and not primarily with a view of how this leads to better practice. These models derive largely from epistemologies and methodologies which deliberately separate the observing subject from the observed object. The adoption of such a position enforces also a separation of theory from practice which is ultimately counter-productive for social work, as it locates the realm of theory formation outside

119

the actual discipline of social work which then appears as having its 'proper place' only in the realm of practice. As a result of this division, research insights by practising social workers become either mere 'refinements' in the area of application or correctives for certain theoretical assumptions, while their influence on theory formation as such remains limited. What this has meant in many European countries is that in addition to the theory/practice tension a *de facto* divide has operated between on the one hand a socially determined aspiration to become grounded in positivist empirical research which always stops short of informing practice directly, and on the other the development of skills and competences largely in the 'humanist' tradition (client-centred), without critical reflection on the theoretical foundations of the latter. Typical British pragmatism accommodates this tension, as is still evident from recent research by Lyons (2000) whereas in other countries the divide is much greater and often institutionally framed (universities do research, non-university institutions train for practice).

While social science based approaches to social work and social work training, particularly of the positivist kind, are also to be found on the European continent, we find there additionally a strong intellectual counter-force in the form of the hermeneutic tradition, which has influenced the development of 'pedagogical' models of social work. Admittedly, there is a strand within pedagogy that, taking its point of departure from the taken-for-granted societal function of education, also quite pragmatically focuses on improving the efficiency of 'the education system' according to an official political agenda, mainly in the form of didactics as the science of teaching methods. On the whole, however, continental-European pedagogical reflection tends to start from the person of the learner. For this tradition, the 'formation' of people into competent adults and citizens is not a mechanical processing of 'raw products' to a standard pattern, but is rather the process of engaging with the innate inquisitive and creative potential of the learner as an active subject who contributes to the shaping of society at the same time as it shapes him or her (Winkler 1988). This process requires a scientific method of its own, a method of studying and evaluating what happens in the encounters of people as subjects, in the creation of life concepts and social meaning, in the attempts at understanding the process of the formation of synchronic and diachronic cultural differences. Here the separation of theory and practice is much less straightforward and the complexity and immediacy with which this web of meanings is being investigated and conceptualised seems to correspond much more to the complexity and immediacy which characterise social work practice (Hamburger 2003). Seen from this perspective social work need not be apologetic about the 'messy' nature of its theory formation – it can, rather, be proud of the immersion in 'life processes' its discipline represents, as a paradigm even for other disciplines and professions (Parton 2000).

Nevertheless, as shall be shown in the following, there are no grounds for 'glorifying' the social pedagogy model and simply promoting it as the answer to all the problems social work is facing within the applied social science tradition. Social pedagogues are being confronted with exactly the same dilemmas at the theoretical and political level (Thole 1999b). It is therefore more important to explore the intricate interplay between academic and political discourses throughout the history of the social professions. This can help to understand that the answer to more recognition and accountability lies not in social work refining its research agenda but in taking the political aspect of research more seriously, not just as context but as a critical dimension of the methodology itself. The theme of how to 'encounter the other' dealt with in the previous chapter has equal relevance in research as it has in practice. A communicative approach means not taking identities as fixed, essentialist qualities, but as negotiated, emergent sets of social relationships which need to be embedded in political frameworks of rights and obligations. The aim of social work research is not the discovery of pre-existing communities of identity or layers of meaning, but the creation of the conditions for interactive social citizenship in the creation of such meaning, in practice and in research.

There has indeed always been something peculiar about the type of knowledge used by social workers. It is hard to deny that their methods, in all European countries, very much originated in 'plain common sense' being systematically applied by 'no-nonsense people'. These pioneers saw themselves not as soft-hearted almsgivers who did their work for heavenly rewards in the guise of secular martyrs and saints, but as rational beings intent on bringing general and long-lasting solutions to social problems. Their type of common sense was characteristic of a particular class in the industrialising Western societies, a class that had gained its social and economic advantages by applying the particular pragmatic rationality that a capitalist market economy required. This rationality was turned into common sense and thereby assumed also a moral authority, parallel to and interlacing with that rationality of patriotism (see chapter 5). Common sense sees no need to base itself on research – it regards the personal daily success stories of practice experience as its field of research, often encapsulated in proverbs and little practice wisdoms which give the appearance of universal validity. Early social work needed no other way of knowing; in fact the application of common sense had what today would be termed an anti-discriminatory dimension about it: as long as the solution to the problems encountered by recipients of organised charity needed no 'special' knowledge, these clients could be seen as part of 'mainstream society', at least potentially, and it was up to them to prove through their behaviour that they were capable of belonging to mainstream society. 'There can be no doubt that the poverty of the working classes of England is due, not to their circumstances (which are

121

more favourable than those of any other working population in Europe), but to their improvident habits and thriftlessness. If they are ever to be more prosperous it must be through self-denial and forethought' (Charity Organisation Review 1881, vol 10: 50 quoted in Jones 1983: 76). The price of this incorporation was, as with all universal expert systems, the loss of self-defined identity, the imposition of a generic identity which always already knows 'the other'.

Sure enough, these early charity workers did not actually get very far by trying to model their clients' behaviour on their own successful adaptation to shrewd economic thinking, by giving good examples themselves and appealing to reason and its intrinsic rewards. The subsequent rise of Freudian psychology to the position of the decisive paradigm in so many of the early social work courses in the industrialised world and its impact on the development of the casework method can partly be attributed to the ingenious and alluring project psychoanalysis pursues. This is to shed light on the workings of the unconscious and emotion-driven parts of the human mind that are largely responsible for our irrational and unreasonable acts by systematising them and identifying their internal logic. In other words, it claims to succeed by bringing the realm of unreason also under the sway of reason, by completing the great Enlightenment project of gaining insight into the last uncharted territories of the all-too-familiar: human weaknesses, failures and depravities.

Freud's psychological model remains highly controversial and epitomises in many ways the dilemmas faced by all modern, rationality-based and therefore objectifying scientific paradigms when they turn their attention to the enquiring subject, in other words when they try to come to terms with the phenomenon of human reflexivity. Freud himself was very clear about his goals and the consistency of his method when he extended his scientific medical training and his research experience in neurology into the realm of human behaviour. For him the world he discovered, the world of unconscious drives and of the mental apparatus, revealed their logic to the explorer with such regularity that he felt able to deduce scientific laws of nature from his observations with which he could explain the genesis of mental illnesses such as neuroses with the same consistency as the models of causality which physicians had used to understand physical illnesses like cholera and smallpox and treat them effectively. And yet Freud's findings are not verifiable in the same empirical way, and terms like the Id, the Ego and the Superego remain ambivalent. Do they signify 'actual' structures of the mind or are they best thought of as metaphors whose substance can never be confirmed in the same way as the metaphor of an atom or a bacillus can be verified under the microscope? Much of the validity of research done on Freudian findings depends on the perspective of the observer.

It is interesting to note how this ambivalence in Freud's method was then given opposite 'spins' in the context of different prevailing national and political cultures. In England Freud's method, and the security and prestige it promised to practitioners in the 1920s on account of its positivist implications, was treated as a direct parallel to the social enquiries that had been conducted earlier by figures associated with the Fabian Society. Statistical investigations into the prevalence of poverty in certain districts, as conducted by Joseph Rowntree in York and Charles Booth in London, had found clear evidence that poverty was not the result of individual failings, weakness of character, or lack of motivation, but of structural causes such as the absence of work opportunities, poor housing conditions and lack of educational opportunities (Jones 1983). For the Fabians, the factors accounting for social problems were quantifiable and the moral appeals, the principal instrument of the early charity workers, though being based largely on reason rather than on religious or other ideological prescripts, were therefore misplaced.

Although an ardent controversy characterised these contrasting positions in the early phase of the search for theories to underpin social work practice, reflected in the contrast between the Charity Organisation Society which advocated individual case-work and the Fabian Society seeking to establish the basis for social improvements in the reform of social conditions, they were united in the quest for the establishment of objective criteria for their actions (Briggs 1961). The responsibility of the expert or the professional was expressed in a fund of knowledge which was acquired through systematic studies with individuals or sections of the whole society as their objects. The objectivity of such knowledge was regarded as a safeguard against arbitrary or interest-led interference and manipulation in the lives of people, whose interests were taken care of in an impersonal manner by the quality and detachment of the knowledge base. The compromise was reached in the classic textbook of the time, Mary Richmond's *Social Diagnosis* (Richmond, 1917), which advocated the systematic investigation of all pertinent factors affecting a person's problematic situation. Its title makes conscious reference to diagnosis as the defining tool of medicine. This served not only as a practical guide for the complex social and psychological indicators to be taken into consideration by the practitioner but also to enhance the status and prestige of the profession as a respectable, science-based activity.

But what are the underlying assumptions of this kind of practice and this kind of knowing? It basically continues the line of development which since the Renaissance and the Enlightenment had installed science, defined in the form of the systematic application of reason, as the dominant and most powerful paradigm of understanding the world, freed from the impositions of dogma and the hierarchy of learning that was passed down the line of illustrious and revered authorities. Knowing was now in the hands of anybody who followed the method and used the power of thinking linked to the accuracy of observation. It was in this sense a democratic tool, paralleled in religious terms by the Reformation which set out to liberate believers from the grip of the Church hierarchy and gave them direct access to the truth in the form of the Bible translated into the vernacular. Reason promised to establish its authority not by coercion or persuasion but by revealing the universal self-evidence of the truth as contained within the laws of nature. Science was set to make its spectacular conquests, closely accompanied by the military conquests by the West that culminated in colonialism: rationality, the superiority of Western science and technology, functioned as the decisive element of legitimation for these displays of power, force and violence. For rationality admits only one universe, one truth, and one authority, a realm within which there is really no room for diversity. 'The other' is an object of investigation until it is incorporated into the codex of 'the known' and hence robbed of its qualities of 'otherness'.

Western rationality simply had no room for pluralism, and even where it came face-to-face most directly, vividly and inescapably with plurality, namely when dealing with human beings and their diverse interests, life-styles and cultures in politics, the political and legal systems that emerged in the process of democratisation based on reason showed a precarious propensity to help reason along with coercion and violence. Democracy became the formal instrument with which to reconcile the divergence of interests that exists in every society. But it had severe limitations: first of all it involved only a highly selected group of citizens who were entitled to vote, at least at the beginning, secondly it was only a formal device which in itself did not promote the substance of social and legal values, and thirdly it posed the question of representation that brought with it political parties and their 'objectified' class interests (Mouffe 1996).

With the advent of industrialisation and the development of nation states, but also with the spread of movements for greater representation, democracy and liberation, societies in Europe began diversifying structurally and not just culturally. At the same time industrialisation and the agendas of nation states required homogenisation and standardisation of knowledge, behaviour and attitudes (Gellner 1983). Reconciling these conflicting demands became partly the task of the emerging social welfare systems; partly it was also the function of education systems, with compulsory schooling playing a central role in the creation and standardisation of national cultures and national languages. In both the educational and the social field two fundamentally divergent approaches could be (and were in fact) taken; one that treated the learner or the recipient of a social service as an object, as the material to be formed and processed so that it would take the required shape, and one that started from the inalienable personhood of the learner and his or her right to

124

self-realisation, be that in situations of need (for social problems can be conceptualised as life-long learning opportunities), or in the course of a continuous process of the improvement of an individual's innate potential.

This latter direction can be exemplified with the reception of Freud on the European continent and particularly in Germany, which took a different course within this pedagogical tradition from that within Anglo-Saxon positivism. Pedagogy as an academic discipline was keen to develop an epistemology that differed from the positivism prevailing not only in the natural but also in parts of the social sciences. In the latter part of the 19th century the 'human sciences' generally ('The Arts' or *Geisteswissenschaften*) had put up resistance against the threatened dominance of the positivist model of scientific enquiry over all disciplines and argued that they required instead a methodological basis of their own (Dewe and Otto 1996, Hamburger 2003). The understanding of historical or literary texts required involvement in the lifeworld to which they referred and of which they were part rather than analytical abstraction and neutral distance as was the case with the objects of the natural sciences. The academic tradition which consolidated around these hermeneutic concerns asserts that human beings are characterised first and foremost by their ability to give meaning to their world and their actions and that these meanings cannot be understood 'objectively' and from the outside; the learner, the researcher, has to participate in them, albeit systematically and consciously. Hermeneutics therefore proposes an at first sight paradoxical approach to understanding, namely that recognising the possibility that both the observer and the observed occupy separate subjective worlds and therefore cannot really understand each other is the decisive step that will eventually lead to some kind of understanding between both persons/worlds. Of course, such understanding cannot come about if both parties, both partners in this dialogue, remain static, even where written texts are concerned. The relationship has to be made dynamic and entails by necessity a process of interaction and of communication.

In this regard the reception of Mary Richmond's textbook *Social Diagnosis* on the European continent was indicative (see above chapter 5). Alice Salomon, a leading figure in the development of German professional social work and social work education (Kuhlmann 2001), published a textbook under the same title, arguing that diagnosis (or *Recherche*, as she terms it significantly) does not amount to the amassing of mere data but involves their 'evaluation, comparison and interpretation. The total picture does not result from the addition of details' (Salomon, 1926: 7). Social workers research by involving themselves rather than by staying detached, by being moved and by recognising the affective processes that evolve from every encounter (cf Treptow 1995). Salomon, in seeking to become engaged in a holistic process of *Verstehen,* does abandon neither the concern for

125

finding a universal reference point in the process nor her fascination with positivism; she develops a version of subjectivity-cum-universality that is most intriguing in as much as it appears to us today to be at one and the same time hopelessly dated and acutely modern (Treptow 1996). For her the subject of the social worker/observer is indeed not neutral. Her concern is the professional and academic training of *women* as social workers and it is to their womanhood, to their specifically female qualities, that she takes recourse as the guarantee for a non-partisan, non-ideological approach to 'caring'. Alice Salomon believed that the construction of an ideal of 'motherliness' could provide a point of encounter and of reference that not only gave individual clients directions for the improvement of their situation without feeling threatened by the ideological, party-political agendas of a welfare state and a powerful class within it, but could also provide a blueprint for a better society in general beyond the self-interests of political factions and interest groups.

The texts of Alice Salomon give the impression that this form of feminism, which she uses very much for hermeneutic purposes, was constantly verging on the edge of total subjectivity. Yet she recoils from its relativist consequences to seek reassurance in almost 'mystic' universal reference points. Motherhood was one such universal heuristic; the idealised national community became another. This latter was the pathway taken, perhaps typically for a male scholar, by the prime exponent of German social pedagogy of the time, Hermann Nohl. He had been a student and assistant of Dilthey, the 19th century philosopher who had laid the foundations for the hermeneutic approach, and largely as a result of the experience of the First World War brought his philosophical studies to bear on practical concerns about the state of German society. He, like many 'reform pedagogues' before him, regarded pedagogy as the vital ingredient for the formation of a nationally integrated 'folk' community, an encompassing entity which in turn was vital for the moral formation of individuals in the face of party-political divisiveness and the alienation caused by industrialisation. For Nohl the universalising element in the pedagogical process is the encounter with 'life' in which a Hegelian Spirit has a guiding presence for those who do not rely on abstract reflection but on 'experiencing life as such' (Blickenstorfer 1998).

Both Salomon and Nohl wanted to avoid at all costs ending up with subjective relativism for their discipline, despite the value they placed on subjective meanings and their historical construction and reconstruction in intervention. Motherliness and the formation of a national folk community for them were not elements in the formation of particular, exclusive, superior identities, but reference points for a universal societal community capable of accommodating the diversity of 'the other'. They were also agreed in setting their pedagogical programmes in opposition to party politics, although Nohl

126

pessimistically had to admit that all pedagogical reform programmes ended up being subverted by party politics (Nohl 1982). Nevertheless, these proposals sound to present day listeners at best like hopelessly idealist, nostalgic and romantic sentiments, at worst folk- and motherliness-promoting ideologies that paved the way for Nazism. Neither Salomon nor Nohl were in any way propagandists or apologists for the Nazis—quite the contrary: both lost their positions under Fascism, although the latter had for a time seemed ready to give the 'community appeal' of Nazism the benefit of the doubt. But Nazism imposed its positivist reading on their intended hermeneutics.

For just as social work was gingerly feeling its way towards an appropriate epistemology through the dilemmas of detachment and involvement and of universalism and particularism, in both research and practice, the political vulnerability of both the positivist and the hermeneutic approach was exposed devastatingly in the context of Nazi totalitarianism in Germany. The extent to which the status and knowledge insecurity of the social professions contributed to their incorporation into Nazi welfare ideology and their role in the selection of people destined by the system for segregation, incarceration and eventual elimination remains very much under-researched (Sünker and Otto 1997, Schnurr 1997). The subjectivist approaches, in either their hermeneutic or in their identity-centred versions, amounted easily to a kind of naïve idealism that 'went with the stream of history', especially when the Nazi regime glorified motherliness, community, and the infusion of meaning into the coldness and senselessness of modern urban and industrial life. Heidegger himself, the chief exponent of hermeneutic philosophy in the 1930s, displayed very obvious leanings towards the regime. But although after the defeat of Germany this naïve enthusiasm was held mainly responsible for the unprofessional, ideology-driven conduct of the social (and indeed the medical and other) professions, it has to be recognised that positivism fared no better. When diagnostic decisions were made of 'unsocial behaviour' or of 'hereditary defects in social skills' in families with alcoholism, in populations with an itinerant life style etc., the majority of professionals firmly believed that they applied 'objective criteria' and distanced themselves thereby from the consequences of their impartial diagnosis (Sünker and Otto 1997). In both epistemological traditions of the social professions the ethical and particularly the political questions had either been externalised or had been raised far too uncritically. Both could be fused and brought in line with political ideology without this triggering much by way of effective resistance. Universalism and particularism had both failed to represent and protect adequately the excluded 'other'.

The social reconstruction and re-education programme which the United Nations and the Western Allies instituted in post-Fascist Europe which relied heavily on social work training as a means of 'democratising' the world (Altmeyer 1955) failed to come to grips with the full extent of this crisis of

127

confidence that the Holocaust had caused for all sciences and humanities. Conceptually, it put all its faith in positivism and the creation of 'neutral' professionals bounded only by the precepts of self-determination and human dignity (Lorenz, 1994). Universalism was the unquestionable consensus in social work methodology, applying science-based methods without distinguishing (and thereby discriminating) on account of the recipients' identity. From this perspective the only valid type of research was quantitative, and most of that was not undertaken within social work itself but within sociology and psychology, so that the discourse in social work really did not advance much beyond the point it had reached in the case work models in of the 1920s.

The fundamental crisis of uncertainty in the social sciences was to occur later. It was not triggered, as might have been expected, by the turmoil of war and a world rent apart by the Cold War, but by the slow but steady exhaustion of the project of modernity in its failure to deliver the promised progress through reason (Nicholson 1999). The civil rights and women's movements of the 1970s and 80s exposed not just the emptiness of the promise of universality and thereby equality contained within the project of modernity, but above all the highly subjective, power-driven interests vested in this type of universalism. Yet the impact of that crisis on social work and social work research was slow to arrive and was masked by the still prevailing endeavour of the social professions to gain prestige and status by operating to positivist principles regardless of their suitability to social work situations (Rojeck et al. 1988). This can be seen in the continuing prevalence of quantitative over qualitative studies undertaken in social work, despite some seminal qualitative work, most notably in the UK that of Mayer and Timms (*The Client Speaks*, 1970). As Sherman and Reid state, 'There was also a recognition that the study and analysis of what goes on in the actual process of practice had been shortchanged in favor of measurable outcomes' (Sherman and Reid 1994: 3). Even in the contemporary German context, where so much more primary work has been done on hermeneutic pedagogical theory, a recent review of trends in social work research found an overwhelming preponderance of empirical/evidence based practice (Thole 1999a, 1999b).

This amounts to a very strong indication that social work's quest for autonomy and respectability is being conducted not from within the perspective of the discipline's own requirements and parameters, but that it follows a political agenda of 'scientific management' and 'bureau-professionalism' (Harris 1998). This is understandable given the ever more explicit and overt political pressure on social work. Neo-liberal governments in Europe everywhere tended to consider the profession at best a necessary evil that had its social uses only when it was kept in a subordinate position. They achieved this by reminding the profession of its inefficiency as

128

measured by quantitative criteria and thereby installed quantitative measures as the prime outcome criterion. Social work had to prove its worth within the criteria of efficiency and effectiveness set. Subsequently, a new agenda set during the late 1990s by centre-left governments in Europe of the New Labour type used the efficiency criterion as a means of incorporating social work more firmly in its welfare agenda of 'activation' and case management for which only quantitative measures were declared relevant (Lorenz 2001, Dahme and Wohlfahrt 2002). In these circumstances, having a research basis of its own would assist social work in distancing itself from ideological impositions and many sought in evidence-based approaches a means of regaining autonomy. This alone, however, is insufficient since the objectivity implied in this label is deceptive and fails to address the fundamental question, in whose interest and from which value basis such evidence is being collected (Humphries 2004).

In the over-reliance on quantitative research designs highlighted above, the parameters of what is to be known have already been defined (Silverman 1993). The prescription of 'evidence based practice', which corresponds to this research preference and which is gaining ground in social services across Europe today, only accentuates the dilemma for social workers over their social and political position and needs to be placed therefore in a much wider context: on the one hand they are to take account of the concerns of clients first and foremost, for which the criterion of 'what works best' would give clear direction. On the other hand they have to complete this task within socially and politically already defined criteria of acceptability and cost efficiency. 'We believe that the reasons for the current hegemony of the idea of "evidence-based practice" in regard to social work education have more to do with the political agendas of New Labour than with the needs of practitioners' (Jordan and Parton 2004: 31). How can the personhood of the client be constituted as that of a real partner in a context, in which socially, culturally and indeed ethnically distinct identities and hence needs are pre-defined bureaucratically and differentiation is used only for purposes of categorisation? How can social work develop a coherent mandate when the very notion of a welfare consensus is disappearing from the agenda, to be replaced by the fragmentation and privatisation of social services (Khan and Dominelli 2000)?

The dilemma is further aggravated by developments in the practice field which are generating their own agenda for practice and research, in the wake of the growing importance of social movements in all areas of welfare. These take up the critique levelled against professions and their hold on social and political power generally, and strive to apply research designs that reflect the interests and views of service users (Beresford, 2000). Qualitative research models are an obvious choice when the aim is to represent users' authentic voices and this has indeed inspired a proliferation of methods which offer alternatives to positivism. This development has been facilitated by the 'exhaustion' of the project of modernity in the social sciences mentioned above, and their general 'turn towards the subjective'. But it needs to be examined whether 'the other' actually has a better chance of being represented in this way or whether new distortions and forms of exclusion result from these trends. The call for client self-representation could be regarded as a kind of return of 'common sense' (as the alternative to expert systems), however in its subjective, fragmented version, valid not for a 'common universe' of meaning but only for distinct universes of people who share the same identity characteristics. As Williams and Popay state in relation to the development of a new framework for welfare research:

> 'The development of new social welfare movements based on the politics of identity has drawn attention to the particular, and often overlooked, needs of social groups and challenged the "false universalism" of welfare. ... However, they (i.e. these movements) also run the risk of freezing or fixing people into single unitary identities, when in fact, their self- identities may be quite complexly and multiply constituted (in terms of class, race, ethnicity and so on)' (Williams and Popay 1999: 170).

Hence for social work the split in the consensus on validity criteria is not solely an academic question over the detached choice of research methods; underlying that is the struggle for social work's position in society, the conflicting forms of legitimation of its actions, and above all the ethical foundations of various research and practice options. While the post-modern critique has helped to weaken the dominance of the positivist position, the alternatives it has to offer have to be treated with caution. When Seidmann states that

> 'postmodernity may renounce the dream of one reason and one humanity marching forward along one path towards absolute freedom but it offers its own ideal of a society that tolerates human differences, accepts ambiguity and uncertainty, and values choice, diversity and democratisation' (Seidmann, 1998: 347)

it must be asked whether this ideal simply emerges by letting go of other strictures or whether toleration and acceptance can only be achieved by means of a systematic process of reflexivity which itself has to be systematically conducted. Mere deconstruction, mere reflexivity and subjectivity, as Parton rightly points out in his critique of Schön's (Schön 1987) proposal of the 'reflective practitioner' (Parton 2000), is not enough and could, indeed, lead to the same kind of 'detachment' that paved the way for 'ideology-prone' practice of scientific detachment that was ideologically misused in the Nazi era.

Social work has to confront a bigger challenge than merely the ambiguity and uncertainty arising from matters concerned with research. As the previous chapter sought to demonstrate, it is centrally and generally concerned with creating the possibility of understanding others across the chasms of

130

'difference' that are opening up in a globalised yet fragmented society. Or to put it another way round, it is the possibility of creating such understanding on which efforts in practice and in research need to converge. This proposed comprehensive project, and the type of research that would follow from it, does indeed connect with the hermeneutic tradition and with the perspectives opened up by the discipline of social pedagogy on the European continent, which so far have had only a marginal impact on English-language discourses in social work. Hermeneutics in the version of critical theory elaborated by the Frankfurt School and in particular by Jürgen Habermas opposes the post-modern indifference to universal ethical questions while at the same time addressing issues of identity and diversity very explicitly (Ashenden 1999). Meaning and identity for Habermas are not just given entities but are being continuously constituted communicatively in what he terms 'the lifeworld' (Habermas 1987). In engaging in a process of communication, in the course of which we want to be understood and to understand, we all ('experts' and 'lay people' alike) give an implicit commitment, however minimal, to rules and conditions without which communication cannot happen successfully.

Genuine communication can only take place and be defended against all the interference of games-playing, manipulation and oppression which threaten understanding if in the act of communication the transcendental, anticipated conditions for understanding prevail and are upheld with at least a minimal commitment to the possibility of understanding. In communication as in genuine research the precise outcomes are open, but the enterprise only makes sense ultimately if it is constructed as a means of finding truth. The discovery of deception afterwards is so devastating because it violates this commitment. Just as the encroachments on the lifeworld by 'the system', whose rationality is imposed through the media of power and money, constitute the true crisis of the welfare state and need to be reversed (Habermas 1994), the processes distorting communication in research also need to be reversed in the search for socially meaningful, critical and emancipatory approaches.

The lifeworld in which these processes happen cannot be researched from a situation of detachment but only from one of involvement, albeit of critical involvement (Fook 1999, Humphries 2004). This means designing approaches that create mutual respect for differences and yet commitment to a common cause between the communicators, establish rules in the process of communicating, and aim at achieving consensus on the aims, scope and uses of the research. The identification and gradual reduction and elimination of threats and distortions, which will inevitably occur but which constantly subvert communication, are very much part of the research process. But this means considering and acting upon the social context within which research takes place rather than accepting it and carrying out research only within politically defined parameters. Out of this kind of action research identities can be constituted in the process not as sets of individually separate identities or as given group identities, but as emergent communities, fleeting and yet stable enough on account of the rules which inform and govern them, rules which in themselves expand to unwritten and indeed written rights and in that sense to political commitments, penetrating out from the lifeworld back into the system (Habermas 1990). The 'community of understanding' which this process and commitment constitutes is therefore ultimately a political entity, and the participants consequently need to confirm each other as citizens, as people who do not just tolerate each other's differences but negotiate them towards common, and this means now consensually agreed, elements.

To elaborate on a scenario used already in previous chapters on intercultural practice: the very serious concern over the level of child sexual abuse which is being voiced in practically all European countries converges ever more strongly on the exclusion and incarceration of perpetrators as the only effective means of safeguarding the wellbeing and integrity of children. Social workers and other 'liberal-minded' professionals get accused of having wasted too much effort on understanding the minds of paedophiles and thereby on finding 'excuses' for them which lead to them being given second chances inappropriately and dangerously. This seems to constitute a straight forward call for better diagnostic tools to identify the dangerous from the acceptable person. From a pedagogical perspective, however, the issue needs to be stated the other way round: the mind of a person who is not being understood, who is placed outside the potential community of those who seek to share a common language, is a very dangerous phenomenon indeed because we can never be sure of 'catching' all perpetrators and, when they are arrested and treated, of eliminating their influence lastingly.

This understanding cannot be derived solely from objective criteria obtained from the distanced scrutiny of the person's behaviour but requires at least a degree of 'involvement'. Sure enough, there are psychological profiles of abusers, there is an array of evidence that accumulates about general precipitating factors, there are legal criteria—but all these represent 'the system' as formalised and abstracted realms of power. They have to be scrutinised in terms of their real relevance to the understanding of each specific situation, their *meaning,* and such understanding needs to be created again and again in each 'case'. The 'truth' about a person rests not with the expert; it emerges from the communicative choreography of something like a courtroom, in which all the people affected participate and strive to determine rules that are meaningful to the specific situation. And the process of establishing the truth only comes into its own when it leads to change, to a situation in which the actual and potential damage is not externalised (in the form of procedural avoidance or routine) but where the relationships which turned so harmful and damaging are yielding to the possibility of being fundamentally re-worked. The child victim remains linked to the father who has caused harm, no matter how far and for how long the perpetrator is removed or imprisoned, just as the traumatic events need to be worked on rather than just ignored. Social workers can supply the vital link between these separate and yet connected worlds, and their ability to ford the divide depends vitally on their communicative competence which is in turn related to the kind of research that helps to articulate the internal world of both victim and perpetrator.

This process therefore does involve rationality at the same time as it acknowledges the limitations and indeed the destructiveness of rationality. It constitutes 'the other' as different at the same time as it aims at establishing a consensus over universal principles and criteria (Dewe and Otto 1996). This is more than a mere pragmatic and eclectic bringing together of quantitative and qualitative research methods, of positivist/empirical and constructivist/ subjectivist principles, of theory and practice. Instead it spells a research agenda that is simultaneously an academic and a pedagogical task, precisely not in the sense of teaching the other party 'a lesson' but of trying to initiate a shared learning process. It is aimed at constituting social bonds that do not exist or have been disrupted and reaches therefore beyond the mere determination of exclusion and inclusion of 'categories of people' such as 'perpetrators' and 'deviants'. It is a research task that strives for accountability in the face of the complexity of societies; it seeks to connect and include through the creation of communities of communication while at the same time imposing safe limits to the degree of 'inclusion' in such re-connected, safeguarded communities. But these limits need to be found at the level of lifeworld communication; ultimately they cannot be imposed via criteria formulated entirely at the level of the system, yet they have to render the lifeworld safe and reliable.

Social work's apparent difficulties with research, and the tangled history of its epistemology, just like the entire uncertainty over what actually constitutes its subject matter, are indications that the discipline occupies a critical point in society at the intersection of system and lifeworld. Hermeneutic reflection on this position and the forms of research and practice that follow from it can not only give the social profession more confidence, but can also assume paradigmatic significance for other professions caught up in the current crisis of confidence over professional knowledge and expertise. Accountable practice is inseparable from the quest for reliable knowledge, which is in turn dependent on processes of legitimation within a democratically constituted community. There is indeed validity in seeking 'common sense' as the basis for social work intervention; not, however, common sense as a fixed, already given form of wisdom that allows no further questioning, but as something always yet to be constituted and negotiated, a common task

133

in which all parties have a stake. Social work research must face up to its political responsibilities in this comprehensive sense rather than delegating and externalising them, no matter how uncomfortable this burden is. The quest for knowledge is and remains an ethical task, and as such its pursuit is to be assessed in terms of how it reaches 'others', rather than how consistent it is in itself.

In this situation it seems epistemologically helpful for social work that a starker polarisation has set in between universalism and positivism-inspired empiricism on the one hand and a new self-confidence in subjectivism and constructivism on the other. 'Experience' came to be taken seriously again as a subject of and as a vehicle for welfare research, particularly in studies inspired by feminism, which simultaneously challenged the alleged neutrality of conventional approaches. 'Because gender-absence and gender-neutrality in social science is impossible to obtain, presentations in these traditions do not eliminate power relations between women and men, but rather only serve to obscure them' (Hanmer and Hearn 1999: 107). Other social movements, notably those of black people, people with disability, psychiatric illness, social care users and trauma survivors, add their voice to the critique of 'top-down research' and seek to re-claim the right to their authentic representation in research (Beresford and Evans 1999).

With those challenges questions of identity move centre stage once more, not just in terms of the identity of service users, but also of that of service providers, individually and collectively. The movement promoting emancipatory, user-led research has a very distinct agenda of challenging the professional power of established professions which they see as being maintained not least by means of 'authoritative' research. Here the interplay between intellectual, professional and political factors comes into play again and a shift in emphasis and orientation really only becomes effective in the wake of social policy changes aimed at altering the role and structure of public social services fundamentally (Gibbs 2001). It appears like a curious and dangerous coincidence for social work that the agendas to 'de-construct' its power and structure are coming from both those directions, from neo-liberal policies and from user movements, which makes it very difficult for social work to respond to these demands in a non-defensive manner. It might hold sympathy for the 'emancipatory' approach to research as it concurs with some of its central values, but such sympathy is going to be short-lived if this results in the gradual erosion of social work's recognised place in society. But once this conflict is seen in line with social work's straddling position between system and lifeworld new, less defensive responses become possible, not least in terms of research strategies.

Seen from an historical perspective, the sharp divisions over the choice and function of research in social work today are not a new phenomenon. However, they present themselves with unprecedented force (Gibbs 2001), and this indicates not that social work per se is in a confused state but that the rupture between system and lifeworld and the processes of differentiation within each of those domains have become more acute. Social work is unavoidably caught up in this process and finds its role and identity threatened by the bewildering plurality of demands and of reference points in this debate. What seems therefore to be more important than making decisions on whether to pursue this or that research methodology is to relate the discourse on research back to fundamental reflections on the place and role of social work in society. The plurality of forms of social work referred to in the introductory chapter can serve as a heuristic device to a better understanding of the dilemmas it faces. On the one hand there are many parallel ways of interpreting this role on account of the historical nature of the profession, and this means its dual mandate between system and lifeworld. On the other hand it also provides a basic understanding for the shared themes connecting those different manifestations. In its vibrant and immediate link to lifeworld processes, despite their often contradictory effects on epistemology and practice, social work keeps open its potential for communicative action, action that engages with conflicting norms, wishes and aspirations in such a way that it creates the conditions for a consensus. In this context starting from a position of unassailable certainty would actually be counter-productive. Social work research can ultimately only make sense as research that considers the complexity of factors impinging on social problems and develops its approach as communicative action. The many attempts at framing social work research as a reflexive process which are currently under debate are hopeful signs in this direction (e.g. Fook 1999). This debate needs to be linked, however, to a critical theory of society in order to prevent its function and its results from becoming absorbed into the system with its pursuit of instrumental action, thereby risking to effect unintended consequences of tighter and more powerful social control. In this sense it is necessary for both social work practice and research to take stock of the changing social policy context in which social work operates in Europe, and to explore the interplay between political, cultural and scientific developments as they affected social work during the formative stages of European nation states and now during the decline of the nation state as a seat of governance. This task will be the subject of the following chapter.

8. Digital capitalism and globalisation—challenges for social work in Europe

From the middle of the 1990s onwards social workers in all parts of Europe encountered a perplexing similarity of experiences almost regardless of the welfare regime under which they worked: While the demand for social services is undiminished or even growing as reflected in the number of staff employed (Rauschenbach 1999), all social services seem to be placed under severe financial constraints and are being regarded as an unnecessary drain on public resources. The responses to this dilemma are organisational changes which imply the delegation and privatisation of large sectors of the public social services, accompanied by methodological changes in the form of the new concept of social management (Badelt 1997). These developments indicate that the function of social work within the prevailing economic system of capitalism is changing universally as the nature of capitalism is changing. Whereas social work was once keen to place itself professionally outside the realm of economics, the better to perform its function of compensating clients for the adverse effects of economic inequality in areas not covered effectively by social policies it is now becoming increasingly and explicitly enmeshed in economic matters and more specifically in helping to secure the success of the new form of capitalism. In this sense it is also becoming more directly enmeshed in carrying out explicit functions of social policy implementation. This change manifests itself both in terms of their mandate in adjusting clients to the economic conditions of global capitalism, and in the organisational changes of social service structures which become subjected to the prevailing efficiency drive

The dialectics of labour and capital change towards what has been described as 'digital capitalism' and with this the nature of 'the social' as the interlacing arrangements of social solidarity within the nation state is also being subjected to a fundamental revision. The nation state as a territorially defined unit, which was potentially always in conflict with capitalism but functioned in effect as a stabilising and motivating influence on the development of capitalism, is losing its powers of governance and hence its role as central reference point for the organisation of the relationship between labour and capital (Böhnisch and Schröer 2002). With the help of new electronic means of communication and cheaper transport costs transnational companies form, in contrast to merely multinational companies of the past. These new entities are now capable of forming entire independent economic networks and aree intent on breaking their link to distinct locations as 'bases' for their operations in the interest of the total flexibilisation of the production process and hence of labour. They thereby re-create the 'local' instead as mere sites of consumption.

The new features of capitalism enlist social work in a potentially very different way in the project of economic and social transformation: it is becoming directly involved in making the new economic system work more smoothly and in giving it the appearance of legitimacy. Whilst social work owes its existence to its capacity to play an auxiliary role to capitalism it never before had experienced the dominance and pervasiveness of capitalist economics as explicitly as under the conditions of globalisation. Gone is the political will to create free spaces and 'protectorates' in which the commodification of social relations was held at bay or could even be suspended, which had been a central feature of welfare state developments in all their national forms (Esping-Andersen 1990). So far the profession and the operations of social services within the various constructs of the welfare state were always somehow exempt from the strict application of market principles, whereas they now become increasingly incorporated into them. Social work is becoming an instrument of commodification, of increasing the market value of human labour and personal transactions, even care itself. Social relations are to be transformed into commodity transactions on which a globalised digital capitalism depends, and the absorption of social services themselves into a limitless commodity market is but one sign.

Part of these global economic and social changes is the re-structuring of the nation state as the mediating institution between welfare and economics. The 'hollowing out' of the state (Jessop 2000a) and especially the reduction of its steering capacity through social policies is one of the effects of the phenomenon of globalisation which can be taken here as the complex interaction of developments at the technological, cultural and social, political and economic level:

- The technological changes are perhaps most apparent in everyday experience as they have offered media access and communication links beyond borders on a vast scale causing a decisive shift in the social perception of the relative positions of core and periphery in global geographic relations.
- Cultural changes had already been set in motion by the mobilisation of ethnic and gender identities in social movements and follow now in the wake of these technological possibilities, particularly in the dissemination of cultural markers such as music, writing, fashion and general life styles. There now ensues a new counter-flow of homogenisation and differentiation, explored already in chapter 2, which constantly pulls down and re-

138

establishes cultural boundaries and barriers and sets identities in a permanent state of flux.
- Linked to that are therefore new social phenomena around these processes of identity formation and re-construction which become geared towards a much wider variety of reference points. Identities are no longer contained within national and regional geographical entities and established cultural patterns, but offered as infinite, seemingly unlimited choices which are, however, simultaneously denied to most on account of resource and power criteria.
- Politically, the nature of the nation state is changing profoundly 'not only in the greater significance of globalisation, triadization, regionalization, transnational urban networks, cross-border regions and so on, but also in the state's denationalization (or "hollowing out") as specific state powers and capacities are moved upwards, downwards and sideways' (Jessop 2000a: 180).
- Economic changes, which by many are regarded as the driving force of all the other changes despite the relative autonomy of several of the other flanking developments, amount to a pervasive liberalisation of the market economy from statist policies resulting in a much greater 'inter-penetration (of economies) through a variable mixture of extraversion, inward investment and an expanding international division of labour. This weakened the "taken-for-grantedness" of the national economy as an object of economic management and reduced the effectiveness of Keynesian policies' (Jessop 2000a: 174f).

It is crucial to regard these economic transformations not as 'inevitable necessities', akin to natural processes, natural catastrophes perhaps, to which one can merely adapt and over which one has ultimately no control. Instead, there are political choices at the heart of these developments and this gives reason to re-focus on the political mandate of social work, on the political organisation of social solidarity, and not to delegate responsibility to the 'invisible hand of the market'.

First indications that the impact on social work of changes in the economic process are indeed still mediated by the state and by politics can be derived from the observation that while there are common definite shifts in the nature of social service delivery in all European countries, there are marked differences in those shifts, differences that are very much in line with the political cultures of the respective countries (Esping-Andersen 2002). In addition, changes that appear identical in direction can in fact have very different effects and connotations. For instance, social work methodology across Europe seems to be infused with concepts of 'activation' and 'empowerment' which can be regarded as positive or negative developments.

In fact the decision over the merits of these interventive principles, which are by no means completely new anyway in the history of methodological discourses in social work (Kessl and Otto 2003), cannot be made at the methodological level alone; instead everything depends on the political context in which they are being applied, as Torfing demonstrated with the example of 'activation' in the Danish context (Torfing 1999). What can be identified as a common feature in all welfare systems, however, is the greater polarisation between parts of the social service delivery systems that provide 'care' and those responsible for ever more restricted areas of 'control', the latter lying chiefly in the hands of public agents whereas the former are ever more being 'contracted out' to the non-statutory sector (White 2003). This growing polarisation is evidence of the weakening of the various compromises that had been part of the nation state project in the form of the respective welfare regimes, so that the elements that constituted those compromises assume greater independence and become increasingly detached from an overall concept of social solidarity.

From these preliminary observations concerning the importance of social work's continuous and inescapable embeddedness in history and politics follows also that the changes confronted by social work today do not mark a total rupture, a discontinuity, a sign of social work having also arrived in the land of post-modernity or post-structuralism, where the end of history has been proclaimed and may even have to be celebrated. On the contrary, they are meant to highlight just how important it is to examine any changes that have occurred within an historical context and not outside it. This has not the aim of establishing continuities within the apparent discontinuity as a means of demonstrating the unchanging sameness and status of the profession, but to utilise the political and at the same time the methodological potential that derives from recognising those historical connections not as incidental to social work but as its very medium through which it operates its special version of professionalism. This is the point where a wider European perspective on social work is particularly instructive not only academically but for the actualisation of practice perspectives in the face of the different historical and political meanings of the similarities and dissimilarities we can observe. Rather than retreating into abstract universals that are supposed to describe social work 'in essence' or 'social work as it really was meant to be' these observations are meant to lead back to detailed historical reflections as the basis for contemporary social work practice. Social work remains an historically contingent profession, perhaps more than any other professions, and to abandon the sensitivity to history, to recast social work as an activity that determines its own parameters with no reference to any political or historical context, is to abandon its social dimension, to declare the social, in the words of Agnes Heller and Ferenc Fehér, as a mere artefact (Heller and Fehér 1988).

As shown in chapter 2, the history of social work in Europe is intricately bound up with the history of the European nation states. They in turn owe their existence partly to the accumulation of military power in the hands of a new political elite, and partly to an arrangement with the emerging principles of capitalism and to the careful harnessing of its power (Flora 2000). The fervour of national movements that swept across Europe in the 19th century found its realisation predominantly in those political units that had command over an economically viable territory, with the exception perhaps of those curious smaller units like Luxembourg, Lichtenstein, Monaco, San Marino, Andorra. Nationalist sentiments without a viable economic basis did not come to fruition. To what extent capitalism itself needed an arrangement with the nation state is a difficult historical and economic question and this is not the place to enter into the highly controversial debate about the origins of capitalism (see Frank and Gills 1993). Suffice it to say that capitalism, since the formulation of its core principle of the commodification of goods and labour power beginning with the adventurous enterprises of mercantile families in the Renaissance and culminating in the industrial revolution (Wallerstein 1993), had on the one hand a very strong international and, for the standards of the respective transport and communication means of the time, global dimension. On the other hand it always needed an arrangement with localised political power centres to secure the 'fair' and unimpeded operation of the market as the place for commodity exchanges and hence latched on to the nascent nation states to form national economics. It needed this alliance for two basic reasons: for the protection of the liberal principles on which it is founded, the legal and, if necessary military enforcement of contracts between private individuals, and, in its industrial form, for the reproduction and educational preparation of a civilised labour force. The emerging social protection systems of the nation state, covering gradually all aspects from compulsory education to health care and social insurance, were therefore a direct response to the exigencies of capitalism (Leibfried und Rieger 2001). At the same time, the commodity principle of capitalism meant that the costs of social integration and protection were being 'externalised', did not feature in the profit calculations of the market and became the burden of nation states or of civil society from whose confines and obligations capitalism sought to set itself free to pursue profit maximisation across boundaries.

This particular arrangement between the nation states and capitalism, in which organised welfare in whatever mix between governmental and non-governmental agencies and later explicit social policies featured quite prominently, in turn contributed to the formation of a series of social and political compromises that became characteristic of the nation state as a welfare state. These therefore required compromises, and these compromises were the framework within which social work forged its own characteristic methodological and organisational compromises according to the specific political cultures of the different versions of nation and welfare states in Europe which gave it its diverse professional forms and traditions that seem so incompatible. Granted this perspective of welfare and social work as a series of arrangements with capitalism mediated by the nation state, what we are witnessing today is the breaking apart of those compromises centred on the nation state, and this paradoxically as a result of the very stability and success which welfare policy measures had produced for the market economy (Rieger and Leibfried 2001). In the contemporary scenario social work's own compromises are coming under pressure as the nature of its association with the state changes, and this regardless whether social services in a particular European country are being delivered predominantly through governmental or through non-governmental agencies.

The following is therefore an attempt to make evident the divisive effects on social work training and practice of the dissolving of the compromises contained within the nation stateconstruct and hence within traditional functions of social work, with the intention of underlining the impossibility of divorcing social work practice from social policy considerations and competences.

Of the numerous compromises that were forged in the formation of this modern, ambiguous, effective and yet inherently unstable entity of the nation state, the following have special relevance for social work, and this not in any particular order of priority, since they have to be seen as cyclically interconnected :

1. At the **political level** the most prominent compromise was between the ideas of liberalism and the various forms of communalism as the two legs on which, according to Bauman, modernity was founded (Bauman 1995b). In a sense both these principles were a threat to the stability and the legitimacy of the modern state unless they were brought aboard and formed part of the crew of political ideas steering the nation state project. The former wanted to limit the state's functions to an absolute minimum, to those of a custodian of rights, while communalism, particularly in its socialist form, sought to merge the contractual functions of the state with those of 'brotherhood' and hence of affective social bonds which made the state ultimately 'superfluous'. Communalism emphasised the existence of a common cause, if not the existence of a common 'essence', in a broad spectrum of social categories from ethnicity to gender and class position, that constitutes a deep sense of belonging beyond any contractual arrangements as envisaged under liberalism. It manifested itself in internationalist forms such as the labour or the women's movement on the one hand, both of which were accused of lacking in commitment to the nation, and as nationalism on the other, which also

142

presupposed a common 'substance', derived from historical, ethnic and biological-racialist arguments, as the basis of a sense of belonging which ultimately also obviates the state as a political instrument. The nation states managed more or less to tie both tendencies down to a commitment to a national project in which liberal democratic principles played a central though feebly developed role side by side with the fostering of emotional attachments and a sense of obligation to the national unit mainly through the education system and social institutions. The two world wars that erupted in and devastated Europe and large parts of the world during the 20th century bear witness to the inherent instability of this compromise.

Implied in this nation state solution was therefore also the class compromise, and this in a dual sense: The nation state based its politics quite explicitly on class differences in as much as the liberal construct of the autonomous individual came to benefit particularly the bourgeois elite which subsequently used it as the key principle of moral education and commercial conduct, while communalism, in a tamed and carefully controlled form, was applied to the masses, in an oppressive form once the sting of internationalism and self-determination had been removed (Bauman 1995a). These politics thereby simultaneously acknowledged and denied the existence and relevance of class, holding out the promise for the masses that individuals would one day be capable of leaving the confines of communal bonds, securities and constraints and distinguish themselves economically and socially as individual 'climbers' who benefited individually from the mechanisms of the market while relying on the fact that this system would allow only a few to succeed whereas 'the anonymous masses' would remain excluded from such opportunities of personal improvement.

2. This particular political settlement was backed by developments at the **cultural level** which probably more than anything else gave the nation states their particular character. Nation states are distinctly modern phenomena, not just in the sense that they are mostly of quite recent origin, having emerged in the latter part of the 19th and the early parts of the 20th centuries, but also in the sense that they mark a break with traditional societies and the political and social principles that had constituted them, which Durkheim summed up as 'mechanical solidarity'. Their basis is that of a society characterised by the division of labour and hence of a differentiation of roles that strive ever more evidently towards rational assumptions as enshrined in commerce, bureaucracy and the democratic formation of the general will of the people derived from an enlightened set of freedoms. And yet culturally, the social bonds that constitute and symbolise these modern creations are, in the European

context, not grounded only on rational, universal and hence abstract principles but are invariably also being portrayed as ancient, as mythical in origin, as based on a collective yearning for cultural unity and homogeneity (Delanty 1996). This of course marks the compromise of nationalism, in its emancipatory and at the same time its oppressive form. National identity, promoted through a uniform national education system and a standardised national language, became the carrier of not just 'traditional' social values, but of their recast modern version tailored not least to the requirements of industry and the free market economy (Gellner 1983). Through the device of this ambiguity identities could be manipulated, could be made operational for particular political purposes, particularly in the romantic version of a national identity which re-worked the process of incorporation into a national cultural identity as the release from serfdom (Giesen and Junge 1991).

Chief among these applications was the work ethic, which aimed at bringing the traditional notion of pride in one's work across the historical threshold of the onset of the division of labour. The work ethic, detached from its artisan context, upheld pre-modern principles and conditions as the ethical basis for the formal identity with and self-worth in a job while allowing none of the traditional contents to be preserved on which personal pride and identification with a product were once premised. 'The moral crusade recorded as the battle for the *introduction* of the work ethic ... was in fact an attempt to *resuscitate* basically pre-industrial work attitudes under new conditions which no longer made them meaningful' (Bauman 1998b: 7, original emphasis).

The other compromise between pre-modern and modern social claims and conditions, based on the same mechanisms, was the creation of a hierarchy of standards of moral conduct generally by treating personal/cultural and collective/national identities as products of quasi-biological mechanisms of evolution and cultural development. This extension of Darwinian principles from the biological to the social and cultural domain gave rise to racist constructs of national superiority which in effect formed tautologies of community bonds immune to critical argument (see chapter 2). As Giesen and Junge observe, 'the very impossibility of meaningful objections allows for the staging of communalism which cannot find any immediate backing in modern structures of society' (Giesen and Junge 1991: 297). With this device, claimed and applied by different European nationalities simultaneously, nationalism was exported globally in the form of colonialism, legitimating a hierarchical, exploitative world order on the grounds of a spurious replacement of subjective cultural criteria with seemingly objective, scientific indicators.

3. This latter achievement was based on a third level of compromises, the **organisation of the scientific enterprise** of enquiry, learning and application within the national framework. The liberation of scientific curiosity from dogma which had been initiated by the renaissance movement and had given the project of the Enlightenment its characteristic stance steered science on a universalising course which saw no sense and justification in national boundaries and irrational cultural traditions. Yet Enlightenment has its dialectically mediated negative side, as Horkheimer and Adorno point out in their pioneering analysis.

'We have no doubt that societal liberty is inseparably connected to the process of thinking that promotes enlightenment. However, we also believe, that the very concept of this way of thinking, no less than the concrete historical forms, the institutions of society, into which it is interwoven, contain the germinal point of this regression which is happening all around us today' (Horkeimer and Adorno 1947: 7f, own translation).

Foucault's perspective (Foucault 1992) on the development of modern science indicates similarly that this enterprise, though being geared at the liberation from the arbitrary power of traditional institutions, brought with it tremendous accumulations of power which were eagerly taken up by new regimes of governance harnessed also partly in the form of the nation states. Science became committed to the national cause, or at least its organisation in universities and its application in technology constantly created this pull towards a national orientation once universities became national institutions. As Bollenbeck states in relation to developments in 19th century Germany:

'The emperor, high ministry officials and university professors promote, not without contradictions and resistance, a reorganisation of the system of formation in favour of "realism". This is grounded not just in the success of natural sciences and technology, but also in the new situation of growing competition in world markets and imperial claims. The guidelines produced by a high level conference on school curricula in 1890 state "the number of hours in the curriculum devoted to ancient languages has to be restricted in order to do justice to the growing demands of other areas of knowledge created by the new world position of Germany' (Bollenbeck 1996: 227).

The interests of the nation state combined the national scientific enterprise with the emerging national economies to launch the competitive race of steamboats, of patented inventions and of warfare technology. While the autonomy of professors and of scientific research was safeguarded by the state in a system defined most explicitly by Humboldt, this safeguard depended on the usefulness of the universities for the national cause and remained therefore a fickle compromise, and

145

not only in the natural sciences, but also in the Arts, where for instance the German concept of '*Geisteswissenschaften*' implied a Hegelian universalism of '*Geist*' which in reality manifested itself most clearly in the national cultural enterprises (Lohmann 1998).

All these different levels of compromises have in common that they stabilised a particular relationship between universalism and particularism at the level of the nation state. The nation state made the universal particular, it nationalised universal features in the economy, in culture and in science, while at the same time making the particular universal, declaring its own values, standards and identities as superior to all others with the implicit or explicit claim that sooner or later other nations would have to recognise the hierarchy it set up as valid and binding and hence submit to the dominance of one victorious nation state.

In the context of these historical arrangements social work also forged its own compromises in close affinity to the political developments of the nation state. These parallel compromises could be summarised in the following way:

1. **Politically,** early social work in the form of organised charity in the emerging industrial slums was on the one hand confronted with Malthusanism, the extreme form of liberalism which espoused the principle of non-interference with the self-limiting process of poverty. This limited charitable efforts to a margin where the threat of destitution was always to be maintained rather than eliminated even though 'deserving' cases hat to be protected. On account of their bourgeois background the pioneers of what was as yet rather unreflected practice regarded squalor, destitution, depravity, quite rightly, as mass phenomena, signs of 'another world' or indeed of 'another nation', a nation of the excluded, from which it was possible and necessary to escape into a promised land of dignity only through particular individual efforts (Bommes and Scherr 2000). On the other hand the settlement movement related to a kind of political collectivism that eschewed extreme individualism and liberalism and fostered links with other social movements, notably the women's movement. This gave rise to early projects of community work and community education in which the poor and destitute were recognised in their capacity to act for themselves and collectively (Jones and Nowak 2000)). The 'masses' therefore appeared in two forms, as a threat from which it was necessary to escape and as an educational object which had to transform itself, and early social work methodology attempted to come to terms with this by vacillating between both poles and settling on giving help centred on the individual and

146

rescuing systematically (rather than indiscriminately) while not excluding some forms of group and community work, with 'client self-determination' acting as a moral and methodological indicator of the ambiguity. The tension between both starting positions remained (figure 7).

political level

nation state	liberalism		collectivism
		class compromise: only the elite can afford **individualism**; workers become **'the masses'**; **political citizenship** conceded selectively	
social work	**Malthusian-ism** (poverty relief is counter-productive)		**settlement movement** (bottom-up renewal of society)
		rescue of individuals from faceless squalor, self-determination also in groups and communities	

Figure 7

2. At the **cultural level**, social work's individualism underwent a series of transformations, in line with the prevailing political trends highlighted above and the advancement of a scientific paradigm, which will need to be dealt with in the next section. On the one hand, charitable assistance was an expression of and aimed at maintaining distinct cultural identities and allegiances and was being provided from within the confines of distinct religious or humanist organisations each with their own value

orientation. Charity workers were their ambassadors and acted as shining examples of the benefits of living a life according to those precepts. However, the social commitment of charities, in contrast to proselytising church missions, converged on the other hand on universal principles of rationality and of insight into the necessity of acting prudently and sensibly. In bridging the gap between those potentially contrasting demands social work chimed in with the fundamentals of the national project, the building of an integrated, stable nation guided by both rationality and yet culturally distinct from other nations. Charity Workers therefore offered their personal example and commitment as a unifying, universal identity that could absorb differences of origin and of material means under the umbrella of patriotism. The emerging social profession provided a kind of 'national curriculum' of values equivalent to that which standardised the school system, but adjusted to the various cultural deficits it identified in the objects of their attention (Kunstreich 1997). This massive exercise in the assimilation to, or rather in the construction of a national identity provided the fine-tuning of symbolic solidarity on which the unstable political entities of nation states so utterly depended. In every European country the criteria governing the distinction between the deserving and the undeserving poor were made up of a mix of economic factors (the work ethic) and appeals to national pride. Notably, this assimilation programme was not delivered by state officials primarily on account of the rigidity of institutions in delivering exclusion and segregation 'on principle', but by organisations of civil society which were committed to national integration as a cultural project. Their way of delivery always sought to make reference not so much to coercion, but to the voluntary, self-generated efforts by clients in determining their own destiny (figure 8).

cultural level

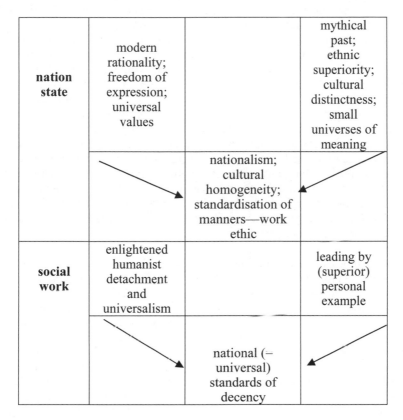

			mythical past; ethnic superiority; cultural distinctness; small universes of meaning
nation state	modern rationality; freedom of expression; universal values		
		nationalism; cultural homogeneity; standardisation of manners—work ethic	
social work	enlightened humanist detachment and universalism		leading by (superior) personal example
		national (– universal) standards of decency	

Figure 8

3. At the **level of scientific activity and legitimation** early social work also forged a compromise. In recognition of the sheer ineffectiveness of appeals to morality (without coercion) and in the light of the cultural compromise emerging on the cultural horizon early social work training was on the one hand keen to align itself broadly with the scientific project of the 19th century which affirmed positivism, value neutrality and the instrumental use of knowledge for the purpose of solving problems not only of nature, but also of human behaviour and of society (Scherr 2000). The new disciplines of sociology, pedagogy and psychology represented these principles and became key reference points for systematically derived methodological knowledge. On the other hand, subjective

149

reflections on the various dimensions of the acting and intervening self also played an important part in the origins of social work training. These dimensions included not just practice experience ('learning by doing'), but also gender identity as the majority of members of the new profession were women. Again, social work epistemology and subsequent training patterns represent a compromise (figure 9) Particularly those methods gained prominence in which the 'self' of the worker remained central and in which individual solutions prevailed. But this 'self' was now also recast in terms of a universal willingness to listen, to be non-judgemental, and to act rationally and purposefully. This happened for instance, in the affirmation of female qualities of motherliness, which had served the German pioneer of social work education, Alice Salomon, as a central reference point for her pedagogical programme for the purpose of raising social work above party- and class-political subjectivity (see chapter 5). This stance made the profession acceptable to modern sensitivities, even though the status of an 'independent profession' was ultimately denied (Giesen and Junge 1991), and it made it no less attractive to the nation state project, as outlined above.

These highly ambivalent and initially quite fluid arrangements consolidated themselves in the decades after WWII when the European nation states really came into their own as welfare states. As Rieger and Leibfried, among many others, note, 'The welfare state marks a high point in exclusive nation-statism...The welfare state represents the primacy of domestic social and economic policy vis-à-vis the world market and international politics. This constellation is a result of the social as well as political integration of the working class into the nation-state' (1998: 367). It was during that period that the 'bureau-professional' breakthrough for social work (Harris 2003) was prepared in quite a number of countries, albeit with significant variations. As demonstrated in chapter 3, arrangements varied according to the type of welfare regime that became established. A universal regime, such as it prevailed in Nordic countries, emphasised very much the entitlements of all citizens to state welfare services and lessened the degree to which stigma resulted from intervention. This model implied a high degree of state control over the economy, but also a high degree of homogeneity among service users, which made it difficult to articulate issues of identity and difference.

scientific level

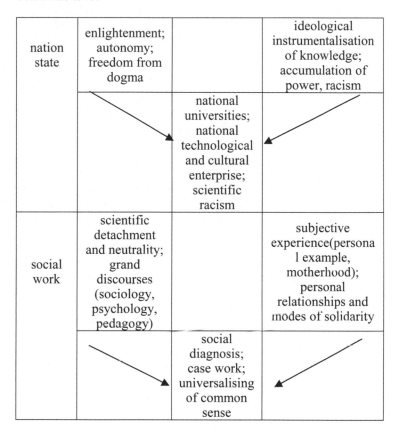

nation state	enlightenment; autonomy; freedom from dogma		ideological instrumentalisation of knowledge; accumulation of power, racism
		national universities; national technological and cultural enterprise; scientific racism	
social work	scientific detachment and neutrality; grand discourses (sociology, psychology, pedagogy)		subjective experience(personal example, motherhood); personal relationships and modes of solidarity
		social diagnosis; case work; universalising of common sense	

Figure 9

The corporatist model, prevalent in the Bismarckian tradition of Germany but also in the Netherlands and Austria, delegated welfare services to agencies of civil society. This entailed a higher degree of differentiation and nominally a better chance for the articulation of cultural difference, but the effects were kept within bounds by the agencies' commitment to preserving a framework of national identity. It is interesting to note that in those countries the state made a much greater effort at negotiating and fostering the social responsibilities of capital and industry. Without this the brand of 'pluralism' in social service provisions it promoted through the principle of subsidiarity would

151

have been too susceptible to deep social and economic divisions threatening the stability of the whole construct. Social workers in corporatist welfare regimes are not placed at the forefront of social divisions and of conflicts between the private and the public sphere as they are in residual models, because the dividing line between both spheres is much more diffuse and multi-layered. This is certainly one of the implications of social work in a residual welfare regime such as in the UK, that it magnifies the significance of the border between the private and the public sphere as an immensely political issue because of the divided role of welfare it promotes. The state deliberately uses social services as a defence against the de-stabilising effects of a pronounced polarisation between capital and labour, which is why in the UK 'bureau-professional hierarchies were as much a basis for the power exercised by social workers as the basis for the exercise of power over social workers' (Hugman 1991: 62). Welfare is divided between those who have to rely on state services and those who have the means to 'care for themselves', or at least out of other private means. This system has stigma and conflict built into it, no matter how careful social workers are in playing this down with the help of sensitive working methods.

In view of the fundamental changes dealt with at the start of this chapter which alter the nature and function of the nation state profoundly it is no wonder that these historical compromises, concluded within the confines of each political culture, are splitting up again to make way to new versions of the old polarisation. The disaggregation of factors, of conflicts and contradictions that had been bundled and contained within the politics of the nation state itself, sets free a whole range of forces which in turn affect also the nature of social work. What can be observed on the whole is that the mediating function of the state is weakening and that social services are therefore exposed more directly to economic influences than they were during the heydays of the welfare consensus. The changes witnessed in social services can only be understood against the background of the changing relationship between state and capitalism.

At the level of the nation state the following separations and polarisations have set in:

1. Politically, the balance between liberalism and communalism has been upset, releasing both tendencies into separate fields of gravity no longer related centrally to the nation state concept. The increasing liberalisation of the capitalist market economy gave rise to a revival of ideological positions that pick up on selected ideas of classical liberalism but mix them with extreme forms of individualism and a calculated disregard for anything primarily 'social' although this was never part of classical liberalism as such. At the same time, communalism also re-emerges, but in

fragmented form and no longer primarily under the umbrella of nationalism. It is perhaps indicative, that communitarianism for instance, while continuing a theme that can be traced back through the collective movements of the 19th century to pre-modern notions of community, today makes little reference to the state either. Where it does, it regards the state as a metaphor of a bigger community, but communities get equally constructed as non-geographic interest groups, and indeed the politics of single issue social movements have become a strong national and particularly international force, cutting across the party alliances that had been formative for the nation state period. Communalism also becomes the receptacle of resentment at the threatened loss of identity which aims at re-constituting the nation state as a one-sided interest community of tribalism and xenophobia (figure 10a).

As a consequence, the organisation of class relations mediated by the nation state between both poles also breaks down. This has the effect that individualism, in the form of a 'bootstrap ideology', reaches much further into areas formerly protected by the bonds of collective class solidarity forged in the classical industrial confrontations between capital and labour. Elite and mass, entrepreneurs and collectivists, capital and labour no longer confront each other within an awareness of their interdependence but have become split off from one another. To those keen to exercise the choices that an unencumbered market capitalism suggests (no matter what their 'classical' class position is) the rest, those left with no choice, simply do not matter any longer, not as a reserve pool of labour, not even as a serious social threat of instability. Perhaps they interest remotely as consumers of leisure of which they have acquired an endless but unusable supply, but their consumer potential is always financially limited. They need to be contained and controlled and for that purpose private security businesses are moving into this market, diluting the state monopoly on policing. The uncoupling of the political process from the mediation of the nation state makes the creation of solidarity and cohesion more and more a commercial matter. 'Earning' the status of citizenship refers no longer to a mere moral quality but has assumed a highly material ring.

2. Equally, the ruptures in the construction of a uniform national cultural identity are all too obvious. Usually this phenomenon gets discussed from the perspective of the increases in immigration which have affected Europe (see chapter 4). This view makes it easy to blame the immigrants for having caused the allegedly homogeneous national cultures to become heterogeneous and the ordinary citizen to be plunged into an identity crisis. This view fails to recognise that all nation states are complex cultural compromises or impositions which pursued the ideal of

homogeneity for political purposes. Today a new arrangement between the nation state and capitalism necessitates labour mobility on a global scale and this makes the maintenance of the myth of a homogeneous national culture untenable. The alleged new crisis of identity is the old crisis of the construct of a national identity. It is the dictate of a globalising economy which compounds this crisis by giving consumers of life-style attributes, which replace cultural referents, a conflicting message: that they should be part of a unified world culture, and that they should also create their own individual style and personality. The national culture is hence merely one reference point among numerous others (figure 10b).

3. Scientific and educational agendas are also changing in line with the altered role of the state vis-à-vis the economy. Many academics who find themselves exposed to the winds of quality assessment and competitive research tendering in subject areas that never had anything to do with commercial considerations wake up to the realisation how cosy the arrangements with the nation state had been. Universities have to learn to operate more like commercial enterprises in order to maintain their market share and their usefulness for a national agenda no longer guarantees state funding. But it is not just the organisational framework of research and knowledge creation that is affected by the loss of a national horizon, the disciplinary boundaries of discourses themselves begin to disappear and admit a sense of relativity and subjectivity, particularly in the arts, that references post-modernism and post-structuralism (figure 10c). The trend is exemplified by the growth of 'cultural studies' as the new umbrella discipline that incorporates hitherto disparate disciplines, avoiding the claims to universality once expressed by the concept of the *Geisteswissenschaften* (cf. Oesterle 1991) but setting new standards for a 'universal relativity' of equally valid positions. True, the deconstruction of national certainties, the exposure of regimes of power that masqueraded as truths was long overdue. However this has the effect of splitting research and academic discourses into one camp that is utilitaristically concerned with 'what works' and another that suspends truth claims in mere aestheticism that can then be used for all kinds of purposes.

Disaggregation of Nation State compromises

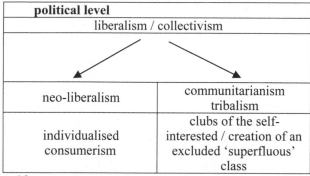

political level	
liberalism / collectivism	
neo-liberalism	communitarianism tribalism
individualised consumerism	clubs of the self-interested / creation of an excluded 'superfluous' class

Figure 10a

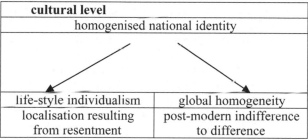

cultural level	
homogenised national identity	
life-style individualism localisation resulting from resentment	global homogeneity post-modern indifference to difference

Figure 10b

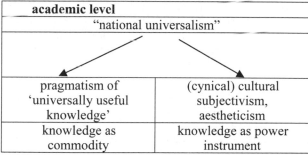

academic level	
"national universalism"	
pragmatism of 'universally useful knowledge'	(cynical) cultural subjectivism, aestheticism
knowledge as commodity	knowledge as power instrument

Figure 10c

155

Now the main changes in contemporary European social work can be explained in the context of all these changes. A brief review of the effects of the disaggregation processes open a way of seeing what possibilities, but also what dangers they entail.

1. The political changes heighten the tension along the individualism–communalism axis for social work. With the re-orientation of social policies towards more efficiency and social control on the one hand the individualised focus of case work narrows even further down to the perspective best exemplified by case management, and this in most European countries. Case or care management can imply that only certain functions of a person, not even the individual person as a whole, are of concern. Used uncritically, this perspective has the tendency to narrow people down to particular collections of need in relation to available resource packages. On the other hand with the change of perspective from 'clients' to 'consumers of services' new forms of collective action open up, particularly in the field of welfare rights, lobbying by user groups and community action. Nevertheless, the overall steering effect of the state's influence on the social work mandate is being replaced or at least being equally affected by economic considerations, budgetary constraints, cost-benefit calculations, purchaser mentalities. State agencies set up quasi-market conditions which inevitably alter the nature of the relationship with service users towards a purchaser/provider axis, even where those terms are not being used (figure 11). However, nowhere has the influence of the state disappeared entirely and nowhere has social work become a free commercial service agent—on the contrary, the state has increased its interest in and control over social work in certain fields, notably child protection (see chapter 9). But it is precisely in the differential effects of these changes that a fundamental transformation becomes apparent: the mandate of social work is shifting away from at least potentially democratic controls mediated or guaranteed by the national state towards the force field of commercially negotiated, ultimately private transactions which bypass democratic mediation. While the drift is in a similar direction in all countries, the effects of these changes are much more pronounced in a residual welfare system like the UK (Aldridge 1996). Both the universalist and the corporatist welfare regimes seem to reflect a greater willingness by society to accompany this 'marketisation' with democratic controls. Here the changes are subjected to much more intensive public debate and scrutiny than seems to be the case in the UK. In those countries this offsets to an extent the commodifying effect of contracting out and of managerialism that has become a strong feature of social work for instance in the Netherlands where service providers have to bid for contracts annually on very clearly defined efficiency criteria (Laan 1998).

political level

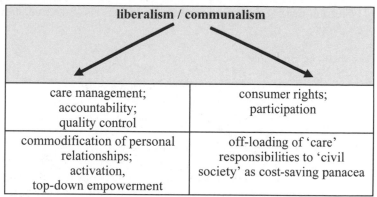

liberalism / communalism	
care management; accountability; quality control	consumer rights; participation
commodification of personal relationships; activation, top-down empowerment	off-loading of 'care' responsibilities to 'civil society' as cost-saving panacea

Figure 11

2. The new 'cultural' emphasis on identity meets social work largely unprepared. As noted in chapter 5, the 'colour-blind approach' to social work methods as a sign of its scientific orientation had been very firmly established in all countries. The break-up of the universalism on which it was based was spearheaded by the women's movement and the black liberation movement and had a salutary but also a dangerous effect. Because the historical link of social work approaches with the universalism of a national orientation had largely been ignored or taken for granted as the actual frame of reference for issues of equality and solidarity across gender, ethnic and cultural divisions, it is now hard to reconcile the identity discourse with a concern for equality. With the fading of this national reference point issues of 'difference' and also of equality have to be grounded differently and this exposes a 'weak spot' in social work's linking of methodological and ethical questions (Banks 2006). The uncertainty over how to establish criteria for identity other than through reference to national culture invited false reassurances in the form of essentialism on the one hand and often also in the form of cultural racism. Where before national identity had been assumed to have been simply given, so the re-discovered ethnic and cultural differences were now frequently also treated as simply given (figure 12). Furthermore, concern over identity in social work was relegated to specialised areas, such as work with immigrants and refugees, and the attempt at bringing anti-racism on the agenda run into a barrage of opposition rallying under the banner of equality, and this not just in Britain. At the same time, the

weakening of the national agenda did help to articulate not just the right
to cultural self-definition and the 'right to be different', but also a whole
range of methods aimed at fostering skills of individuation and personal
decision-making, of which 'life coaching' is but one fashionable
example.

cultural level

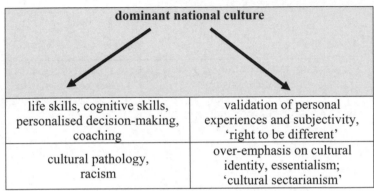

dominant national culture	
life skills, cognitive skills, personalised decision-making, coaching	validation of personal experiences and subjectivity, 'right to be different'
cultural pathology, racism	over-emphasis on cultural identity, essentialism; 'cultural sectarianism'

Figure 12

3. Scientifically and professionally, the disappearance of grand
narratives in social work, when read against the background of the disaggregation of nation state compromises, also leads to new dichotomies.
Yes, the end of a 'gladiatorial approach' to methods (Rojek, Peacock and
Collins 1988) comes as a relief, and post-modern deconstruction, the
laying bare of the hidden power agendas at the core of theory models,
may help to reactivate social work's emancipatory claims (Howe 1994).
Post-modern critique in social work methodology has triggered a new
discussion on reflective practice (Fook 2004, Healy 2005, Parton 2004).
But one of the dangers with this project of post-modern reconstruction is
the replacement of methods with procedures: different situations require
different forms of intervention and the choice is either arbitrary or fixed
on procedural, legal or managerial grounds. There are signs of the
'competence road', the assessment of outcomes of training courses rather
than curricula contents being taken by social work courses in quite a
number of European countries. This shifts the emphasis in training and
education from 'input' (the package of course elements and subject areas)
to 'output' (the ability to perform to agreed standards and requirements).
There are clear indications that this trend matches the general re-
definition of social issues as risks, with all the concomitant implications

of the instrumentalistion of professional—client relationships. In some instances however, the competence discourse is more pronounced, as for instance in the UK where it dominates the qualifications and exam system in social work (figure 13). As Dominelli and Hoogvelt (1996) have shown, the technocratisation of UK social work follows a political agenda, which in turn is a response to a new arrangement between the state and capital. The political significance of methodological considerations is becoming ever more apparent and requires close attention in the profession. The retreat to detached scientific methods is not a solution to the uncertainties created at the methodological level. Only the fundamental re-examination of the foundations of accountable practice can clear a way beyond the potential indifference of ethical and methodological relativism and eclecticism and protect practice against political misuse.

academic level

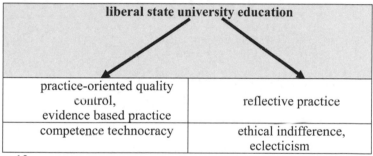

Figure 13

These effects of disaggregation triggered by the weakening of the nation state and with it of the welfare state in the wake of globalisation call for a new orientation in the social work methods discourses in Europe. The hope of constructing a 'Social Europe' hinges centrally on the ability of the European Union to integrate the divergent cultural traditions under a strong social rights and equality agenda in its own social policy initiatives. This poses the challenge of developing a model of 'European Social Work' that would contribute to this process, not just through political lobbying but also through the re-orientation of its methods towards the realisation of various dimensions of European citizenship (Meehan 1993). This will be the subject of the next chapter.

What requires attention is therefore not just the differences in theory frameworks in social work but their significance within a particular political agenda. In every intervention of social work the entirety of social relationships gets negotiated and this is particularly acute in a period of considerable re-organisation in European welfare regimes, as will be discussed in the following chapter.

9. Neo-liberal policies – prospects for social work

Issues of cultural difference discussed in the previous chapters have relevance also in relation to the differences in political cultures prevailing in different countries. As discussed in the opening chapters, social work is bounded very closely by social policy decisions and needs to take position towards recent fundamental developments if it is to remain true to its social and professional mandate. The emphasis lies in this chapter on the fact that there are indeed differences between social service delivery systems in different European countries, differences which depend partly on the nature and tradition of the respective 'welfare regimes' and partly on the extent to which social work methodology, in relation to these regimes, has itself contributed to the shaping of a 'welfare culture. It is hypothesised that these professional responses are expressions of a highly differentiated array of academic discourses, which often threaten the unitary appearance of the professional field and indeed its very professionalism when the groups' close links to 'volunteering' and its rootedness in social movements is taken into account. But this diversity can be regarded in many ways as a unique reservoir of creativity, resistance and ultimately autonomy precisely under the impact of ever more powerful political and monetary sanctions (Lorenz 2001). This creativity can be harnessed to form the nucleus of the epistemology and methodology of a European model of social work that comes to terms with diversity and negotiates cultural differences communicatively while engaging critically with social policy developments.

There is an increasing awareness among social work practitioners in all European countries that international comparisons of developments in welfare are not just a matter for social policy analysts, but are of direct relevance to practice (Payne 1998). Whether the actual changes in welfare systems which characterise contemporary social policy developments all over Europe are directly linked to the mechanisms of economic globalisation is a moot question, but there is no denying that policy trends, particularly those of the neo-liberal ilk, have traversed national boundaries with astonishing ease (Penna et al. 1999). The last decades of the 20th century have brought about decisive shifts in the orientation of welfare systems away from states playing (or at least aspiring to play) a prominent role in the provision or regulation of welfare services and towards delegation, de-regulation, privatisation and political targeting of specific groups of receivers. There is, however, no actual convergence discernible in these trends and this is not only hampering the development of a consistent social policy approach at the level of the European Union but shows also that the nation states have retained a good deal of their autonomy and are likely to hold on to this for the foreseeable future (Rieger and Leibfried 1998). Welfare is still far too important a source of political legitimation, precisely at a time when autonomy and thereby the visibility of 'governance' are being curtailed at the economic level, to be sacrificed to trans-national bodies. On the contrary, welfare measures and programmes, in an intriguing parallel to their origins during the height of industrialisation, are again used as a means of reaching citizens directly and individually with a moral appeal to their responsibility that emphasises obligations rather than entitlements. In distinction from those early welfare programmes however, which heralded the development of ever more comprehensive social policies, these measures are having the effect of furthering social fragmentation rather than integration as the entire relationship between capital and labour and between capitalism and the state changes (Böhnisch and Schröer 2002). Welfare programmes are no longer carriers of the promise of social justice and equality but tools for the re-distribution of opportunities according to principles of justice which are based on the willingness by subjects to adjust to the demands of the new economy for totally flexible workers and indeed for the trouble-free exclusion of 'no-hopers'. The changes across different European 'welfare regimes' gave rise to the expectation that neo-liberal doctrines would sooner or later prevail and that the state would eventually cede its welfare functions to the market wherever possible

The selective use of welfare measures which often no longer amount to a comprehensive social policy, corresponds closely to the changing role of the state overall or, more precisely, to – in Balibar's words – the 'privatisation' of the state: 'The "state" as an institution of power-concentration, to which responsibilities for policy-making can be attributed and which mediates publicly between interests and social forces, this kind of state has a tendency to vanish in Europe' (Balibar 1993: 153). Beyond that, the main thrust of the social policy changes affected the perception of the concept of 'the social' itself which looked as if it was losing all significance, to be replaced by rampant individualism, tempered only by the emphasis neo-liberalismplaced on family solidarity and mutual support. This context is bound to have profound implications for social work methods which had been linked to a specific role of the state in relation to society (see chapter 2), directly and indirectly.

In most European countries the re-structuring of the welfare state according to neo-liberal principles had first been promoted by centre-right governments during the 1980s. Although in no country were the changes as pronounced and as ideologically symbolic as in the United Kingdom, neo-liberal principles did not remain the hall-mark of conservative governments. There was a brief period in the mid-1990s when the majority of the countries

162

of the European Union had elected social-democratic governments and there were considerable expectations that these governments would re-dress neo-liberal welfare politics, hopes that were soon to be thwarted. By March 2001 the following countries of the EU could be said to have centre-left governments: Apart from the UK, only Greece, Portugal and Sweden were governed by social-democratic parties without the need to form coalitions, although in electoral systems of proportional representation these parties achieved only between 36.4 and 44.6 per cent of the popular vote. In Denmark a coalition between Social-Democrats and Liberals held power whereas the German Social-Democrats governed in coalition with the Green Party. Complex coalition arrangements applied in Finland, France, Italy and the Netherlands where centre-left parties had at best marginal leads over other coalition partners. Ireland had a coalition government between the 'republican party' Fianna Fail and the Progressive Democrats, a former break-away party who gave the coalition a right-of-centre direction although this would not necessarily be the political home of the major partner. Only Austria, Belgium and Spain were governed by declared Conservative or Right Wing parties, although the close ties between Blair of the UK's New Labour and Aznar as Head of the conservative Spanish Partido Popular and subsequently also with Berlusconi of Italy's Forza Italia signify further fluidity of the left-right spectrum in Europe. As Dahrendorf (1999) points out in his critique of the 'authoritarian streak in Europe's new centre', 'twenty years ago these parties had twice their current support in Europe. Social democrats are distinctly minority parties in most European countries' (1999: 14). In purely electoral terms, the swing away from conservatism in Europe has not been decisive and on this basis alone the differences particularly in terms of welfare policies between centre-left and centre-right governments were minimal.

In view of this some politicians began to talk of The Third Way to characterise new departures in welfare policies as alternatives to the 'classical' positions of left and right. Anthony Giddens, himself one of the chief intellectual architects of this project, traces what he sees as an emergent consensus back to the 'new progressivism' with which the American Democrats sought to give their social policies profile and appeal (Giddens 2000). Its emphasis on 'equal opportunity, personal responsibility and the moblizing of citizens and communities' (Giddens 2000: 2) had a decisive influence on Blair's New Labour concepts and led to a transatlantic dialogue on what then came to be termed 'third way politics' in which originally Clinton and Blair as well as Schröder of Germany, Kok of the Netherlands and d'Alema of Italy were involved. The decisive European impetus for the attempted launch of a 'Third Way' platform for Social Democrats was to have come however from a joint paper between Blair and Schröder published in 1999 under the title 'Europe – The Third Way – die Neue Mitte' (Blair-

Schröder 1999). In it the two leaders reaffirm what they consider to be core principles of social-democratic policies such as fairness, social justice, freedom, equality of opportunity, solidarity and responsibility for others. However, they re-define the social-democratic understanding of the role of the state as supporting and not hindering the market economy with the catch-phrase 'the state should not row, but steer: not so much control, as challenge' (Giddens 2000: 6). The welfare state is to be 'modernised', not abolished. The old principles therefore call for a new interpretation commensurate with the conditions of a changed global environment so that social justice must no longer be geared towards 'equality of outcome'. Instead, rights need to be balanced by responsibilities, aspirations for a secure, life-long workplace need to give way to an affirmation of flexible markets. The state's role is to invest in 'social and human capital' (Blair-Schröder 1999), which means motivating and supporting citizens in vocational training and re-training, in life-long learning, and to foster solidarity not just towards the recipients of benefits but also towards those who pay for them. As concrete social policy measures the paper mentions the fight against poverty and exclusion, against criminality and for urban renewal through the strengthening of the community spirit. The paper explicitly calls for a commitment by social democratic governments 'to examine all recipients of social benefits, including people of working age ... as to their ability to earn a living and to reform state institutions to render them capable of supporting those able to work in finding suitable jobs' (ibid.).

Although this initiative was designed as an appeal to all social democratic parties of Europe to join this project none of the other centre-left parties in Europe felt comfortable enough with the proposal to rally around this Third Way or Middle Ground notion of welfare. Prime Minister Jospin of France and his social-democratic Parti Socialiste explicitly distanced themselves from the proposals (Chambers 2000). This is not to say that their policies did not in effect amount to very similar measures. Both the divergence and the similarities highlight a noteworthy aspect of current processes of social policy making: on the one hand there is pressure on all governments to 'service' the market more explicitly and more indirectly with social services in the broadest sense which produces a kind of convergence of policies. On the other hand there are distinct welfare traditions at both the cultural and the political level which offer sufficient resistance against whole-sale and unimpeded changes being imposed. This observation adumbrates the margin of social work's autonomy in relation to social policies and also possibly the arena in which allies in a more active shaping of social policies 'from the bottom up' can be enlisted. This is the arena in which critical cultural politics and the recognition of identities matters directly to social work practice.

The evaluation of more specific social work responses to new social policies in European countries needs to start therefore from a brief re-statement of the fundamental and, to some extent irksome fact that social work practice in no country managed to overcome completely its dependency on the prevailing welfare regime, no matter how strong professional aspirations tried to elevate their practitioners to a level of greater autonomy. As demonstrated in the introduction, the way social work practice comes across to service users does not depend solely on the professional methods applied but on a complex set of expectations and relationships between citizens and society, mediated by the state, which make instrumental use of social professionals. Research has shown that responses by practitioners from different countries to a 'given' social case such as suspected child abuse are only partly the result of a scientifically based and professionally conducted analysis of 'the problem' (e.g. Hetherington et al. 1997; Baistow and Hetherington 1998). For the most part social professionals enact and represent the type of citizenship that characterises the political culture of a country generally.

However, the extent to which nation states are characterised by their own brand of social policy and are capable of maintaining their autonomy to do so has become severely curtailed. In the context of Europe two interlocking factors are responsible for this in the form of globalisation and the process of European integration. The former manifests itself in the intensification of competition between market players formerly bounded by national economic interests and now strong enough to dictate their own terms to governments. A coalition of interests in turn provides an incentive for national governments to lower social costs of employers and to abandon the aspiration of creating full employment while putting more pressure on employees and on the unemployed to seek employment. Neo-liberal ideologies fully exploit and further contribute to this economically driven phenomenon which in turn triggers the sets of political expectations mentioned above.

Europe as the economic, political and social project of the European Union with the 'old' western European member states and the countries of Central and Eastern Europe who have now joined stands at the intersection of the forces of globalisation and those re-affirming the importance of state-centred governance, albeit at collective and probably federalist level. 'European integration is a process that facilitates and accelerates a process of economic internationalisation while inhibiting ... a parallel process of regulatory transnationalisation or the "spontaneous" appearance of a transnational European governing capacity' (Offe 2000: 25). It therefore provides both a vehicle for a globalising economy and a supra-national defence against its unregulated impact which the nation states are no longer able to mount effectively themselves. While the EU member states are anxious to retain a degree of autonomy in devising and pursuing social policies and the European Union as such limits its own social policy proposals largely to the area of employment protection and the fight against exclusion, this national autonomy is clearly prescribed by economic market principles aimed at 'liberating' the famous 'invisible hand' of the market from the influence of the state to allow it to self-regulate the encounter of commercial and consumer interests. Steek describes the effects as a growing 'voluntarism': 'National politics are increasingly finding themselves forced to ... move away from hard obligations to soft incentives, from regulation to voluntarism, and from social-interventionism to liberal democracy' (Steek 1995: 58).

A wider diversity of actors in politics and of levels of policy making, ranging from the regional to the supra-national, therefore comes into operation inevitably, especially in matters of creating social cohesion through welfare. This widening field of operators enhances the ambiguity of social policies generally as highlighted in the European social policy project. The inter-play between traditional national and emergent European social policies as well as the shifts in social policy resulting from changes in governments after elections therefore produce widely differing effects, not so much perhaps in the appearance of individual measures but above all in the sub-texts of social contracts as they are being re-drawn. As already mentioned, it is not just that the categories of 'left' and 'right' become fragmented in themselves and meaningless as far as the comparison between whole sets of policies are concerned (Spicker 2000), this disaggregation also corresponds to the emergence of much more localised, pragmatic and temporal groupings of mutual support at all levels, ranging from families, business partnerships and political parties to international alliances. Social work can no longer occupy a secure and taken-for-granted space in these scenarios and the study of the differential effects of these changes and the dynamics behind them becomes essential for the re-orientation of social work practice.

In the case of Germany the welfare consensus that had prevailed in the post-World War II era under both Christian Democrat and Social Democrat governments had shown remarkable continuity with both the Weimar and the Bismarckian model of social provisions. The German Basic Law (Grund-gesetz) declares (article 20 (1)), 'The Federal Republic of Germany is a democratic and social federal state'. However, the combined effects of globalisation, demographic shifts, European Integration and German Unification issued in the following principles as guidelines for a 're-structured social state' *(Umbau des Sozialstaats)* (Offe 2000), which became even more apparent during the second term of office of the centre-left coalition government in Germany under Schröder which culminated in the controversial 'Hartz IV' policies: reduction of costs of public social security to protect jobs and prevent further unemployment; relaxation of controls over wages, particularly at the lower end to bring in more people from unemployment; cutting of tax-financed social costs such as long-term unemployment and social security payments. After many years of mere technical changes in social policy the effects of these goals upset the finely balanced interplay of interests on which the corporatist system depended and cause a fragmentation of established collective actors into new, short-term and opportunist alliances of interests. Organisationally this means that the dominant position held by the major non-governmental welfare organisations as the main players in the provision of social services under the principle of subsidiarity and social responsibility is no longer secure. Although the German government is slow to dismantle the undoubted privileges these organisations enjoyed (as it could—and should—by way of implementing the EU principle of 'freedom of movement of services' between European countries and the liberalisation of trade in services under the GATS agreement) there is nevertheless more emphasis on efficiency and competitiveness between the services. Some analysts interpret this as a shift away from subsidiarity towards the implementation of market conditions (Münder 1998). In terms of the mode of service delivery it means that social policy 'assumes increasingly the character of a supportive infrastructure assisting service users in the management of individual biographical transitions, ruptures and crises for broad sectors of the population (*Lebenslaufpolitik*, 'life trajectory politics')' (Olk 2000: 107). This comes close to the 'life politics' concept proposed by Giddens (1994) and calls for an 'activating' dimension of welfare provisions (Dahme and Wohlfahrt 2002), summed up in a much used metaphor that the welfare state should stop providing a safety net but offer a trampoline instead which catapults recipients back to a level of independent functioning (Butterwegge 1999).

These new politics do not work 'automatically' and their in-built ambiguities allow for a considerable margin of discretion in their implementation. Their operationalisation depends on the whole range of social professionals playing their part in the practical realisation of these new departures and adjusting their methodologies accordingly. Chamberlayne and Rustin (1999) found a close correspondence between British and German social policy approaches under New Labour in terms of their emphasis on making the receipt of certain types of welfare payments conditional on clients receiving individualised casework. In the case of Germany they showed that the methodological focus on 'activation' did not take account sufficiently of the actual biographical trajectories of the recipients of such casework interventions, and this despite the avowed attention to individual life and career concepts. Implementing this policy fully would have required a much more open acknowledgement of the lack of correspondence between the stated policy objectives on the one hand and the actual structural restrictions with the concomitant 'habitualised but now inappropriate patterns of orientation' displayed by recipients on the other (Chamberlayne and Rustin

1999: 116). This leads to a growing discrepancy contained within the principle of subsidiarity, so central to German social policy, the discrepancy between a 'liberal' interpretation which emphasises the self-organising potential of civil society and indeed of the individual, and a 'paternalistic' version in which the state maintains tight control over the conduct of its subjects along the chain of devolved service providers. In this tradition social work does not need to change paradigm to comply with the requirements of an 'activating state' (Kessl and Otto 2003) and the profession in Germany has hence put up much less resistance against the new social policy pressures than for instance that of the UK.

The Dutch welfare model was originally based on a slightly different interpretation of corporatism from that prevailing in Germany. Here civil society was expected to be organised and represented in the provision of welfare (as in other public services) through clearly defined institutions reflecting the main ideological 'blocks' of society, such as the churches and humanist and labour organisations, in a form of 'institutionalised pluralism' (Spicker 2000). It was therefore all the more astonishing that in a 'Copernican Revolution' (Voogt and Wiertsema quoted in Laan 2000: 89) the influence of these 'pillars' declined steadily and quite radically during the 1980s to give way to a much more unencumbered quasi-market re-grouping of interests (on the side of the providers and of the users) than in the German case. Clients have been re-constructed as customers to such an extent that the category of 'needs' has been replaced by that of 'demand', expressed in their 'purchasing power', to which agencies have to respond by delivering and managing packages of service products (Laan 2000). Welfare services and in particular social workers were deployed more directly and more unambiguously in order to implement the principle of the 'activating welfare state'. This principle is not only geared towards motivating more clients to take up paid employment (instead of relying on welfare benefits and social assistance) but also towards motivating welfare providers to produce measurable results and to stick to targets that form the basis of a contractual agreement with funding authorities (Laan 1998). There are no longer any 'privileged' service providers as agencies get selected for funding on a competitive, product- and efficiency-oriented basis (Bekkers 1999).

Central to social policy in France have always been the family and the 'constant refusal of the French state to create a large public welfare institution' (Bouget 1998: 156), social protection having been modelled on Bismarckian principles. Nevertheless it regarded the family not as a private institution but as the mediator of citizenship. Its employment-based contributory reliance was bound to lead to serious fiscal difficulties as France experienced mass unemployment and a steep increase in poverty levels during the 1980s. Thus the 1988 reforms of the centre-left government of Rocard created the guaranteed minimum income scheme RMI (*Revenue*

Minimum d'Insertion) as a family policy while it in fact benefited mostly isolated individuals without family support (Levy 1999). Juppé's plan for reform of the entire social welfare system was an attempt to even out the inconsistencies of the system without unifying it under one universal principle and it therefore earned approval and critique on both the political right and the left. The Jospin reforms in the late 1990s symbolised a state of French social-democratic thinking on welfare which was concerned with social integration but tried to avoid both unifying centralisation and rampant marketisation. It further strengthened the family orientation of French social policy by restoring universal family allowances while at the same time shifting the financing of social welfare from contributory to tax-financed income transfers (Bouget 1998). The fundamental link of social policies with citizenship rights in France is not least illustrated by the public impact of demonstrations and protests that spontaneously accompany policy changes and that are a vivid reminder to French politicians that social cohesion cannot be a matter of rhetoric but requires a solid political basis. This is also reflected in social work responses to the reformed welfare scenario. It was evident in Chamberlayne's and Rustin's research on the biographical meaning of 'exclusion' that while the French programme of 'social insertion' might appear as the re-affirmation of an individualised casework approach, it balances individual action with a focus on the assembling of a comprehensive range of relevant services which together constitute a practical form of social citizenship in Marshall's sense (Chamberlayne and Rustin 1999).

The principle of 'activation' also became particularly important in the transformation of one of the Scandinavian welfare models in the case of Denmark where 'the social-democratic coalition government, which came into power in 1993, has certainly produced a "miracle" as unemployment has diminished while the inflation rate remains low' (Torfing 1999: 6). On the face of it this success was accompanied by 'workfare' measures similar to those characterising social benefit conditions in the UK and the USA. But while the 'welfare reforms' of the 1980s in Denmark under the conservative Prime Minister Schlütter had aimed mainly at the reduction of public spending, the new activation policies rely heavily on individualised social work support for welfare recipients in their intended transition from economic exclusion to work participation. The Danish approach does not leave it to the 'didactics' of market consequences (making people 'learn' from the threat of their benefits being cut off) but invests heavily in raising skills levels and in designing specific counselling programmes that enhance the effectiveness of the measures. It also remains within the ambit of the Nordic welfare state tradition which values positively the central role of the state despite the arrival of neo-corporatist elements of regional and privatised devolution. The image of the state as a guarantor of equality and social integration accounts in no small measure for the acceptance such activation policies receive in Denmark among the population, including those most directly affected by them (Torfing 1999), in contrast to the resistance they evoke in liberal, residual welfare regimes where service users perceive the role of the state as surveillance and infringements of liberty (King 1995).

This impression is confirmed by developments in other Nordic countries. Sweden embarked on a wide-reaching reform of its 'institutional' welfare state during the late 1980s and 90s, largely under the impact of mass unemployment which undermined the entire basis of a system built on full employment being the first responsibility of the state. Despite the central role played by the state it would be wrong to regard the Swedish welfare system as monolithic even before the advent of 'New Public Management' and its emphasis on decentralisation and 'out-contracting' since the welfare state itself was the product of strong popular movements in Swedish civil society of which not all traces were lost (Sunesson et al. 1998). Nevertheless, the recent changes in social policy introduced many quasi- and actual market conditions into the social service delivery system while still attributing to the state the overall responsibility for the setting of standards. Selectivity increases by design and by default, with many service users seeking alternative sources of support, a sign that the strong welfare state in Sweden had by no means generated a paralysing dependency for recipients. Citizens are concerned about the ensuing inequalities but their concern will be negotiated at both the political and the market level (Lundström and Wijkström 1997). Comparative studies again emphasise the absence of highly polarised antagonism in the Swedish case of 'marketisation' which is so typical of the UK's residual legacy (Bryntse 2000). However, social workers in Sweden also see little option but to 'arrange' themselves within the new welfare environment although their role in 'activation' is less directly defined than in Denmark. Inevitably, their range of methods and activities is diversifying and they encounter greater competition from members of other social professions.

This is also the case in Finland where the economic crisis in the mid-90s had been much more pronounced and decentralisation of welfare responsibilities to municipal level has been introduced pervasively. On both the political right and the political left notions of 'active citizenship' in conjunction with a renewed emphasis on the merits of a strong civil society gained prominence (Anttonen 1998). But the programme of delegation of services and the introduction of quasi-markets did not obliterate the strong social policy orientation in social work, despite the simultaneous increase in attention on problems requiring 'therapeutic' interventions (Hämäläinen and Niemelä 2000, 2005). The profession's commitment to finding a synthesis between both traditions rather than being driven into a polarisation reflects the wider social policy context in which the differentiation of services is nevertheless carried by a broad consensus on social citizenship and equality

170

which the country strives hard to defend in the face of pressures from globalisation demanding a weakening of these principles. In contrast to its reputation as leading to dependency and inertia there is evidence that 'welfare statism has meant a thorough democratisation of Finnish society' (Anttonen 1998: 363) and all parts of society in Finland realise that welfare, democracy and social integration need to remain connected, no matter what forms the delivery of services is going to take.

Post-WWII Italy had largely been governed by centre-right coalitions under the dominant influence of the Christian Democrats. With constantly unstable majorities and consequently frequent elections a highly 'polarised, particularistic-clientelistic welfare state' (Ferrera 1996) became established which offered generous protection to privileged groups while leaving excluded those without political access and clout. Fundamental changes in the 1990s gradually took shape under the threat of Italy's failure to qualify for EU monetary union and in the course of the exposure of widespread corruption in all sectors of the political system. Explicit neo-liberalism made a brief appearance during the short life of the first right-wing Berlusconi government in 1994 while subsequent coalition governments, formed mainly by re-constituted parties on the left, pursued a course not just of reform but of the establishment of a coherent social policy approach in the first place. This represented ultimately an attempt at a changed relationship between citizens and the state that was no longer mediated almost exclusively through intermediary institutions of civil society but through public, professional services. While social policy is only beginning to matter in this relationship and the emphasis is on the reduction of unwarranted privileges, these reforms 'have done little to address the gaps in coverage or upgrade the benefits of Italy's most disadvantaged citizens' (Levy 1999: 257). This applies also to the introduction of Law 328 of 2000 which promoted devolution of social services and closer cooperation between private and public organisations. Efficiency criteria and quality controls in Italian social services find acceptance only slowly (Corposanto and Fazzi 2005) and inequalities in service levels across the country remain pronounced. This illustrates the continued importance of the relationship between political and social participation in all welfare systems. Regardless of the political orientation of governments in Italy the political and social significance of the social professions is being discovered and developed (Fasol 2000) but professional and political notions of client orientation and devolution frequently clash.

Given the wide discrepancies between the different routes charted by social policy reforms in countries across Europe it is difficult to identify common features and definite trends in social work under changing social policy conditions. The dissolving of the contours of distinct welfare regimes, initiated largely but not exclusively by centre-right governments, continued unabated under New Labour and social-democratic governments. However,

171

their policies tended to affirm that social cohesion cannot be achieved as a by-product of the market oriented behaviour of individuals but requires explicit political measures on behalf of society as a whole constituency. This insight seems to prevail also under the more recent swing back to centre-right governments in Europe which in practice appear to mitigate their avowed neo-liberalismconsiderably, particularly in the area of social policy. At the same time the relationship between economic and political activity generally has become highly contentious and the translation of new policies into social action requires the active participation of a whole stratum of social professionals.

The New Left everywhere in Europe faces a dilemma. It is conscious that the specific character and value of its policies is always going to be judged by its social policies and its commitment to social justice and equality, but also that the views of international capital on a government's economic principles, policies and performance have become an equally if not more important source of legitimation. As Offe remarks in relation to his analysis of the state of welfare in Germany during the Schröder years,

> 'leading office holders of the new Social Democratic administration have stressed, perfectly in line with "Third Way" and "New Labour" doctrines of how to mobilize, activate and make more "self-reliant" the labour force, the need for technical as well as institutional "innovation". Unburdening employers from some of the costs of security and protection is an imperative that unions and Social Democrats no longer seriously resist' (Offe 2000: 22).

Neo-liberal welfare policies in most European countries originally aimed at the individualisation of risks and the privatisation of social solidarity (Pierson 2001). The increased inequality and social instability that resulted from this have mobilised the electorate into reminding governments that 'the social' cannot be cancelled with impunity. Social workers, despite the sporadic resistance shown to neo-liberal changes, were ultimately in danger of themselves becoming victims of the abolition of 'the social' or at least of seeing their jobs being passed on to other actors in the field ready to provide what the new welfare markets demanded. They had resigned themselves to making the most of the changes for themselves personally and professionally either by concentrating more on counselling and therapeutic skills which suited a privatised market much more readily or by equipping themselves with managerial competences and qualifications to become active players (and winners) in the production of service packages. The lack of a constituency to support their actual professional interests among service users, politicians or the general public left them little alternative.

Overall the transition from neo-liberal to New Labour and social-democratic influences on European welfare systems appear to have heightened the pressure on and the fundamental dilemma for social work. Neo-liberalism had sought to reduce the function and contribution of this professional group largely to a residual role in the sense that its interventions

172

would be confined to the margins of society, only to where extreme circumstances call for the control and containment of 'deviants'. In relation to the labour market this ideology had accepted that the most useful deployment of social work would be for the control and containment of the 'superfluous and the "unintegrateable", in other words not for the achievement of social inclusion but the management of exclusion' (Scherr 1999 p 21). Neo-liberalism sought to transform 'mainstream' users of social services into consumers who would seek to cut out the mediation provided by social workers and demand a new, direct market in services or resort to pre-professional voluntary and self-help efforts. New Labour has recognised that there are advantages in 'bringing the state back' into the mix of organisational and conceptual arrangements for social service provisions. It therefore needs social workers much more centrally again as the transmitters of the 'message' contained in its welfare concepts. It requires the social professions as public educators, as mediators of a managerial culture that modernises social services and allows therefore resources to be rationed. Their tasks and therefore their professional scope are tightly prescribed by an agenda that seeks to 'activate' people threatened or already affected by poverty to becoming re-connected into a flexible market and thereby probably into society, although this goal is much more removed. They are to simultaneously maximise the efficiency of services by managerial and quantitative criteria. Potentially this offers the social professions once more a position of importance and higher status which a whole generation of social workers had not known or which had never been achieved in the first place in particular countries.

On the other hand playing this prescribed new role effectively requires a fundamental readjustment of the profession's methodological and political orientation from a concern with an ideal-typical state of well-being defined within the – often hazy – parameters of the profession's own history of criteria ('coping', 'maturity', 'autonomy') towards largely externally pres-cribed goals (adjustment, economic usefulness, conformity with contractual conditions of welfare payments, but also risk elimination and procedural cor-rectness). The value of the interventions of these recast professionals will be measured by criteria of efficiency and effectiveness within given parameters which are of an explicitly political nature. The new political parameters also give new connotations to professional and methodological core principles such as 'empowerment', a concept which had stood for a person-centred, emancipatory programme and which now carries more functional notions of consumers being enabled to make 'sensible' choices. While this is reminiscent of the 'colonisation' of terms like 'community' through the neo-liberal attack on notions of society and 'the social' and had always been a feature of a controlling 'incorporation' of critical concepts into hegemonic discourses, this latest shift seems to grip social professionals much more inescapably. Social workers are all too conscious that their very future as a profession might depend on their willingness to deliver on the terms set by the new agendas – the market might otherwise favour different or newly emerging operators which go under titles like care managers or life coaches.

The 'neo-social' tendencies in politics and their attempts at incorporating social work into 'New Welfare' strategies draw heavily on the methodology of case management as management generally has become a paradigm for solving complex issues. This is reminiscent of these origins of the professionalisation of social work, which had also modelled itself on an already established profession in the form of medicine. What is more, spearheaded by New Labour in Britain all governments across Europe tend to legitimate their programmes now with strong moral references, expecting social professionals to be capable of becoming the carriers of this moral mandate without having to appear moralistic themselves. In this sense, the motto of the 'activation of citizens', precisely because it combines elements of rational economics and of therapy, has a highly symbolic function well beyond its functional use – it is a moral crusade. Whether it is in the interest of clients to be activated and empowered or whether their willingness to be active and seek work of any kind is a test of their being a 'deserving case' for social assistance remains conveniently ambiguous and depends still very much on the political culture of a country. In those countries where the state is ultimately perceived by citizens to be an alien, threatening power the controlling element of interventions will always trigger suspicion and resistance by recipients of such programmes, and this despite all efforts by social workers to overcome the legacy of class divisiveness in their methodology.

Despite the continued emphasis on de-regulation, privatisation and the Third Sector, welfare measures are still of political interest to the state for whose implementation social work services are crucial. This means that despite the appearance to the contrary as if social work through the use of management paradigms had become more detached from politics, all social work interventions and methods need to be seen in a wider political context. Furthermore, it means that conflicts and social problems that arise at the personal and local level need to be related back to a wider political process precisely because the state is seeking to eliminate public fora and institutions in which such issues could be raised effectively (Böhnisch, Schröer and Thiersch 2005). The political nature of social work practice is borne out not so much in political campaigning, appropriate though this might be particularly in the context of renewed and invigorated community action programmes (Popple and Redmond 2000), but in giving direct, personal interactions with service users a 'citizenship dimension' so that they become an element in the re-creation of social solidarity as inter-locking networks of rights and obligations.

174

This approach seeks to reverse the trend towards the privatisation of responsibilities without underestimating the importance of non-governmental organisations. The social domain, where the private and the public sphere meet and interact, has always been the domain for social work interventions because here social bonds get negotiated. The withdrawal of the state from a commitment to this social domain makes it even more necessary for social work to emphasise the importance of a public sphere in the resolution of all social problems, even when they present themselves initially as totally private. In this such an approach to social work differs not only from neo-liberal concepts that deny the importance of 'the social', but also from the conservative and communitarian evocation of 'community' into which individuals have to be integrated and to whose values they have to adjust. A citizenship approach to social work practice does not pre-suppose the existence of such given communities but emphasises the necessity to create new communal structures with sets of mutual responsibilities within binding frameworks of rights and entitlements. The approach also goes beyond a concept of individualised 'life politics' as a viable framework for post-traditional social work methodology although such politics of 'personal mastery' (Ferguson 2001) can form an important element within the construction of citizenship. It marks instead an approach that operates at the micro and the macro level simultaneously and enhances not just people's personal but also their political coping capacities, which are being so badly neglected. Coping requires reliable and sustainable structures that can be openly negotiated, otherwise 'coping' can easily turn into forms of social deviance that create their structures and habits without reference to rights and ethics. There are indeed warning signs that such alternative private structures are emerging, not just in the field of organised international crime, but in no-go zones of urban areas and in the spread of illegal economies..

The quantitative growth of the professional field at a time when party politics appeal to voters with the promise of constant fiscal reductions in public and particularly in social spending bears witness to the profession's political significance. Yet this very importance limits the profession's scope in defining its own priorities as responses to the needs and requirements of service users. The autonomy of the social work profession was never defined or definable in absolute terms. Its enmeshment with the state is not a relict that stops social work from realising its actual potential, but it prescribes the essential parameters for the development of its competences. The contemporary situation of social work in Europe and particularly the lack of preparation for the rapid changes that face the profession on all fronts reflect the relative underdevelopment of its political analysis and action competence. There appears to be ample scope within the political agenda of 'activation' set for social work by neo-liberal governments to formulate a differentiated and sophisticated response which takes on the challenges posed in the name of accountability in terms of effectiveness and yet constructs its independent set of value criteria. To achieve this goal social work needs to operate with cross-national comparisons in order to recognise the political nature of the changes it becomes embroiled in. It also needs to build cross-national and cross-cultural alliances in order to play an active part in these transformation processes in the interests of and in collaboration with those most immediately affected by them. The diversity of traditions in Europe, at political, cultural and methodological level is an enormous pool of resources which is best being harnessed by social workers in Central and Eastern Europe where a pioneering spirit prevails and where conflicting social and political developments trigger a much more immediate engagement with these kind of processes than in those parts of Europe where social work carries the burden of being an 'established' profession.

The different conceptions of organised social solidarity under the conditions of industrialised modernity which the European nation states developed have left strong cultural traces at the level of the lifeworld which account for the remarkable resistance against the threat of neo-liberal homogenisation. Like all cultural traditions they have to be regarded, however, as dynamic processes in whose shaping all members of these communities need to have a share. Social policies are not being made exclusively at the level of the system but also within the networks of informal and indeed professional engagements and commitments in situations where people are threatened with marginalisation and exclusion. There is no doubt that European societies east and west are engaged in momentous transformation processes which challenge the very foundations of social solidarity. But after the demise of the totalitarian communist state in Europe in 1989 and the first decades of the neo-liberal backlash and its ideological promotion of the market as a panacea it is becoming clear that none of the institutions of the state, of the market and of civil society can have a monopoly on the production and delivery of welfare. They act instead as correctives of each other and the proportion to which each can make its particular contribution has to be worked out in every regional and historical context afresh but with reference to the prevailing traditions. New and challenging is at the start of the new millennium the changing role of the state in terms of its strategies and capacities to govern. The shift from government to governance is fraught with dangers as power can escape the established but insecure controls of democracy to accumulate in new centres of influence, particularly in the economy and in the media. But the shift has also released new capacities of governance and participation in other parts of civil society. Self-help initiatives abound, social movements are a force to be reckoned with, consumers claim their rights to quality services. While social work will always have to carry functions of social control, it also needs to engage critically with these new forms of governance. Its historical roots in social movements like the women's movement as well as its grounding in theoretical discourses that emphasise social justice, human dignity and empowerment should make it well prepared to make a constructive contribution to the development of a 'governmentality' aimed at solidarity across differences rather than exclusion. In this sense social work practice becomes explicitly social policy practice as in every single moment of intervention the right of the participants to belong and the form in which that belonging can be realised are at stake. Ultimately the future of the European project, of transforming competitive and belligerent nation states into co-operative open communities, hinges on the strengthening of the development of a social dimension from below. This is where an intercultural, anti-racist and in that sense European form of social work has its place and its role which it can only fulfil by developing its core methods as competence in intercultural communication.

'Europe's special quality is the emancipation of the individual, liberation from the compelling authority of religious-ideological modes of thought which were deemed obligatory. Rule that is ideological, nationalist, communist, fundamentalist, theocratic – in a word, rule governed by ideas discriminates on the basis of loyalty to the ideas themselves, and does not ensure equal rights for citizens. A society that is enlightened, realistic, worldly, pluralist, and willing to negotiate is the result of a long process: it is a slow-growing plant. The reliability of the civilized citizen denotes an inner value system for whose survival fear of punishment is insufficient. Europe was united by community of reflection (my emphasis).' (Konrád 2001: 370)

Bibliography

Abye, T. (2001), Social work education with Migrants and refugees, in L. Dominelli, W. Lorenz and H. Soydan (eds.), Beyond Racial Divides – Ethnicities in social work practice, Aldershot: Ashgate, pp. 117-133.

Adams, A., Erath, P. and Shardlow, S. (1999) (eds.), Key Themes in European Social Work; Theory, Practice, Perspectives, Lyme Regis: Russell House.

Adams, A., Erath, P. and Shardlow, S. (2000) (eds.), Fundamentals of Social Work in Selected European Countries – Historical and political context, present theory, practice, perspectives, Lyme Regis: Russell House.

Aldridge, M. (1996) Dragged to market: being a profession in the postmodern world, British Journal of Social Work 26, pp. 177-194.

Altmeyer, A. (1955), Training for international responsibilities, in A. Myrdal, A. Altmeyer and D. Rusk, America's role in international social welfare, New York: Columbia University Press.

Aluffi Pentini, A. (1996), The specific and complementary nature of inter-cultural and anti-racist pedagogical approaches, in A. Aluffi Pentini and W. Lorenz (eds.), Anti-racist work with young people, Lyme Regis: Russell House.

Aluffi Pentini, A. and Lorenz, W. (2006); Globalisation between universal sameness and absolute divisions: Creating shared pedagogical border zones as an antiracist strategy, in D. Macedo and P. Gounari (eds.), The Globalisation of Racism, Boulder / London: Paradigm Publishers, pp. 165-183.

Aly, G., Ebbinghaus, A., Hamann, M. Pfäfflin, F. and Preissler, G. (1985), Aussonderung und Tod. Die klinische Hinrichtung der Unbrauchbaren, Berlin: Rotbuch Verlag.

Anderson, B. (1983), Imagined Communities, London: Verso.

Anttonen, A. (1998), Vocabularies of citizenship and gender: Finland, Critical Social Policy 18;3, pp. 355-373.

Ascoli, U. (1987) 'The Italian welfare state: between incrementalism and rationalism', in R.R Friedmann, N. Gilbert, M. Sherer (eds.) Modern Welfare States: a comparative view of trends and prospects, Brighton: Wheatsheaf, pp. 110-150.

Ashenden, S. (1999), Habermas on discursive consensus – Rethinking the welfare state in the face of cultural pluralism, in P. Chamberlayne, A. Cooper, R. Freeman and M. Rustin (eds.), Welfare and Culture in Europe – Towards a new paradigm in social policy, London: J. Kingsley, pp.216-239.

Ashenden, S. (2003), Governing Child Sexual Abuse: negotiating the boundaries of public and private, law and science, London: Routledge.

Auernheimer, G. (2001), Migration als Herausforderung für pädagogische Institutionen, Opladen: Leske and Budrich.

Badelt, C. (1997) Sozialmanagement – Ein kontroverses Konzept zur Integration von wirtschaftlichem und sozialem Denken, Soziale Arbeit 46, 10/11, pp. 326-337.

Baine, S., Benington, J. and Russell, J. (1992) Changing Europe, London: NCVO Publications.

Baistow, K. and Hetherington, R. (1998), Parents' experiences of which welfare interventions: an Anglo-French comparison, Children and Society 12; pp. 113-124.

Balibar, E. (1991), The nation form: History and ideology, in E. Balibar and I. Wallerstein, Race, nation, class: ambiguous identities, London: Verso.

Balibar, E. (1992), Les frontières de la démocratie, Paris: la Découverte.

Balibar, E. and I. Wallerstein (1991), Race, nation, Class: Ambiguous Identities, London: Verso.

Balibar, R. (1985), L'Institution du français: essai sur le co-linguisme des Carolingiens Paris: la République.

Banks, S. (2006), Ethics and Values in Social Work, Basingstoke: Palgrave, 3rd ed.

Bastenier, A. (1994), Immigration and the ethnic differentiation of social relations in Europe, in J. Rex and B. Drury (eds.), Ethnic mobilisation in a multi-cultural Europe, Aldershot: Avebury.

Bateson, G. (1942), Social planning and the concept of 'Deutero-learning', Conference of Science, Philosophy and Religion, Second Symposium, New York: Harper, 1942, pp. 81-97.

Bateson, G. (1951), Information and Codification: A philosophical approach, in J. Ruesch and G. Bateson, Communication —The social matrix of psychiatry, New York: Norton.

Bauman, Z. (1989), Modernity and the Holocaust, Cambridge: Polity Press.

Bauman, Z. (1992), Soil, blood and identity, The Sociological Review 40.4: pp. 675-701.

Bauman, Z. (1995a), Life in fragments, essays in postmodern morality, Oxford: Blackwell.

Bauman, Z. (1995b), Searching for a centre that holds, in M. Featherstone, S. Lash and R. Robertson (eds.) Global Modernities, London: Sage.

Bauman, Z. (1997), Schwache Staaten; Globalisierung und die Spaltung der Weltgesellschaft, in U. Beck (ed.), Kinder der Freiheit, Frankfurt: Suhrkamp, pp.315-332

Bauman, Z. (1998a), Globalisation: the human consequences, Cambridge: Polity Press.

Bauman, Z. (1998b), Work, Consumerism and the New Poor, Buckingham: Open University Press.

Beck, U. (1992) Risk Society, London: Sage.

Beck, U. (1994), Nationalismus oder das Europa der Individuen, in U, Beck and E. Beck-Gernsheim, Riskante Freiheiten, Frankfurt: Suhrkamp, pp.466-481.

Becker, S. (1987) 'How much collaboration?', Community Care 26 March: pp. 23-24.

Bekkers, J.J.M. (1999), De vergeten infrastructuur? Over vraaggerichte sturing en lokaal sociaal beleid, Openbaar bestuur 9, pp. 22-25.

Beresford, P. (2000), Service users' knowledges and social work theory: conflict or collaboration? British Journal of Social Work 30; 4, pp. 489-503.

Beresford, P. and Evans, C. (1999), Research note: Research and empowerment, British Journal of Social Work 29, pp. 671-677.

Bernstein, B. B. (1971), Class, codes and control, London: Routledge & Kegan Paul.

Blair-Schröder Paper (1999), Der Weg nach vorne für Europas Sozialdemokraten. Ein Vorschlag von Gerhard Schröder und Tony Blair, quoted in http://www.amos-blaetter.de/AR-blair-schroeder-papier.html

Blickenstorfer, J: (1998), Pädagogik in der Krise: hermeneutische Studie, mit Schwerpunkt Nohl, Spranger, Litt zur Zeit der Weimarer Republik, Bad Heilbrunn: Klinkhardt.

Bock, G. (1983) Racism and sexism in Nazi Germany: motherhood, compulsory sterilization and the state, Signs: Journal of Women in Culture and Society 8;3 pp. 400-421.

Böhnisch, L. and Schröer, W. (2001), Pädagogik und Arbeitsgesellschaft. Historische Grundlagen und theoretische Ansätze für eine soziapolitisch reflexive Pädagogik, Weinheim: Juventa.

Böhnisch, L. and Schröer, W. (2002), Die soziale Bürgergesellschaft – zur Einbindung des Sozialpolitischen in den zivilgesellschaftlichen Diskurs, Weinheim: Juventa.

Böhnisch, L., Schröer, W. and Thiersch, H. (2005), Sozialpädagogisches Denken – Wege zu einer Neubestimmung, Weinheim: Juventa.

Bollenbeck, G. (1996), Bildung und Kultur – Glanz und Elend des deutschen Deutungsmusters, Frankfurt: Suhrkamp.

Bommes, M. and Scherr, A. (2000), Soziologie der Sozialen Arbeit, Weinheim and Munich: Juventa.

Bouget, D. (1998), The Juppé plan and the future of the French social welfare system, Journal of European Social Policy 8;2, pp. 155-172.

Branckaerts, J. (1983), 'Belgium', in D. Pancoast, P. Parker and C. Froland (eds.), Rediscovering Self-Help, London: Sage.

Brenton, M. (1982), Changing relationships in the Dutch social services, Journal of Social Policy 11; pp. 59-80.

Briggs, A. (1961), The welfare state in historical perspective, European Journal of Sociology 2;2, pp. 221-258.

Brown, W. (1995), Wounded Attachments: Later modern oppositional political formations, in J. Rajchman (ed.), The Identity in Question, London: Routledge, pp. 199-227.

Brubaker, W. R. (1989), Immigration and the Politics of Citizenship in Europe and North America, New York / London: University Press of America.

Brubaker, W. R. (1990), Immigration, citizenship, and the nation-state in France and Germany: a comparative historical analysis, International Sociology 5;4, pp. 379-407.

Brubaker, W. R. (1996), Nationalism reframed, nationhood and the national question in the New Europe, Cambridge: CUP.

Bruner, J. (1984), Interaction, communication, and self, Journal of the American Academy of Child Psychiatry 23;1, pp. 1-7.

Bryntse, K. (2000), Kontraktsstyrning i teori och praktik, Lund: Lund Studies in Economics and Management.

Butterwegge, C. (1999), Der Sozialstaat in der „Globalisierungsfalle"?, Die neoliberalistische Ideologie und die Realität, Neue Praxis 29;5, pp. 435-447.

Campanini, A. and Frost, E. (2004) (eds.), European Social Work – Commonalities and Differences, Rome: Carocci.

Cannan, C. (1991), 'Seine Policies', Social Work Today 14 March 1991; pp. 25-26.

Carter, J (1998), Postmodernity and the fragmentation of welfare, London: Routledge.

Castles, S. and Miller, M.J. (1993), The age of migration—International population movements in the modern world, London: Macmillan.

Chamberlayne, P. (1992), New directions in welfare? France, West Germany, Italy and Britain in the 1980s, Critical Social Policy 11; 3, pp. 5-21.

Chamberlayne, P. and Rustin (1999), From Biography to Social Policy, Final Report of the SOSTRIS Project, London: Centre for Biography in Social Policy, Sociology Department, University of East London.

Chambers, G. (ed.) (2000), European social democracy in the 21st century, London: Friedrich Ebert Stiftung, electronic edition http://www.fes.de/fulltext/bueros/london/00711.htm

Christie, A. (2002), Responses of the social work profession to unaccompanied children seeking asylum in the Republic of Ireland, European Journal of Social Work 5;2, pp. 187-198.

Cigno, K. (1985), The other Italian experiment: neighbourhood social work in the health and social services, British Journal of Social Work 15; pp. 173-186.

Commission of the European Communities (2004), Proposal for a Directive of the European Parliament and of the Council on Services in the Internal Market. COM(2004) 2 final/3.

Corby, B. (1991), Sociology, social work and child protection, in M. Davies (ed.), The Sociology of Social Work, London: Routledge.

Corposanto, C. and Fazzi, L. (2005), Introduzione, in Corposanto, C. and Fazzi, L. (eds.), Il servizio sociale in un'epoca di cambiamento: scenari, nodi e prospettive, Rome: Edizioni EISS, pp. 9-13.

Culpitt, I. (1992), Welfare and citizenship: Beyond the crisis of the welfare state? London: Sage.

Dahme, H.-J. and Wohlfahrt, N. (2002), Aktivierender Staat – ein neues sozialpolitisches Leitbild und seine Konsequenzen für die soziale Arbeit, Neue Praxis 32;1, pp. 10-32.

Dahme, H.-J., Otto, H.-U. und Trube, A. (2003), Soziale Arbeit für den aktivierenden Staat, Leske and Budrich: Opladen.

Dahrendorf, R. (1992), The New Europe, Journal of European Social Policy, 2; 2, pp. 79-85.

Dahrendorf, R. (1999), The Third Way and Liberty – an authoritarian streak in Europe's new centre, Foreign Affairs 78;5, pp. 13-17.

Delanty, G. (1995), Inventing Europe. Idea, identity, reality, London: Macmillan.

Delanty, G. (1996), Beyond the nation-state: national identity and citizenship in a multicultural society, Sociological Research Online 1;3.

Dewe, B. and Otto, H.-U. (1996), Zugänge zur Sozialpädagogik, Reflexive Wissenschaftstheorie und kognitive Identität, Weinheim and Munich: Juventa.

Diehl, K. and Mombert, P. (eds.) (1984), Sozialpolitik, Ausgewählte Lesestücke zum Studium der politischen Ökonomie, Frankfurt.

Dingwall, R., Eekelaar, J. and Murray, T. (1995), The Protection of Children: State Intervention and Family Life, London: Avebury, 2nd ed.

Dominelli, L. (1998), Multiculturalism, anti-racism and social work in Europe, in C. Williams, H. Soydan and M. R.D.Johnson (eds.), Social Work and Minorities, London: Routledge, pp. 36-57.

Dominelli, L. (2006), Racialised identities: New challenges for social work education, in K. Lyons and S. Lawrence (eds.), Social Work in Europe: Educating for Change, Birmingham: Venture Press, pp. 81-101.

Dominelli, L. und Hoogvelt, A. (1996), Globalisation and the technocratization of social work, Critical Social Policy 47, pp. 45-62.

Donati, P. and Colozzi, I. (1988), Institutional reorganisation and new shifts in the welfare mix in Italy during the 1980s, in A. Evers and H. Wintersberger (eds.) Shifts in the Welfare Mix—their impact on work, social services and welfare politics, Vienna: European Centre for Social Welfare Training and Research, pp. 63-96.

Donzelot, J. (1979), The Policing of Families—Welfare versus the state, London: Hutchinson.

Durkheim, E. (1984) (orig. 1893), The Division of Labour in Society, Basingstoke: Macmillan.

Dyson, K.H.F. (1980), The State Tradition in Western Europe, Oxford: Martin Robertson.

Ellemers, J. E. (1984), Pillarization as a process of modernization, Acta Politica 19; 1, pp. 129-144.

Erath, P., Littlechild, B. and Vornanen, R. (2005) (eds.), Social Work in Europe – Descriptions, Analysis and Theories, Strassfurt: BK Verlag.

Ergas, Y. (1982), Allargamento della cittadinanza e governo del conflitto: le politiche sociali negli anni settanta in Italia, Stato e Mercato 6; pp. 429-464.

Esping-Andersen, G. (1990), The Three Worlds of Welfare Capitalism, Cambridge: Polity Press.

Esping-Andersen, G. (1996), After the golden Age? Welfare state dilemmas in a global economy, in G. Esping-Andersen (ed.), Welfare States in Transition – National Adaptations in Global Economies, London: Sage, pp 11-32.

Esping-Andersen, G. (2002), Why we need a New Welfare State, Oxford: Oxford University Press.

Fasol, R. (2000), Social Work in Italy, in A. Adams, P. Erath and S. Shardlow (eds.) Fundamentals of Social Work in Selected European Countries, Historical and political context, present theory, practice, perspectives, Lyme Regis: Russell House, pp. 65-81.

Ferge, Z. (1979), A Society in the Making—Hungarian Social and Societal Policy 1945-75, Harmondsworth: Penguin.

Ferguson, H. (2001), Social Work, Individualization and Life Politics, British Journal of Social Work 31;1, pp. 41-55.

Ferguson, H. and Kenny, P. (1995) On behalf of the child: child welfare, child protection, and the Child Care Act, Dublin: A & A Farmar.

Ferrera, M. (1996), The 'Southern' model of welfare in Social Europe, Journal of European Social Policy 6;1, pp. 17-37.

Flora, P. (1986), Growth to Limits: the Western European Welfare States since World War II, Vol. 1, Berlin: de Gruyter.

Flora, P. (2000), Stein Rokkan: Staat, Nation und Demokratie in Europa, Die Theorie Stein Rokkans aus seinen gesammelten Werken rekonstruiert und eingeleitet, Frankfurt: Suhrkamp.

183

Fook, J. (1999), Critical reflectivity in education and practice, in B. Pease and J. Fook (eds.), Transforming Social Work Practice – Postmodern critical perspectives, London: Routledge, pp. 195-208.

Fook, J. (2001), Emerging ethnicities as a theoretical framework for social work, in L. Dominelli, W. Lorenz and H. Soydan (eds.), Beyond Racial Divides – Ethnicities in social work practice, Aldershot: Ashgate, pp. 9-22.

Fook, J. (2004), Critical reflection and transformative possibilities, in L. Davies and P. Leonard (eds.), Social Work in a Corporate Era – Practices of power and resistance, Aldershot: Ashgate, pp. 16-30.

Foucault, M. (1972), The Archaeology of Knowledge, London: Routledge.

Frank, A.G. and Gills, B.K. (1993), The World System: Five hundred years or five thousand? London: Routledge.

Fraser, D. (1973), The Evolution of the British Welfare State, London: Macmillan.

Fraser, N. (1995), Politics, culture, and the public sphere: toward a postmodern conception, in L. Nicholson and S. Seidman (eds.), Social Postmodernism—beyond Identity Politics, Cambridge: Cambridge University Press, pp 49-68.

Fraser, N. (1998), From redistribution to recognition? Dilemmas of justice in a "post-socialist" age, in C. Willett (ed.), Theorizing Multiculturalism, Oxford: Blackwell, pp. 19-49.

Fritz, Th. and Scherrer, C. (2002), GATS: Zu wessen Diensten? Hamburg: VSA-Verlag

Fryer, P. (1984), Staying Power: The History of Black People in Britain, London: Pluto Press.

Geisen, T. (2001), Sozialstaat in der Moderne. Zur Entstehung sozialer Sicherungssysteme in Europa, in K. Kraus, T. Geisen (eds.), Sozialstaat in Europa, Geschichte, Entwicklung, Perspektiven, Wiesbaden: Westdeutscher Verlag, pp.21-42.

Gellner, E. (1983), Nations and Nationalism, Oxford: Blackwell.

Gibbs, A. (2001), The changing nature and context of social work research, British Journal of Social Work, 31, pp. 687-704.

Giddens, A. (1984), The constitution of society, Cambridge: Polity Press.

Giddens, A. (1985), Reason without Revolution? Habermas' Theorie des kommunikativen Handelns, in R. J. Bernstein (ed.), Habermas and Modernity, Cambridge: Polity Press, pp. 124-163.

Giddens, A. (1991), Modernity and Self-Identity—Self and Society in Later Modern Age, Cambridge: Polity Press.

Giddens, A. (1994), Beyond Left and Right—the future of radical politics, Cambridge: Polity Press

Giddens, A. (2000), The Third Way and its Critics, Cambridge: Polity Press.

Giesen, B. and Junge, K. (1991) Vom Patriotismus zum Nationalismus, Zur Evolution der "Deutschen Kulturnation", in B. Giesen (ed.) Nationale und kulturelle Identität Studien zur Entwicklung des kollektiven Bewusstseins in der Neuzeit, Frankfurt: Suhrkamp pp. 255-303.

Gilgun, J. (2005), The four cornerstones of evidence-based practice in social work, Research on Social Work Practice 15;1, pp. 52-61.

Gilroy, P. (1992), The end of anti-racism, in J. Donald and A. Rattansi (eds.), 'Race', Culture and Difference, London: Sage, pp. 49-61.

Ginsburg, N. and Lawrence, S. (2006), A changing Europe, in K. Lyons and S. Lawrence (eds.), Social Work in Europe: Educating for Change, Birmingham: Venture Press, pp. 17-36.

Gori, C. (ed.), (2004), L'eredità della legge 328/00. Un bilancio, Rome: Carocci.

Greenfeld, L. (1992), Nationalism. Five roads to modernity, Cambridge: Harvard University Press.

Haarmann, H. (2001), Babylonische Welt - Geschichte und Zukunft der Sprachen, Frankfurt / New York: Campus.

Habermas, J. (1981), Theorie des kommunikativen Handelns, Frankfurt: Suhrkamp.

Habermas, J. (1984), The Theory of Communicative Action Volume I: Reason and the Rationalization of Society (translated by T. McCarthy). London: Heinemann.

Habermas, J. (1987), The Theory of Communicative Action Volume II: Lifeworld and System (translated by T. McCarthy). Cambridge: Polity Press.

Habermas, J. (1990), Moral Consciousness and Communicative Action, Cambridge: Polity Press.

Habermas, J. (1996) Between Facts and Norms: Contributions to a Discourse Theory of Law and Democracy, Cambridge: Polity Press.

Hämäläinen, J. and Niemelä, P., (2000), Social Policy and Social Work in Finland, in A. Adams, P. Erath and S. Shardlow (eds.) Fundamentals of Social Work in Selected European Countries, Historical and political context, present theory, practice, perspectives, Lyme Regis: Russell House, pp. 25-36.

Hämäläinen, J. and Niemelä, P. (2005), De- and reconstruction of social welfare in Finland: Impacts on social work, in B. Littlechild, P. Erath, J. Keller (eds.), De- and Reconstruction in European Social Work, Stassfurt: BK Verlag, pp. 79 93.

Hamburger, F. (1990), Der Kulturkonflikt und seine pädagogische Kompensation, in E.D. Dittrich, F.-O. Radtke (eds.), Ethnizität, Opladen, pp. 76-92

Hamburger, F. (1993), Erziehung und Sozialarbeit im Migrationsprozess, in M.J. Gorzini and H. Müller (eds.), Handbuch zur interkulturellen Arbeit, Wiesbaden: World University Service, pp. 93-106.

Hamburger, F. (2001), The Social Pedagogical Model in the Multicultural Society of Germany, in L. Dominelli, W. Lorenz and H. Soydan (eds.), Beyond Racial Divides – Ethnicities in social work practice, Aldershot: Ashgate, pp. 89 – 104.

Hamburger, F. (2003), Einführung in die Sozialpädagogik, Stuttgart: Kohlhammer.

Hamburger, F., Hirschler, S., Sander, G. and Wöbcke, M. (2004, 2005, 2006) (eds.), Ausbildung für Soziale Berufe in Europa, vol. 1 – 3, Frankfurt: ISS Eigenverlag.

Hanmer, J. and Hearn, J. (1999), Gender and welfare research, in F. Williams, J. Popay and A. Oakley (eds.), Welfare Research: A Critical Review, London UCL Press, pp. 106-130.

Harris, J. (1998), Scientific management, bureau-professionalism, new managerialism: the labour process of state social work, British Journal of Social Work 28;6, pp. 839-862.

Harris, J. (1999), Social work sent to market, International Perspectives in Social Work 2: Social Work and the State, pp. 99-108.

Harris, J. (2003), The Social Work Business, London: Routledge.

Harvey, D. (1989), The condition of postmodernity: An enquiry into the conditions of cultural change, Cambridge: Cambridge University Press.

Healy, K. (2005), Social Work Theories in Context: Creating frameworks for practice, Basingstoke: Palgrave Macmillan.

Held, D. (2002), Die Globalisierung regulieren? Die Neuerfindung von Politik, in Lutz-Bachmann, M. and Bohman, J. (eds.), Weltstaat oder Staatenwelt?, Frankfurt: Suhrkamp, pp. 104-124.

Heller, A. and Fehér, F. (1988), The Postmodern Political Condition, Cambridge: Polity Press.

Hering, S. and Waaldijk, B. (2003) (eds.), History of Social Work in Europe (1900-1960), Female pioneers and their influence on the development of international social organizations, Opladen: Leske and Budrich.

Hetherington, R. (1998), Issues in European child protection research, European Journal of Social Work 1;1, pp. 71-82.

Hetherington, R., Cooper, A., Smith, P. and Wilford, G. (1997), Protecting Children: Messages from Europe, Lyme Regis: Russell House.

Hilgenfeld, E. (1936), Die Volksgemeinschaft als Ausgangspunkt und Ziel im heutigen Deutschland, in H. Althaus, Soziale Arbeit und Gemeinschaft. Ein Beitrag zur III. Internationalen Konferenz für soziale Arbeit, London 1936, Karlsruhe: G.Braun, pp. 1-14.

Hill, O. (1883), Homes of the London Poor, London: Macmillan, second edition.

Hobsbawm, E.J. (1977), The Age of Revolution, London: Abacus.

Hobsbawm, E.J. (1990), Nations and nationalism since 1780: programme, myth and reality, Cambridge: Cambridge University Press.

Hoffman, E. (2001), Inclusive thinking and acting, in L. Dominelli, W. Lorenz and H. Soydan (eds.), Beyond Racial Divides – Ethnicities in social work practice, Aldershot: Ashgate, pp. 59 – 86.

Horkheimer, M. and Adorno, T. W. (1947), Dialektik der Aufklärung, Frankfurt: Suhrkamp 2003.

Horsman, M. and Marshall, A. (1994), After the nation-state; citizens, tribalism and the New World Order, London: Harper Collins.

Howe, D. (1994) Modernity, postmodernity and social work, British Journal of Social Work 24, pp. 513-532.

Hroch, M. (1985), Social preconditions of national revival in Europe, Cambridge: Cambridge University Press.

Hroch, M. (1993), From national movement to fully formed nation, New Left Review 198, March 1993, pp. 3-20.

Hugman, R. (1991), The segregation of women and their work in the personal social services, Critical Social Policy 15, pp. 21-35.

Hummrich, M., Sander, G. & Wöbcke, M. (1997) Annotated bibliography. Social work with immigrants in Germany. Mainz: Johannes Gutenberg-Universität, Pädagogischen Institut.

Humphrey, M. (1996), Civil War, identity and globalisation, New Formations 31; summer, pp. 67-82.

Humphries, B. (2002), From welfare to authoritarianism: The role of social work in immigration controls, in S. Cohen, B. Humphries, E. Mynott (eds.), From Immigration Controls to Welfare Controls, London: Routledge, pp. 126-140.

Humphries, B. (2004), Taking sides: Social work research as a moral and political activity, in R. Lovelock, K. Lyons and J. Powell (eds.), Reflecting on Social Work – Discipline and Profession, Aldershot: Ashgate, pp. 113-129.

Jessop, B (2000a), From the KWNS to the SWPR, in G. Lewis, S. Gewirtz, J. Clarke (eds.), Rethinking Social Policy, London: Sage, pp. 171-184.

Jessop, B. (2000b), The Future of the Welfare State, Cambridge: Polity.Press.

Jones, C. (1983), State Social Work and the Working Class, London: Macmillan.

Jones, C. and Novak, T. (2000), Class struggle, self-help and popular welfare, in M. Lavalette, G. Mooney (eds.), Class Struggle and Social Welfare, London: Routledge, pp. 34-51.

Joppke, C. (1999), Immigration and the Nation State, Oxford: Oxford University Press.

Jordan, B. (1978), A comment on "theory and practice in social work", British Journal of Social Work 8;11, pp. 23-25.

Jordan, B. and Parton, N. (2004), Social work, the public sphere and civil society, in R. Lovelock, K. Lyons and J. Powell (eds.), Reflecting on Social Work – Discipline and Profession, Aldershot: Ashgate, pp. 20-36.

Jouhy, E. (1984) Diachrone und synchrone ... in U. Menzemer, A. Moreau, L'emprise du social—Perspectives françaises et allemandes sur la jeunesse et le travail social, Paris: A. Colin.

Kaldor, M. (2001), New and Old Wars – organised violence in a global era, Cambridge, Polity Press.

Kant, I. (1968) Beantwortung der Frage: Was ist Aufklärung? in Werke, Darmstadt: Wissenschaftliche Buchhandlung, Vol. 9, pp. 51-61 [orig. 1783]

Kantowicz, E. (2004), Poland, in A. Campanini and E. Frost (eds.), European Social Work – Commonalities and Differences, Rome: Carocci, pp. 171-181.

Kappeler, M. (2000), Der schreckliche Traum vom vollkommenen Menschen Rassenhygiene und Eugenik in der Sozialen Arbeit, Marburg: Schüren.

Kessl, F. and Otto, H -U. (2003), Aktivierende Soziale Arbeit, Anmerkungen zur neosozialen Programmierung Sozialer Arbeit, in H.-J. Dahme, H.-U. Otto, A. Trube and N. Wohlfahrt (eds.), Soziale Arbeit für den aktivierenden Staat, Opladen: Leske und Budrich, pp. 57-74.

Khan, P. and Dominelli, L. (2000), The impact of globalisation on social work in the UK, European Journal of Social Work 3;2 pp. 95-108.

King, D. (1995), Actively Seeking Work, Chicago: University of Chicago Press.

Klee, E. (1985), ‚Euthanasie' im NS-Staat. Die ‚Vernichtung lebensunwerten Lebens', Frankfurt: Fischer.

Konrád, G. (1977) The Case Worker, London: Hutchinson.

Konrád, G. (2001), The special quality of Europe is culture, in W. Beck, L.J.G. van der Maesen, F. Thomése and A. Walker (eds.), Social Quality: A Vision for Europe, The Hague, Kluwer Law, pp. 369-373.

Krafeld, F. J. (2001), Gerechtigkeitsorientierung als Alternative zur Attraktivität rechtsextremistischer Orientierungsmuster, in: Deutsche Jugend, 7-8, pp. 322-332.

Krafeld, F. J., Möller, K. and Müller, A. (1993), Jugendarbeit in rechten Szenen – Ansätze, Erfahrungen, Perspektiven, Bremen: Ed. Temmen.

Kronen, K. (1978), Sozialpädagogik: Zu Entstehung und Wandel des Begriffs, Sociologia Internationalis 16, pp. 219-234.

Ksiezopolski, M. (1987), Polish social policy in a situation of economic crisis—is there a choice of alternatives? in A. Evers, H. Nowotny and H. Wintersberger, The Changing Face of Welfare, Aldershot: Gower, pp. 220-234.

187

Kuhlmann, C, (2001), Alice Salomon (1872 – 1948), European Journal of Social Work 4;1, pp. 65-75.

Kunstreich, T. (1997) Grundkurs Soziale Arbeit, Sieben Blicke auf Geschichte und Gegenwart Sozialer Arbeit, Hamburg: Agentur des Rauhen Hauses, 2 Vols.

Kushner, T. and Knox, K. (1999), Refugees in an Age of Genocide: global, national and local perspectives during the twentieth century, London: Frank Cass.

Laan, G. van der (1998) The professional role of social work in a market environment, European Journal of Social Work 1;1, pp. 31-40.

Laan, G. van der (2000), Handlungsspielräume von Sozialarbeitern unter Marktbedingungen – das Beispiel Niederlande, in Otto, H.-U. and Schnurr, S. (eds.), Privatisierung und Wettbewerb in der Jugendhilfe: Marktorientierte Modernisierungsstrategien in internationaler Perspektive, Neuwied: Luchterhand, pp. 87-110.

Lash, S., Heelas, P. and Morris, P. (eds.) (1996), Detraditionalisation, Oxford: Blackwell.

Leibfried, S. (1992), Towards a European Welfare State—on integrating Poverty Regimes into the European Community in Z. Ferge and J. K. Kolberg (eds.), Social Policy in a Changing Europe, Boulder/ Colorado: Westview and Frankfurt: Campus Verlag , pp 34-58.

Leibfried, S. and Pierson, P. (1992) 'Prospects for Social Europe', Politics and Society 20; 3, pp. 333-366.

Leibfried, S. and Pierson, P. (1994), The prospects for social Europe, in A. de Swaan (ed.), Social policy beyond borders. The social question in transnational perspective, Amsterdam: Amsterdam University Press, pp. 15-68.

Leibfried, S. and Rieger, E. (2001), Grundlagen der Globalisierung, Perspektiven des Wohlfahrtsstaates, Frankfurt: Suhrkamp.

Levy, J.D. (1999), Vice into Virtue? Progressive politics and welfare reform in continental Europe, Politics and Society 27;2, pp. 239-273.

Lewis, O. (1959), Five Families: Mexican Case Studies in the Culture of Poverty, New York: Basic Books.

Lister, R. (1998), Citizenship on the margins: citizenship, social work and social action, European Journal of Social Work 1;1, pp. 5-18.

Littlechild, B., Erath, P. and Keller, J (2005) (eds.), De- and Reconstruction in European Social Work, Stassfurt: BK-Verlag.

Lohmann, I. (1998), Die Juden als Repräsentanten des Universellen. Zur gesellschaftlichen Ambivalenz klassischer Bildungstheorie, in Gogolin, M. Krüger-Potratz, M. A. Mezer (eds.), Pluralität und Bildung, Oplanden: Leske und Budrich, pp. 153-178.

Lorenz, W. (1994), Social Work in a Changing Europe, London: Routledge.

Lorenz, W. (1996), The education of the nation: racism and the nation state, in A. Aluffi Pentini and W. Lorenz (eds.), Anti-Racist Work with Young People - European Experiences and Approaches, Lyme Regis: Russell House , pp. 1-25.

Lorenz, W. (2001), Social Work in Europe – Portrait of a diverse professional group, in S. Hessle (ed.), International Standard Setting of Higher Social Work Education, Stockholm: Stockholm Studies of Social Work 17, pp. 10-24.

Lorenz, W. (2001), Social Work Responses to "New Labour" in Continental European Countries, British Journal of Social Work 31;4, pp. 595-609.

Lorenz, W. and Seibel F.W (1999), European Educational Exchanges in the Social Professions—The ECSPRESS Experience, in E. Marynowicz-Hetka, A. Wagner, J. Piekarski (eds.), European Dimensions in Training and Practice of the Social Professions, Katowice: Slask, pp. 315-341.

Lundström, T. and Wijkström, F. (1997), The Nonprofit Sector in Sweden, Manchester: Manchester University Press.

Lyons, K. (2000), The place of research in social work education, British Journal of Social Work 30;6, pp. 433-447.

Lyons, K. and Lawrence, S. (2006) (eds.), Social Work in Europe: Educating for Change, Birmingham: Venture Press.

Lyotard, J.-F. (1984), The Postmodern Condition: A Report on Knowledge, Manchester: Manchester Univ. Press.

Lyotard, J.-F. (1993), Europe, the Jews, and the Book, in Political Writings, London: UCL Press.

Macey, M. (1995), Towards racial justice? A re-evaluation of anti-racism, Critical Social Policy 44/45, vol. 15; 2/3: pp. 126-146.

Macpherson, Sir William of Cluny (1999), The Stephen Lawrence Inquiry, London: HMSO Cm 4262-I, http://www.archive.official-documents.co.uk/document/cm42/4262/4262.htm

McVeigh, R. and Lentin, R. (2002), Situated Racisms, in R. Lentin and R. McVeigh (eds.), Racism and Anti-Racism in Ireland, Belfast: Beyond the Pale Publications, pp. 1-48.

Marshall, T.H. and Bottomore, T. (1992), Citizenship and Social Class, London: Pluto Press.

Marynowicz-Hetka, E., Wagner, A. and Piekarski, J. (1999) (eds.), European Dimensions in Training and Practice of the Social Professions, Katowice: Slask.

Mayer, J. E. and N. Timms. (1970), The Client Speaks: Working Class Impressions of Casework, London: Routledge and Kegan Paul.

Mayer, K.U. and Müller, W. (1984), The state and the structure of life course, in A.B.Sorensen, F. Weinert, L. Sherrod, Human Development: Interdisciplinary Perspectives, New York: Academic Press, pp. 94-123.

Medical Post-graduate Education Centre in Warsaw (1978) Social Workers, their Skills, Effectiveness of Work and Training in the Polish People's Republic, Vol. I, Warsaw.

Meehan, E. (1993), Citizenship and the European Community, London: Sage.

Mennicke, C. (1930), Sozialpädagogik und Volksbildung, in: Hauptausschuss der Arbeiterwohlfahrt (ed.), Lehrbuch der Wohlfahrtspflege, Nuremberg.

Miles, R. (1989), Racism, London: Routledge.

Miles, R. (1993), Racism after 'race relations', London: Routledge.

Mills, C.W. (1943), The professional ideology of social pathologists, American Journal of Sociology 49, pp. 165-180.

Mishra, R. (1990), The welfare state in capitalist society. Policies of retrenchment and maintenance in Europe, North America and Australia, London: Harvester Wheatsheaf.

Mommsen, W.J. (1990), The varieties of the nation state in modern history: liberal, imperialist, Fascist and contemporary notions of nation and nationality, in M. Mann (ed.), The rise and decline of the nation state, Oxford: Blackwell, pp. 210-226.

189

Mouffe, C. (1996), Democracy, power and the 'political', in S. Benhabib (ed.), Democracy and Difference: Contesting the Boundaries of the Political, Princeton, Princeton University Press, pp. 246-256.

Mullard, C. (1982), Multi-racial education in Britain: from assimilation to cultural pluralism', in J. Tierney (ed.), Race, Immigration and Schooling, London: Holt Educational, pp. 154-167.

Müller, B. (1995), Sozialer Friede und Multikultur, in S. Müller, H.-U. Otto and U. Otto (eds.), Fremde und Andere in Deutschland, Nachdenken über das Einverleiben, Einebnen, Ausgrenzen, Opladen: Leske und Budrich, pp. 133-147.

Müller, C.W. (1988), Wie Helfen zum Beruf wurde. Eine Methodengeschichte der Sozialarbeit 1945-1985, vol. 2, Weinheim/ Bale: Beltz.

Müller, S., Otto, H.-U., and Otto, U. (1995) (eds.), Fremde und Andere in Deutschland. Nachdenken über das Einverleiben, Einebnen, Ausgrenzen, Opladen: Westdeutscher Verlag.

Münder, J. (1998), Von der Subsidiarität über den Korporatismus zum Markt, Neue Praxis 28;1, pp. 3 -12.

Mynott, E. (2002), Nationalism, racism and immigration control: from anti-racism to anti-capitalism, in S. Cohen, B. Humphries, E. Mynott (eds.), From Immigration Controls to Welfare Controls, London: Routledge, pp. 11-29.

Natorp, P. (1894), Religion innerhalb der Grenzen der Humanität. Ein Kapitel zur Grundlegung der Sozialpädagogik, Freiburg/Leipzig: Mohr.

Nicholson, L. (1999), The Play of Reason – from the modern to the postmodern, Buckingham, Open University Press.

Niemeyer, C. (1998), Klassiker der Sozialpädagogik, Einführung in die Theoriegeschichte einer Wissenschaft, Weinheim /Munich: Juventa.

Niethammer, L. (1991), Die volkseigene Erfahrung, Berlin: Rowohlt.

Nilsson, I. and Wadeskog, A. (1988) 'Local initiatives in a new welfare state—a Fourth Sector approach', in A. Evers and H. Wintersberger (eds.) Shifts in the Welfare Mix—their impact on work, social services and welfare politics, Vienna: European Centre for Social Welfare Training and Research, pp. 33-62.

Nohl, H. (1982), Die pädagogische Bewegung in Deutschland und ihre Theorie, Frankfurt: Schulte-Bulmke, 9th ed..

Nokielski, H. (1989), Organisationswandel sozialer Arbeit in den Niederlanden, Essen (Habilitationsschrift).

Nowotny, H. (1984), Social concerns for the 1980s, Vienna: European Centre for Social Welfare Training and Research.

Oakley, A. (2000), Experiments in Knowing, Cambridge: Polity Press.

Oesterle, G. (1991) Kulturelle Identität und Klassizismus – Wilhelm von Humboldts Enwurf einer allgmeinen und vergleichenden Literaturkenntnis als Teil einer vergleichenden Anthropologie, in B. Giesen (ed.), Nationale und kulturelle Identität, Studien zur Entwicklung des kollektiven Bewusstseins in der Neuzeit, Frankfurt: Suhrkamp, pp. 304-349.

Offe, C. (2000), The German Welfare State: Principles, performance and prospects after unification, Thesis Eleven 63 (Nov.), pp. 11-37.

Ohland, A. (1937), Der Erfolg der deutschen Fürsorgeerziehung – Kritische Darstellung der bisherigen Untersuchungsergebnisse, Deutsche Jugendhilfe (früher Zentralblatt für Jugendrecht und Jugendwohlfahrt) 29, pp. 6-16; 50-61.

Okitikpi, T. and Aymer, C. (2000), The price of safety: refugee children and the challenge to social work, Social Work in Europe, 7 (1), pp. 51-58.

Olk, T. (2000), Der "aktivierende" Staat. Perspektiven einer lebenslagenbezogenen Sozialpolitik für Kinder, Jugendliche, Frauen und ältere Menschen, in S. Müller, H. Sünker, T. Olk, K. Böllert (eds.), Soziale Arbeit: gesellschaftliche Bedingungen und professionelle Perspektiven, Neuwied: Luchterhand, pp. 99-118.

Otto, H.-U. and Sünker, H. (1989), Nationalsozialismus, Volksgemeinschaftsideologie und soziale Arbeit, In H.-U. Otto, H. Sünker (eds.) Soziale Arbeit und Faschismus, Frankfurt: Suhrkamp, 11-28.

Otto, H.-U. and Ziegler, H. (2004), Sozialraum und sozialer Ausschluss, Neue Praxis 34;2, pp. 117 – 135 and 34;3, pp. 271-291

Parton, N . (1991), Governing the Family: Child Care, Child Protection and the State, London: Macmillan.

Parton, N. (1998), Risk, advanced liberalism and child welfare: the need to rediscover uncertainty and ambiguity, British Journal of Social Work 28;1, pp. 5-27

Parton, N. (2000), Some thoughts on the relationship between theory and practice in and for social work, British Journal of Social Work 30;6, pp. 449-463.

Parton, N. (2004), Post-theories for practice: Challenging the dogmas, in L. Davies and P. Leonard (eds.), Social Work in a Corporate Era – Practices of power and resistance, Aldershot: Ashgate, pp. 31-44.

Payne, M. (1998) Why social work? Comparative perspectives on social issue and response formation, International Social Work 41;4 pp. 443-453.

Penna, S., Paylor, I. and Washington, J. (1999), Globalisation, social exclusion and the possibilities for global social work and welfare, European Journal of Social Work 3;2, pp. 109-122.

Philp, M. (1979), Notes on the form of knowledge in social work, Sociological Review 27;1, pp. 83-111.

Pierson, P. (1994), Dismantling the Welfare State? Reagan, Thatcher and The Politics of Retrenchment, Cambridge: Cambridge University Press.

Pierson, P. (2001), The New Politics of the Welfare State, Oxford: Oxford University Press.

Pieterse, J.N. (1995), Europe among other things: closure, culture, identity, in K. van Benda-Beckmann and M. Verkuyten (eds.), Nationalism, ethnicity and cultural identity in Europe, Utrecht: ERCOMER

Pinker, R. (1990) Social Work in an Enterprise Society, London: Routledge.

Pius XI (1931), Encyclical Letter (Quadragesimo Anno) on Reconstructing the Social Order and Perfecting it Comformably to the Percepts of the Gospel in Commemoration of the Fortieth Anniversary of the Encyclical "Rerum Novarum", Oxford: Catholic Social Guild.

Popple, K. and Redmond, M. (2000), Community development and the voluntary sector in the new millennium: the implications of the third way in the UK, Community Development Journal, Vol. 35; 4, pp. 391-400.

Proctor, R.N. (1988), Racial hygiene: Medicine under the Nazis, Cambridge/Ma.: Harvard University Press.

Radtke, F.-O. (1994), The formation of ethnic minorities and the transformation of social into ethnic conflicts in a so-called multi-cultural society: the case of

Germany, in J. Rex and B. Drury (eds.), Ethnic mobilisation in a multi-cultural Europe, Aldershot: Avebury, pp. 30-37.

Rattansi, A. (1994), 'Western' racisms, ethnicities and identities in a 'postmodern' frame, in A. Rattansi and S. Westwood (eds.), Racism, Modernity and Identity—on the western front, Cambridge: Polity Press, pp. 1-12.

Rauschenbach, T. (1999), Das sozialpädagogische Jahrhundert, Analysen zur Entwicklung Sozialer Arbeit in der Moderne, Weinheim/Munich: Juventa.

Rex, J. (1993), Ethnic and class conflict in Europe, Society and Economy, quarterly Journal of The Budapest University of Economic Sciences, 14;3, pp.19-27.

Rieger, E. and Leibfried, S. (1998), Welfare state limits to globalisation, Politics and Society 26;3, pp. 363-390.

Rieger, E. and Leibfried, S. (2001), Grundlagen der Globalisierung – Perspektiven des Wohlfahrtsstaats, Frankfurt: Suhrkamp.

Robertson, R. (1992), Globalisation: Social theory and global culture, London: Sage.

Roebroek, J.M. (1989), 'Netherlands', in J. Dixon and R.P. Scheurell (eds.), Social Welfare in Developed Market Countries, London: Routledge.

Rojek, C., Peacock, G. and Collins, S. (1988), Social Work and Received Ideas, London: Routledge.

Rorty, R. (1992), Cosmopolitanism without emancipation: a response to Lyotard, in S. Lash and J. Friedman (eds.), Modernity and Identity, Oxford: Blackwell, pp. 59-72.

Rowbotham, S. (1977), Hidden from History – 300 years of Women's Oppression and the Fight against it, London: Pluto.

Sabater, J. (2005), The social welfare regimes in Europe (with special attention to the Spanish case), in B. Littlechild, P. Erath and J. Keller (eds.), De- and Reconstruction in European Social Work, Stassfurt: BK-Verlag, pp. 113-130.

Sachße, C., Tennstedt, F. (1998) Geschichte der Armenfürsorge in Deutschland – vom Spätmittelalter bis zum 1. Weltkrieg, Stuttgart: Kohlhammer, 2nd ed.

Said, E.W. (1994), Culture and imperialism, London: Vintage.

Salomon, A. (1919), Die deutsche Frau und ihre Aufgaben im neuen Volksstaat, Leipzig / Berlin: Teubner.

Salomon, A. (1926), Soziale Diagnose, Berlin: Heymanns.

Saraceno, C. (1987), 'Between state intervention, the social sphere and private life: changes in the family's role', in A. Evers, H. Nowotny and H. Wintersberger, The Changing Face of Welfare, Aldershot: Gower, pp.174-191.

Saraceno, C. (2002), Deconstructing the myth of welfare dependence, in C. Saraceno (ed.). Social Assistance Dynamics in Europe – National and local poverty regimes, Bristol: The Policy Press, pp. 235-258.

Schendelen, van M.P.C.M. (1984), 'Consociationalism, pillarization and conflict management in the Low countries', Acta politica, 19 (special edition), pp. 149-163.

Scherr, A. (1994), Kulturelle Jugendbildung – ein Instrument der Gewaltprävention? Neue Praxis 24;5, pp. 427-434.

Scherr, A. (1999), Transformations in social work: From help towards social inclusion to the management of exclusion, European Journal of Social Work 2;1, pp. 13-23.

Scherr, A. (2000), Wissensaneignung als Bildungsprozeß? Überlegungen zur Funktion pädagogischer Studiengänge und zur Rekonstruktion

(sozial)pädagogischer Wissensformen, in: Dewe, B. and Kurtz, Th. (eds.):
Reflexionsbedarf und Forschungsperspektiven moderner Pädagogik. Opladen:
Leske und Burdrich, pp. 187-202.

Schilde, K. and Schulte, D. (2005) (eds.), Need and Care – Glimpses into the
Beginnings of Eastern Europe's Professional Welfare, Opladen: B.Budrich.

Schnurr, S. (1997), Sozialpädagogen im Nationalsozialismus – Eine Fallstudie zur
sozialpädagogischen Bewegung im Übergang zum NS-Staat, Weinheim and
Munich: Juventa.

Schön, D.A. (1987), Educating the reflective practitioner, San Francisco: Jossey-Bass.

Seidmann, S. (1998), Contested knowledge: social theory in the postmodern era, 2nd
ed., Oxford: Blackwell.

Sherman, E. and Reid, W. J. (1994), Coming of Age in Social Work—The
Emergence of Qualitative Research, in Sherman, Edmund A. Reid, William
James, Qualitative research in social work, New York: Columbia University
Press, pp. 1-20.

Silverman, D. (1993), Interpreting Qualitative Data, London: Sage.

Skehill, C. (1999), The Nature of Social Work in ireland: A Historical Perspective.
New York: E. Mellen Press.

Sloterdijk, P. (1983), Kritik der zynischen Vernunft, Frankfurt: Suhrkamp (2 vols.).

Spicker, P. (2000), A Third Way? The European Legacy 5;2, pp. 229-239.

Squires, P. (1990), Anti-social policy: welfare, ideology and the disciplinary state,
London: Harvester Wheatsheaf.

Stathopoulos, P. (1991), Community development in rural areas of Greece, in M. Hill
(ed.), Social Work and the European Community: The social policy and
practice contexts, London: J. Kingsley.

Steek, W. (1995), Neo-voluntarism: A new European Social Policy Regime?,
European Law Journal 1;1 pp. 31-59.

Sunesson, S. (2000), Schweden zwischen staatlicher Wohlfahrt und
Marktorientierung, in Otto, H.-U. and Schnurr, S. (eds.), Privatisierung und
Wettbewerb in der Jugendhilfe: Marktorientierte Modernisierungsstrategien in
internationaler Perspektive, Neuwied: Luchterhand, pp. 231-238.

Sunesson, S., Blomberg, S., Edebalk, P.G., Harrysson, L., Magnusson, J., Meeuwisse,
A., Petersson, J., and Salonen, T. (1998), The flight from universalism,
European Journal of Social Work 1;1, pp. 19-29.

Sünker, H. and Otto, H.-U. (eds.) (1997), Education and Fascism, London: Taylor &
Francis.

Taguieff, P.-A. (1990), The new cultural racism in France, Telos 83, pp. 109-122.

Tampke, J. (1981) 'Bismarck's social legislation: a genuine breakthrough?', in W.
Mommsen (ed.), The Emergence of the Welfare State in Britain and Germany
1850-1950, London: Croom Helm, pp. 71-83.

Taylor, C. (1992), Multiculturalism—Examining the politics of recognition,
Princeton: Princeton University Press.

Taylor, D. (1998), Social identity and social policy: engagements with postmodern
theory, Journal of social policy 27;3, pp. 329-350.

Taylor-Gooby, P. (2001), The politics of welfare in Europe, in P. Taylor-Gooby (ed.),
Welfare States under Pressure, London: Sage.

Therborn, G. (1995), European modernity and beyond—the trajectory of European
societies 1945-2000, London: Sage.

Thiersch, H. (1986), Die Erfahrung der Wirklichkeit. Perspektiven einer alltagsorientierten Sozialpädagogik, Weinheim: Beltz.

Thole, W. (1999a) Zur Methodologie der Konstruktionen „zweiter Ordnung" – Neue Publikationen zur qualitativen Forschung aus erziehungswissenschaftlicher Perspektive betrachtet, Sozialwissenschaftliche Literatur Rundschau 38; 22, pp. 41-49.

Thole, W. (1999b) Die Sozialpädagogik und ihre Forschung – Sinn und Kontur einer empirisch informierten Theorie der Sozialpädagogik, Neue Praxis 29;3, pp. 224-245.

Thole W. (2002), Grundriss Soziale Arbeit: Ein einführendes Handbuch, Opladen: Leske und Budrich.

Thole, W., Galuske, M. and Gängler, H. (eds.) (1998), KlassikerInnen der Sozialen Arbeit, Neuwied: Luchterhand.

Thompson, E.P. (1968), The Making of the English Working Class, Harmondsworth: Penguin.

Thompson, J.B. (1990), Ideology and Modern Culture, Cambridge: Polity Press.

Todd, R. (1991), Education in a multicultural society, London: Cassell.

Tönnies, F. (1887), Gemeinschaft und Gesellschaft. Grundbegriffe der reinen Soziologie, Darmstadt.

Torfing, J. (1999), Workfare with welfare: recent reforms of the Danish welfare state, Journal of European Social Policy 9;1, pp. 5-28.

Touraine, A. (1995), Critique of Modernity, Oxford: Blackwell.

Treptow, R. (1995), Erleben und Urteilen. Wie anstrengend darf Kultur sein? Zeitschrift für Erlebnispädagogik 6; pp. 18 -1.

Treptow, R. (1996), Wozu vergleichen? Komparatistisches Denken in der Sozialpädagogik / Sozialarbeit, in R. Treptow (ed.), Internationaler Vergleich und Soziale Arbeit, Theorie, Anwendung und Perspektive, Rheinfelden: Schäuble, pp. 1-22.

Vasta, E. (1993), Rights and racism in a new country of immigration: the Italian case, in J. Wrench and J. Solomos (eds.), Racism and migration in Western Europe, Oxford: Berg, pp. 161-179.

Veer, G. van der (1998) Counselling and Therapy with Refugees and the Victims of Trauma, Chichester, John Wiley and Sons.

Wallerstein, I. (1991), The construction of peoplehood: Racism, nationalism, ethnicity, in E. Balibar and I. Wallerstein, Race, nation, class: ambiguous identities, London: Verso, pp. 71-85.

Wallerstein, I. (1993), World system versus world systems, in Frank, A.G. and Gills, B.K. (1993), The World System: Five hundred years or five thousand? London: Routledge, pp. 292-296.

Wallimann, I. (1986) 'Social insurance and the delivery of social services in France', Social Science and Medicine 23; 12, pp. 1305-1317.

Waters, M. (1995), Globalisation, London: Routledge.

Webb, B. (1926), My Apprenticeship, London: Longmans.

Weeks, J. (1993), Rediscovering values, in J. Squires (ed.), Principled positions: Postmodernism and the rediscovery of value, London: Lawrence & Wishart, pp. 189-211.

Weiss, A. (2006), The racism of globalisation, in D. Macedo and P. Gounari (eds.), The Globalisation of Racism, Boulder / London: Paradigm Publishers, pp. 128-147.

Wendt, W.R. (1985), Geschichte der sozialen Arbeit, 2nd ed., Stuttgart: Ferdinand Enke.

White, V. (2003), Drei Modi des Managements Sozialer Arbeit, in H.-J. Dahme, H.-U. Otto, A. Trube and N. Wohlfahrt (eds.), Soziale Arbeit für den aktivierenden Staat, Opladen: Leske und Budrich, pp. 419-435.

Wieviorka, M. (1994a), Ethnicity as action, in J. Rex and B. Drury (eds.), Ethnic mobilisation in a multi-cultural Europe, Aldershot: Avebury

Wieviorka, M. (1994b), Racism in Europe: unity and diversity, in A. Rattansi, S. Westwood (eds.), Racism, modernity and identity, Cambridge: Polity Press, pp. 173-188.

Williams, F. and Popay, J. (1994), Lay knowledge and the privilege of experience, in J. Gabe, D. Kelleher and G. Williams (eds.), Challenging Medicine, London: Routledge, pp. 84-101.

Williams, F. and Popay, J. (1999), Balancing Polarities: Developing a New Framework for Welfare Research, in F. Williams, J. Popay and A. Oakley (eds.), Welfare Research: A Critical Review, London UCL Press, pp. 156 – 183.

Winkler, M. (1988), Eine Theorie der Sozialpädagogik. Über Erziehung als Rekonstruktion der Subjektivität. Stuttgart: Klett – Cotta.

Zarago, J.-V. (1991) ‚Gesetzliche Grundlagen sozialer Arbeit in Spanien', in F. Hamburger (ed.) Sozialarbeit in Deutschland und Spanien – vergleichende Analysen und lokale Fallstudien, Rheinfelden: Schäuble.

Zaviršek, D. (2005), "You will teach them some, socialism will do the rest". History of social work education in Slovenia during the period 1940 – 1960), in K. Schilde, D. Schulte (eds.), Need and Care – Glimpses into the Beginnings of Eastern Europe's Professional Welfare, Opladen: B.Budrich, pp. 237-272.

Zimmer, H. (1996), Pädagogik, Kultur und nationale Identität. Das Projekt einer "deutschen Bildung" bei Rudolf Hildebrand und Hermann Nohl, Jahrbuch für Pädagogik 1996, pp. 159-177.

Žižek, S. (1991), For they know not what they do: enjoyment as a political factor, London: Verso.

Index

Notes

Notes

Notes

Welfare History—Wohlfahrtsgeschichte
A Janus-Book – Ein Janus-Buch

Guardians of the Poor –
Custodians of the Public
Welfare History in Eastern Europe.

Sabine Hering
Berteke Waaldijk
Guardians of the Poor—
Custodians of the Public
Hüter der Armen –
Beschützer der Öffentlichkeit
Welfare history in Eastern Europe
Eine Wohlfahrtsgeschichte Osteuropas
2006. 338 pp. Pb 36.00 Euro (D),
US$43.00. ISBN 3-938094-58-3

The bi-lingual book describes the results of case studies about the history of social work in Eastern Europe between 1900 and 1960 in eight countries: Bulgaria, Croatia, Hungary, Latvia, Poland, Romania, Russia, and Slovenia.

Target groups:

Teachers and students of social work/social politics, Researchers in social history, general interest in EU social policy

The authors:

Prof. Dr. Sabine Hering, University of Siegen, Germany

Prof. Dr. Berteke Waaldijk, University of Utrecht, The Netherlands

Verlag **Barbara Budrich**
Barbara Budrich Publishers

Head-office: Stauffenbergstr. 7 • D-51379 Leverkusen Opladen • Germany
Tel +49 (0)2171.344.594 • Fax +49 (0)2171.344.693 • info@budrich-verlag.de
US-office: 28347 Ridgebrook • Farmington Hills, MI 48334 • USA • info@barbara-budrich.net
North American distribution: **International Specialized Book Services**
920 NE 58th Ave., suite 300 • Portland, OR 97213-3786 • USA
phone toll-free within North America 1-800-944-6190, fax 1-503-280-8832 •orders@isbs.com

www.budrich-verlag.de • www.barbara-budrich.net

Welfare History

Kurt Schilde
Dagmar Schulte (eds.)
Need and Care
Glimpses into the Beginnings of Eastern
Europe's Professional Welfare
2005. 296 pp. Pb 33.00 Euro (D), US$34.90
ISBN 3-938094-49-4

The book gives a collection of case studies by
national researchers from the project "History
of Social Work in Eastern Europe 1900–1960
(SWEEP)". This collection is directed at teaching Social Work and
History of Social Work in an international context since it focuses on
Latvia, Russia, Poland, Hungary, Croatia, Slovenia, Romania and
Bulgaria.

Political Science

Linda Shepherd (ed.)
Political Psychology
The World of Political Science—The
development of the discipline Book
Series edited by John Trent &
Michael Stein
2006. 168 pp. Pb. 19.90 Euro (D)
US$ 23.95
ISBN 3-86649-027-5

The book provides detailed information about the development of the
field of political psychology. It describes the evolution of concepts and
theories within political psychology,
international influences in the field,
current concepts and methodology,
and trends that augur for the future of
the enterprise.

Verlag **Barbara Budrich**
Barbara Budrich Publishers

Head-office: Stauffenbergstr. 7 • D-51379 Leverkusen Opladen • Germany
Tel +49 (0)2171.344.594 • Fax +49 (0)2171.344.693 • info@budrich-verlag.de
US-office: 28347 Ridgebrook • Farmington Hills, MI 48334 • USA • info@barbara-budrich.net
North American distribution: **International Specialized Book Services**
920 NE 58th Ave., suite 300 • Portland, OR 97213-3786 • USA
phone toll-free within North America 1-800-944-6190, fax 1-503-280-8832 •orders@isbs.com

www.budrich-verlag.de • www.barbara-budrich.net